CHINA'S
LONG MARCH OF
MODERNISATION

CHINA'S LONG MARCH OF MODERNISATION

Blueprint & Road Map for The Nation's
Full Development 2016-2049

"".. China marches on ..."
- President Xi Jinping
Beijing New China 70th national
01 October 2019"

KHOR ENG LEE - AARON KHOR

To order additional copies of this book, contact:
Xlibris
1-800-455-039
www.Xlibris.com.au
Orders@Xlibris.com.au
803810

CONTENTS

PART (B) A STRONG MILITARY

THE HISTORIC DECEMBER 1978 CPC DECISION

"... The Third Plenary Session of the 11th Central Committee of the CPC (Communist Party of China) made the historic decision (on 22 December 1978) to shift the focus of the Party and the country to economic development and carry out the reform and opening-up program," President Xi Jinping said on the five-day milestone meeting of the CPC at the Jingxi Hotel in western Beijing..

"It also called upon all Party members and people of all ethnic groups to embark on a new march towards socialist modernization.

"This is a transition of far-reaching significance in the history of the Party and the country..."

PROLOGUE

Attaining a High-Income Economy through Innovation-driven Development

Recalling his one-hour meeting in 1979 with Deng Xiaoping in the Great Hall of the People in Beijing, Sony Corporation chairman Akio Morita remarked that his host made him do most of the talking.

In his book **MADE IN JAPAN** (1986), Morita made several significant observations about the situation in China, and he wrote:

"At the end of the seventies, the Chinese push to modernize was done with a great amount of enthusiasm. Their bureaucrats and experts travelled to Japan, the United States and Europe and began buying up factories that could only be utilized by people with skills that were in very short supply in China... (1)

"Quality control would be essential if they really cared about serving their people. But reliability and durability have always been a problem in China, where the stories of breakdown are topics of general conversation... (2)

"I admire Chinese courage and determination. They have learned a lot about modern industry in a short time, but they have a long way to go... (3)

"By 1985 Chinese textile exports had reached four billion dollars...

"But the factor that has energised Japan to produce ever-new and better products, as it energizes large segments of the American industrial and commercial establishment, competition in the local marketplace, is still missing. And without that spur, progress is hard to achieve..." (4)

In 1986, the year of publication of Morita's book, Japan's share of world exports peaked. But the country's economic decline shortly after led to the end of its post-war miracle. After the bubble burst in 1991, the Japanese economic growth took a nosedive.

In 1978 China's GDP was $216.81 billion with its per capita of $227 for a population of slightly over 956 million. (5)

In 1978 Japan became the world's second largest economy.

In 1979 China embarked on a transitional course to a market economy.

In 2009 China emerged as the world's top exporter of goods.

In 2010 China with its GDP of over $6 trillion displaced Japan as the world's number 2 economy, and three years later in 2013 China became the world's largest trading nation with a gross total trade of $4.2 trillion.

In their book (published in 2000) **CAN JAPAN COMPETE?** Professor Michael Porter (described as the world's leading thinker on competitive strategy and authority on global competitiveness) and his Japanese colleagues wrote: "Today, Japan must move beyond just quality competition to competing on **strategy and innovation**... Genuine innovation not only in products but also in approaches to competing will be required..." (6)

"Technological and business-model innovations are nurturing waves of entrepreneurs and formidable competitors in China," Dr Wendy Hong of HK-based Fung Business Intelligence Centre wrote on November 2015. (7)

In the 13th Five-Year Plan (2016-2020), innovation is positioned at the centre and core of China's development, to transition from a high middle-income level to that of high income.

As presented by Lou Jifang of the Ministry of Civil Affairs, the main objectives of the 13FYP include maintaining economic growth, transforming patterns of economic development, promoting innovation-driven and coordinated development, accelerating agricultural modernisation, reforming institutional mechanisms, promoting pro-poor development, quality of life and a good environment. (8)

According to the Innovation-driven development strategy (IDDS) promulgated by the authorities in Beijing on May 2016 to provide a "top-level design and systemic plan" for China's innovations over the next 30 years, the roadmap proceeds in three stages to turn China into a global innovation champion.

For China to become an "innovative country" by 2020, the initial stage of development entails creating an innovative-friendly environment with improved intellectual property (IP) protection, enhanced incentives, and a comprehensive set of policies and regulations.

According to the World Intellectual Property Organization (WIPO), China ranked 17th in terms of comprehensive sci-tech innovation capability in 2018. China seeks to be seeded 15th by 2020.

China's goal is also to increase the contribution of science and technology to economic growth from 58.5% in 2018 to 60% by 2020, as reported online by **CCTV** March 11, 2019.   26.03.2019 17:23

The midcourse goal is to make major breakthroughs in select areas and to reach the top tier of innovation leaders by 2030.

At the 5th Plenum of the 18th Communist Party Congress on November 2015, President Xi Jinping pointed out that a number of strategic industries and research domains have been selected for pursuing breakthroughs. They include aero-engines, quantum communications, intelligent manufacturing and robotics, deep space and deep sea probes, major new materials, and neurosciences.

According to Science and Technology Minister Wang Zhigang speaking in Beijing on 11 March 2019, China plans to "rank among the world leading innovative countries by 2035, and become a world scientific and technological power by 2050."

As reported by **CCTV** March 11, 2019, Wang has stressed that "sci-tech innovation must be placed at the core of China's modernization process and it's an important support and leading force as well as an important driving force for development…"   26.03.2019 17:32

In the third and climatic stage, China's aspiration is to become a strong global innovation power, to lead the world in the manufacturing field by 2049, and to set the pace in science and technology by 2050 – to mark the first centenary of New China. (9)

Window of "Strategic Opportunity"

Since the early 2000s at the dawn of the new millennium, China's leaders have viewed and regarded the first two decades of the 21st century as a "period of strategic opportunity" to attain prime national objectives of sustaining economic growth at a high level and expanding "comprehensive national power" (CNP) to secure China's status as a great power.

It's also seen as a crucial and challenging as well as generative period for the fast-developing country to catch up with the world's most advanced economic and technological leaders.

The development of a prosperous and powerful China is the realisation of Mao Zedong's mission to "make China rich and strong" and President Xi Jinping's "China Dream" of complete modernization and rejuvenation. In Xi's report to the CPC's 19th National Congress on 18 October 2017, China will become "a global leader in terms of composite national strength and international influence" by mid-21st century.

"The 13-5Y Plan stresses that the nation's future as a global power rests on its ability to build an innovation-led economy," Dr Wendy Hong and colleagues have written in their analysis of China's new development paradigm. (10)

The development of a moderately prosperous society with the doubling of the country's 2010 GDP by 2020 will mark the centenary of the founding of the Communist Party of China (CPC) on 1 July 1921.

According to Cai Fang, deputy director of the Chinese Academy of Social Sciences (CASS), China is expected to have a GDP per capita of $12,600 in 2022, making it a high-income country. (11)

With the support of its strong leadership and industrious population of close to one billion working Chinese, fully committed and dedicated to its peaceful development and comprehensive modernization, China is forging ahead on the driver's seat in various fields of human endeavour.

A leading global role is resourceful and resurgent New China's manifest destiny, with the confidence of attaining (and regaining) the world's largest economy within the coming decade.

Holding high the new banner of the Fourth Industrial Revolution IR 4.0, China will continue steadfastly and strongly on its Long March of Modernization.

In the military field, the People's Liberation Army has developed from a ragtag fighting force of some 20,000 troops into a two-million-strong military that's presently rated as the world's third strongest after its counterparts in the US and Russia.

Speaking at a grand rally to mark the 90th anniversary of the People's Liberation Army (PLA) at the Great Hall of the People in Beijing on 1 August 2017, President Xi Jinping said the PLA has transformed itself from a "millet plus rifles" single-service force to one that has fully-fledged services.

> Having basically completed its mechanization, the PLA is moving rapidly toward having "strong" informationized armed forces. (12)

President Xi stressed that China must step up the PLA's transformation into a world-class military that's ready to fight and win wars in defence of its national sovereignty. (13)

To quote from the May 2017 Report by the US Department of Defense: "... The PLA is pursuing an ambitious modernization program that aligns with China's two centenary goals..."

"DIA (Defense Intelligence Agency) director, Lieutenant General Robert Ashley, emphasized that "China Military Power 2019" (published and released by the DIA on 15 January 2019) showed China's evolution from a domestically oriented force to a global one. He told reporters the PLA was changing "from a defensive, inflexible ground-based force charged with domestic and peripheral security responsibilities to a joint, highly agile, expeditionary, and power-projecting arm of Chinese foreign policy that engages in military diplomacy and operations across the globe," Gabriel Black reported on 30 January 2019 on the World Socialist Web Site. (14)

According to President Xi, the PLA's military mechanization will basically be achieved with advanced IT application and much enhanced strategic capabilities by 2020, on the eve of the CPC's centenary on 1 July 2021.

The people's armed forces will be transformed into a world-class military by mid-21st century – to mark the centenary of the founding of New China/the People's Republic of China/the PRC on 1 October 2049.

In his 56-page statement to the Senate Armed Services Committee on 15 March 2018, Adm. Harry B. Harris Jr., then naval head of US Pacific Command (USPACOM), wrote that on the current trajectory, the PLA will likely attain its goals of completing military modernisation by 2033 and achieving "world class" status by 2049 "well ahead of the projected completion dates…"

With the companion volume **CHINA'S RENAISSANCE**, the following narrative adumbrates the saga of **CHINA'S LONG MARCH OF MODERNISATION** and the phenomenal transformation of the world's most populous nation of nearly one and a half billion Chinese -- from abject poverty to its dream of becoming a fully developed and modernized country by mid-21st century. (15)

It's the greatest development story in human history!

13.07.2017 10:41 28.07.2017 03.08.2017 13:42 04.08.2017 13:55 07.08.2017 10:56 10:59 11.08,2018 16:0724.08.2017 13:02 30.08.2017 10:06 29.09.2017 05:46 03.10.2017 15:12 19.10.2017 02:22 19.10.2017 12:33 26.03.2019 18:05 28.03.2019 15:48

Notes NEW CHINA AA PROLOGUE

1. Published by E.P. Dutton, New York, 1986, p. 215.
2. Ibid., p.217
3. Ibid., p. 217
4. Ibid., p. 217
5. **Wikipedia**
6. Michael E. Porter, the C. Roland Christensen Professor of Business Administration at the Harvard Business School, with Hirotaka Takeuchi, Professor and Dean of the new Graduate School of International Corporate Strategy at Hitotsubashi University in Japan, and Mariko Sakakibara, Assistant Professor at the John E. Anderson Graduate School of Management at the University of California, Los Angeles (ULCA) and former Deputy Director at the Japanese Ministry of International Trade and Industry. Perseus Publishing, Massachusetts, 2000, pp. 189-190.
7. **fbicgroup.com** China's Policy Think Piece Series Issue No. 3 Nov 2015
   Dr. Wendy Hong, Denise Cheung, Davit Sit
   China's 13th Five-Year Plan (2016-2020):
   Redefining China's development paradigm under the
   New Normal
8. **CCTV.com** 11-02-2015
9. **PLANNING FOR INNOVATION** A report for the U.S.-China Economic and Social Security Review Commission July 2016, prepared by Tai Ming Cheung and five other colleagues, University of California Institute of Global Conflict and Cooperation. **uscc.gov**

Executive Summary: "... In the global race for economic, technological and innovation leadership, China is a late entrant but has made impressive progress in closing the gap at the top by harnessing abundant resources accumulated through nearly four decades of high-octane growth and a voracious appetite for foreign technology and know-how..."

9(a) "… Technology will decide which country emerges as the world's dominant economic power in the long run. While about 20 percent of per-capita gross domestic product (GDP) growth is driven by labor and capital, the remaining 80 percent is determined by how rapidly an economy is developing and applying new technology to increase production," Ruchir Sharma, the chief global strategist at Morgan Stanley Investment has written 28 June,2018 on The Coming Battle With China in **The New York Times (nytimes.com)**.

"China's ambition to catch up to Western living standards thus depends largely on how rapidly it can match or surpass Western technology…"

Sharma last visited Beijing in May 2018.

9(b) "… Over the past couple of years, Beijing has rolled out plans to drastically raise China's game in around 20 hi-tech industries, including semiconductors, robotics, aerospace, high speed rail, electric vehicles, pharmaceuticals and new materials," Tom Holland, a former SCMP staffer, has written 2 July 2018 in **South China Morning Post**, on China's ambition to leapfrog technologically and to dominate in burgeoning fields such as AI and aerospace.

"Much of the international attention has focused on the old[fashioned import substitution elements of these plans, with Beijing typically aiming for Chinese companies to capture a three-quarter share of the domestic market over the next 10 or so years…

"But Beijing's plans go far beyond import substitution. In semiconductors for example, state planners want Chinese companies to command a third of the international market by 2030. And in artificial intelligence (AI), they are aiming at nothing less than global dominance…"

Holland knowledgeably commented "there is a fair chance Beijing might just succeed in its bid for global technological supremacy, even though it is starting from so far behind (the US)."

9(c) According to the Global Innovation Index 2018 (released in New York 10 July 2018 and as reported by **AP**), China has risen from 22nd in 2017 to 17th in 2018 among the world's top 20 most innovative economies.

Francis Gurry, director general of the UN World Intellectual Property Organization (WIPO), said China's ranking represents a breakthrough for its economy, which is rapidly transforming and prioritizing research and ingenuity.

"China's rapid rise reflects a strategic direction set from the top leadership to developing world-class capacity in innovation and to moving the structural basis of the economy to more knowledge-intensive industries that rely on innovation to maintain competitive advantage," Gurry said.

Describing China's rapid rise in the rankings over the last few years as "spectacular", the GII Report says China's innovative prowess becomes evident in various areas, including some of its greatest improvements in global research and development (R&D) companies, high technology imports, the quality of its publications, and enrolment in graduate education.

"In absolute values, and in areas such as R&D expenditures and the number of researchers, patents and publications, China is now first or second in the world, with volumes that overshadow most high income economies," the GII Report stated.

The annual GII survey is sponsored by the WIPO, Cornell University's SC Johnson College of Business, and INSEAD, one of the world's leading and largest graduate business schools.

Now in its 11th edition, the Global Innovation Index (GII) ranks 126 economies based on 80 indicators ranging from creation of mobile applications to education spending, scientific and technical publications, and intellectual property filing rates.　　12,07.2018 21:39

10. **People's Daily Online** Dec 06, 2016
11. **GLOBAL TIMES** 2017/8/1 10:34:26
12. **PEOPLE'S DAILY** 2017-08-02 18:34:15
13. **2017 China Military Power Report defense.gov/PDF** 2017-06-06
14. **wsws.org**

(15) In a commentary June 26, 2018 in **Global Asia**, policy analyst at RAND Corporation Ali Wyne noted that between 2001 when China joined World Trade Organization (WTO) and 2016, China's GDP grew roughly 9-fold in a decade and a half -- from US$1.3 trillion to US$11.2 trillion, and its per capita income rose almost 8-fold from US$1,053 to US$8,123.

China's share of world economy roughly quadrupled from 4% to just under 16%.

China accounted for some 34% of global growth in 2012-2016.

China overtook Germany as the world's largest exporter in 2009, and displaced the US as the world's largest goods trader in 2013.

Between 2000 and 2017, China's manufacturing expanded from about one quarter of the US in 2000 to more than the US and Japan's in 2017.

As reported online by **CGTN** Dec 18,2018, China's GDP in 1978 was nearly 45% of UK's, 15% of Japan's, less than 7% of that of the US.

Following the launch of China's reform and opening up in late December 1978, China's GDP grew 33.5 times over four decades and by the end of 2017, averaging 9.5% growth per year. In 2018 China's GDP came to US$13.7 trillion with a per capita of US$9,900 (from $156 in 1978).

"... The Third Plenary Session of the 11th Central Committee of the CPC made the historic decision to shift the focus of the Party and the country to economic development and carry out the reform and opening-up program," President Xi Jinping said on the resolution made on 22 December 1978 at the 5-day meeting in the Jingxi Hotel in western Beijing.

"It also called upon all Party members to embark on a new march towards socialist modernization. This is a transition of far-reaching significance in the history of the Party and the country..."

Four years earlier, towards the end of the Cultural Revolution (1966-76), Premier Zhou Enlai (1898-1976) introduced China's new programme of the Four Modernizations at the Fourth National People's Congress meeting in January 1975.

"… The Four Modernizations were Zhou's goals (with Mao Zedong's blessings) for renewal and advance in agriculture, industry, science-technology, and national defense.They were going to be achieved by the year 2000, a quarter century ahead," Harrison Salisbury wrote in **The New Emperors China in the Era of Mao and Deng** (Little, Brown and Company, Boston, 1992, p.332).

At the 12th National People's Congress in 1982, Deng Xiaoping put forward his theory of "Socialism with Chinese characteristics", to modernize China, build a socialist market economy.

On 29 November 2012 when Xi Jinping, elected a fortnight earlier as CPC general secretary and chairman of the CPC Central Military Commission, visited "The Road toward Renewal" exhibition depicting the country's struggles over the past 170 years at the National Museum of China in Beijing, he spoke on attaining the goal of a moderately prosperous society on the Party's centennial in July 2021 and that of a modern socialist country that is prosperous, strong, democratic, culturally advanced and harmonious on the PRC's centenary in October 2049. And, he said: "I firmly believe that the great dream of the renewal of the Chinese nation will come true…"   27.03.2019 05:34

At the 19th National Congress of the CPC in 2018, President Xi presented the new timeline of the great rejuvenation in three stages: (1) building a moderately prosperous society in all respects by 2020, (2) basically realizing socialist modernization by 2035, and (3) making China a great, prosperous, strong, democratic, culturally advanced, harmonious, and beautiful socialist country by 2049 -- to mark the centenary of New China, the People's Republic of China (PRC) in October 2049.   26.03.2019 19:15

11.08.2018 16:39 17:07
11pages 3,396 words 30.08.2017 13.07.2017 10:42 18.07.2017 05:32 28.07.2017 05:45 03.08.2017 14:00 24.08.2017 13:01 19.10.2017 02:19 19.10.2017 12:29 14.01.2018 00:50 12.07.2018 21:39
12.10.2018 23:45 23:50 17.11.2018 22:15 15.12.2018 02:25 26.03.2019 19:19 27.03.2019 05:37

CHINA A(1)
FIVE-YEAR PLAN

New Development Paradigm To Further China's Modernisation

(A) China's Thirteenth Five- Year Plan (2016-2020)

Taking three years and picking the brains of thousands of Chinese scientists, engineers, academics, economists, and military experts, China formulated its new blueprint of national development to lend further momentum in its "Long March" to Modernization – through the development of the country's technological prowess and national self-reliance and self-sufficiency, with a very bold and highly comprehensive development model based on indigenous creativity, ingenuity and innovativeness. What's known as the **Thirteenth Five-Year Plan (2016-2020), or the 13FYP in brief**, was ratified by the National People's Congress and made public in March 2016.

The **13FYP** is strongly underpinned by the **National Medium- and Long-Term Plan (2006-2020) for Science and Technology Development (referred to in short as the MLP)**, drawn up earlier under the aegis of President Hu Jintao (2003-2013) and Premier Wen Jiabao who both saw the first two decades of the 21st century as opening and providing a "window" of extraordinary and strategic opportunity for China to catch up with the world's leading advanced economic, military and technological powers.

The landmark **MLP** has targeted over a dozen megaprojects to promote China's long-term global competitiveness, including (1) core electronics, high-end general chips and basic software, (2) ULSI (Ultra Large Scale Integration) manufacturing technology with complete sets (suites) of technology to match, (3) next generation (5G) broadband wireless mobile communication, (4) high-end CNC (Computer Numerical Control/computer-automated) machine tools, (5) development of large gas fields and coal-bed methane, (6) large-scale advanced pressurized water reactor (PWR) nuclear reactors, (7) water pollution control and treatment, (8) genetic transformation breeding of new plants, (9) new major drugs, (10) prevention and control of infectious diseases, (11) high-resolution Earth observation system, (12) large passenger aircraft, (13) manned space flight and lunar exploration.

On May 2016, the Chinese authorities in Beijing announced the details of China's **innovation-driven development strategy (IDDS)**, which will transform China into a global innovation champion in three stages over the next 30 years: (1) Becoming an "innovation nation" by 2020, through an innovation friendly environment with enhanced property rights, improved incentives, and a comprehensive set of policies and regulations; (2) Strong support for basic research in strategic industries to achieve important breakthroughs by 2025, and to enter the top tier of innovation leaders by 2030, and to attain the capability to compete with the advanced manufacturing powers by 2035; and (3) Becoming a foremost global manufacturer and leading the world in science and technology (S&T) by 2049, to commemorate the centenary of New China (established October 1949).

Addressing the National Science, Technology and Innovation Conference May 2016, President Xi Jinping emphasized the main thrust of the **IDDS** innovation strategy in developing original and cutting-edge innovations, building big science projects, balancing the roles of state and market, and stressing both innovation in science and technology (S&T) and innovation of institutional measures and mechanisms.

"In the global race for economic, technological and innovation leadership, China is a late entrant but has made impressive progress in closing the gap at the top by harnessing abundant resources accumulated through nearly four decades of high-octane growth, and a voracious appetite for foreign technology and know-how," Tai Ming Cheung and colleagues in the University of California Institute of Global Conflict and Cooperation reported on July 2016. (1)

As Cheung and colleagues have reported, the Thirteenth Plan incorporates as well other major blueprints such as **Made in China 2025** (released May 2015) and **Internet Plus Plan** (released July 2015), two strategic development plans for the next crucial decade and beyond, in response to broad trends in global manufacturing and information technology (IT) development under the label of **"Industry 4.0" aka the Fourth Industrial Revolution** after steam, electrical power, and computer.

Industry 4.0 leverages 9 technological areas: (1) autonomous, (2) simulation, (3) horizontal and vertical integration, (4) Internet of Things (IoT), (5) cybersecurity, (6) cloud computing, (7) additive manufacturing (3-D printing), (8) augmented reality, and (9) big data and analytics.

On 5 March 2015, Premier Li Keqiang proposed "Internet Plus" as a development strategy to restructure China's economy and maintain its growth momentum (6%-7% growth per annum), principally through integrating mobile Internet, cloud computing, big data and the Internet of Things (IoT) with modern manufacturing.

"The Internet of Things is like a new kind of language. It will enable everything to 'talk' with us through the Internet, which in turn will spur innovation and generate new business models," said Zhou Hongyi, CEO of Internet security and search company Qihoo 360.

According to Liu Qiangdong, CEO of e-commerce site JD.com, in future no products can be termed commodities unless they are connected and linked to the Internet.

China has reportedly attached great importance to R&D of the IoT. But, according to one recent report, Chinese innovation has contributed to only 30%, as compared with 70% of advanced economies.

According to many experts, if China succeeds in developing its IoT capability, the new technology will create a fresh market worth several trillion yuan.

The 13th Plan (**13FYP**) highlights technological innovation as the backbone and core of China's new development paradigm. According to **MIC 2025**, manufacturing is essential for China to self-build into a global power, organically and doctrinally based on the characteristically and essentially Chinese concept of **CNP (Comprehensive National Power)**.

Speaking at the second World Intelligence Congress (WIC) in Tianjin 17 May 2018, Zhou Ji, President of Chinese Academy of Engineering, said that smart manufacturing must be used widely used by 2025, and intelligent manufacturing should be a leading force in China's manufacturing by 2035.

(B) Innovation and Technology in China's 13th Five-Year Development Plan

At its 18th National Congress held in November 2012, the Communist Party of China (CPC) proposed a comprehensive strategy of **innovation-driven development**, stressing the great significance of scientific and technological innovation in improving productivity and overall national strength.

In a statement released in Beijing on 3 November 2015 relating to the Party's proposal on the 13th Five-year Plan (2016-2020), President Xi said China must upgrade innovation in key areas of science and technology (S&T) to strive for a series of breakthroughs by 2030. (2)

Targeted projects include aircraft engines, quantum teleportation, intelligent manufacturing and robotics, deep space and deep sea probes, new materials, brain science and health-related science.

The prioritized projects will help China break free technologically from foreign dominance. Moreover, they present challenges and opportunities in newly emerging sectors for innovation at the technological frontiers. Xi said China has moved from the stage of "busy catching up" with developed countries to occasionally setting the pace.

Earlier on August 2014, China selected 16 scientific and technological projects of national importance, including universal chips/semiconductors, broadband and mobile telecommunications, digitally controlled machines, and nuclear power (an audacious, if not also controversial, move to take the country to the forefront of a nuclear renaissance, in the wake of the 2011 Fukushima disaster in Japan).

China also needs urgently to build national laboratories with top-notch talent from within and without, with international peer recognition and the capacity for innovation that warrants global influence, Xi said.

On 21 December 2015, the 5th Plenary Session of the 18th CPC Central Committee proposed five guiding developmental principles which subsequently were adopted and incorporated into the 13th Plan. (3)

The five cardinal principles of China's socio-economic development are: **(1) innovation, (2) coordinated growth, (3) green development, (4) opening up (globalisation), and (5) inclusiveness (sustainable and inclusive development for all).**

INNOVATION is the master key word in national development. Whatever impetus is needed to promote growth, has to come from innovation.

"In traditional industries, China must import the best technologies from abroad," said Dr Robert Lawrence Kuhn, American intellectual and China expert, on **CCTV** 14 November 2012, in presenting China's innovation as a national mission. "To leap ahead, China must innovate in areas where all countries are just beginning, where everyone is standing on the same starting line..." (4)

Launched in March 2016, the Thirteenth Five-Year Plan (2016-2020) will run its course until the first quarter of 2021, the centenary of the Communist Party of China (CPC) which was founded on 1 July 1921.

The landmark **13FYP** has two defining major national goals to be achieved by 2020: (1) the doubling of China's 2010 GDP and per capita income to transcend the so-called "middle-income trap" and to transition to high-income economy, and (2) the development of a moderately prosperous society in all aspects (comprehensively), which officially entails eradication of poverty. (5)

The country's economic restructuring will upgrade and transform 8 key areas: finance, agriculture, high-end equipment, strategic emerging industries, informationization, new-type urbanization, regional development, and ocean-related development (including ocean engineering equipment and high-tech vessels). Strategic emerging industries, from 5G communications and advanced sensors to remote sensing satellites, are all slated for large-scale commercial applications.

In his first speech as general secretary on 15 November 2012, Xi noted that China has entered a critical stage of building a moderately prosperous society, which is a key step towards the Chinese dream of the great national rejuvenation (and total modernization).

Fundamentally, Xi said, the task is about development, with emphasis on promoting social and economic development, and improving human capital (human intelligence, talent, creativity, and knowledge as the driving force of society's wealth, strength, and well-being).

According to Xi, comprehensively building a moderately prosperous society is of strategic importance to China's "Four Comprehensives" blueprint, including comprehensively deepening reform, comprehensively advancing the rule of law, and comprehensively strengthening Party discipline. (6)   05.06.2017 20:07

(C)(1) Innovation-driven Development

The message is clear: China's future as a global power rests on its ability to develop and manage an **innovation-driven economy**.

The **13FYP** has 10 main objectives, including maintaining the sustainable momentum of economic growth, restructuring and transforming the pattern of socio-economic development, optimizing and upgrading the country's industrialization, promoting and maximizing innovation-driven development, accelerating agricultural modernization, reforming institutional mechanisms, promoting coordinated growth intra-regionally and inter-regionally, strengthening ecological construction, improving the people's livelihood and welfare, and promoting pro-poor development in the national drive of eradicating poverty.

Innovation-driven development is to turbo-charge the engines of China's growth, to further strengthen the country's innovativeness and Chinese innovative capabilities in science and technology (S&T) as well as to further harness the vast potential of Chinese entrepreneurship and the immeasurable human resource of the world's greatest developing nation.

Mass entrepreneurship and innovation are to leverage China's immense human capital, talent and energy of some 800 million workers on a scale unprecedented in human history. They will further develop the humongous network of commercial and industrial bases of some 70 million small- and medium-sized enterprises (SMEs) to accelerate and grow fresh sources of socio-economic growth. (7)

The mainspring of China's development strategy, innovation and technology are designed to ratchet Chinese manufacturing up the technological ladder and as well up the value-added chain, to enhance the country's global competitiveness and to further hone its technological cutting edge in key sectors of the national economy.   2,025 words
06.06.2017 18:23

The **13FYP** calls for speeding up construction of a new generation infrastructure, development of 5G telecommunication technology, and implementation of the **Internet Plus programme** (released July **2015),** and harnessing the power of connectivity of the Internet technologies to revolutionize production and organization.

Internet Plus will capitalize on China's huge online consumer market. **Internet Plus** will build up domestic mobile Internet, cloud computing, Big Data, and the Internet of Things (IoT) sectors, and help create a class of global competitors by assisting domestic firms to expand and operate abroad.

Artificial Intelligence (AI) will also be harnessed to generate further economic growth driven by innovative, internet-related technologies.   12.10.2018 22:10

The **13FYP** will increase fixed broadband household penetration from 40% in 2015 to 70% in 2020, and mobile broadband subscriber penetration from 57% in 2015 to 85% by 2020.

In June 2016 China had 710 million Internet users. Over 800 million by the end of 2018.

China's Big Data market is expected to grow from RMB 110.5 billion (US$17 billion) to RMB 879 billion (US$135.2 billion) by 2020.

The government has set up 780 investment funds worth nearly $326 billion (RMB 2.18 trillion) by end of 2015.

According to a January 2017 statement issued by the National Development and Reform Commission (NDRC) and Ministry of Industry and Information Technology (MIIT), China will invest $179.1 billion (RMB 1.26 trillion) to improve broadband and mobile networks from 2016 to 2018, for construction of over 56,000 miles (90,000 km) of high-speed fibre optic cables and 2 million 4G base stations.

In the informationization of commerce and industry, its focus is on **quality manufacturing**, rather than sheer quantity or scale, and clean as well "green" production for both product quality and environmental protection.

Released on 25 May 2015, **Made in China 2025 (MIC 2025)** documents a 10-year (2015-2025) development programme and strategy to focus on manufacturing innovations and integration of information and manufacturing technologies, to develop intelligent manufacturing capabilities, and to upgrade 10 key sectors:

(1)   Energy saving and new energy vehicles (NEVs)
(2)   Next generation information technology

(3) Biotechnology, biomedicine, and high-performance medical devices

(4) New materials (8)

(5) Aerospace and aviation equipment

(6) Ocean engineering equipment and high-tech vessels

(7) Railways and rail equipment for an advanced digitally networked world-class rail transportation system

(8) Robotics

(9) Electrical power equipment, mainly nuclear and renewable energy, and

(10) Advanced agricultural production machinery.

Technologically, China is zeroing in on 6 leading-edge technologies for rapid development and eventual large-scale commercialization: (1) Information Technology (IT), (2) New Materials, (3) Advanced Manufacturing with extreme manufacturing technologies and intelligent service advanced machine tools, (4) Marine Technologies for 3D maritime environmental monitoring, fast, multi-parameter ocean floor survey, and deep sea operational technologies, (5) Advanced Energy Technologies including hydrogen energy and fuel-cell technologies, alternative fuels, and (6) Laser and Aerospace Technologies, particularly chemical and solid state laser technologies to eventually field a weapon-grade system for ground-based and airborne platforms.

China aspires to achieve 70% self-sufficiency in high-tech industries by 2025, and to advance to the vanguard in global high-tech manufacturing by 2049 -- the centenary of New China.   11.08.2018 17:41

The government has earmarked 16 "major special items" to develop indigenous capabilities, including core electronic components, high-end universal chips and operating system software, very large-scale (VLS) integrated circuit manufacturing, next-generation broadband wireless mobile communications, high-grade numerical machine tools, large aircraft, high-resolution satellites, and lunar exploration. (9)

The **13FYP** also seeks to deepen China's Energy Revolution by establishing a modern energy system that is clean, low-carbon and efficient.

2,697 words 08.06.2017 19:49

C (2) Coordinated Development and Growth

Coordinated growth is to help resolve long-existing disparities in regional development, redundant construction, industrial duplication, and shortfalls in public services – through improvements in regional intergovernmental coordination of policies, planning and allocation of resources, through accelerated new-type urbanization, *hukou* (household registration) reform, and through construction of city clusters to maximize sustained socio-economic growth and productivity on the scale of greater agglomeration.

The central government seeks intergovernmental coordination to improve public services including education, healthcare and social security, public transport and utilities like electricity and water supply, promotion of innovation, law enforcement, and environmental conservation.

As some 16 million farmers (more than the population of the kingdom of Belgium and over twice the population of the republic of Singapore) migrate annually to the cities and towns, China will continue to build the necessary infrastructure including housing, water and power supply, transportation, and internet services to serve the whole country.

The required measures will be taken to accelerate urbanizing the millions of rural migrants, to accommodate and absorb them into the mainstream of society.

Comprehensive and coordinated development seeks to optimize cooperation, collaboration and coordination between and among regions to address, adjust and balance current and long-term issues of the socio-economic development of China's rural and urban areas.

World-class city clusters will be built strategically in the Beijing-Tianjin-Hebei region to the northeast, Yangtze River Delta in the middle of the country and Pearl River Delta to its south, Chengdu-Chongqing region (in South west and central), and Shandong Peninsula (NE China).

According to a report by Li Yan in **People's Daily Online** May 26, 2017, these three regions have the country's most dynamic economies, with the highest levels of openness, and strongest capacity for innovation.

The strengths of each area will be bonded and meshed synergistically to speed up overall development; for example, Hebei's lower labour costs, Tianjin's good infrastructure and logistics, and Beijing's pulling power as the national capital and centre of government, politics, culture, and technological innovation.

City clusters are designed and destined to become mega-hubs in the montage of national development and growth.

A comprehensive transportation system will be developed. Over RMB 15 trillion (US$2.2 trillion) will be invested to develop domestic transportation from 2016 to 2020.

By 2020, China will have 150,000 km of railway lines including 30,000 km HSR (High Speed Rail) to serve 80% of big cities with a population of one million or more, and 5 million km of roads, including 36 new highways, and 260 airports.

Accelerated new-type urbanisation

"What we stress is a new type of urbanization that puts people in the heart (of it)," Premier Li Keqiang said in March 2013. "It needs the support of job creation and provision of services…"

China's urbanisation will be stepped up from 56.1% in 2015 to 60% by 2020, in tandem with creation of over 50 million jobs, further *hukou* reform, and renovation of "rundown urban areas" with construction or renovation of a total 20 million residential units.

About 260 million rural residents (very close to the entire population of Indonesia, the largest country in Southeast Asia) have migrated to urban areas over the past three decades, many of them without access to urban public housing, education and other public services.

The **13FYP** will increase the registration of permanent urban residents from 39% in 2015 to 45% of the population in 2020.

According to a 2010 survey by the State Council's Research Development Center, the lifetime costs of providing the urban social services system to estimated 260 million migrant workers and their families would come to around RMB 20.8 trillion (about US$3.1 trillion).

Released on March 2014, the **National Plan on New Urbanisation (2014-2020)** incentivizes rural migration to third- and fourth-tier cities by making it easier to obtain *hukou* (national household registration) and providing affordable housing for 100 million current residents through renovation of shanty towns and new construction.

Estimated/expected total costs of 3 major initiatives under the 13th Plan:

Urbanization (2014-2020) RMB 42 trillion (US$6.3 trillion)

Healthcare (2015-2020) RMB 2 trillion (US$298.9 billion)

Green Energy and Environmental RMB 10 trillion (US$1.5 trillion)

3,336 words 09.06.2017 19:21

C (3) Green Development

The green light of development focuses on the national commitment to redressing severe environmental degradation, and signals China's shift to clean production, low carbon economy, conservation of resources, and sustainable growth.

The 13th Plan (**13FYP**) highlights environmental quality as a core issue. **13FYP** emphasizes 19 ecological and environmental projects to protect the environment and to enhance efficient use of resources: 5 energy conservation and recycling, 6 environmental rehabilitation and protection, and 8 projects to restore mountains, lakes, rivers, and forests.

Out of 25 FYP targets, 10 are environmental and binding as well — to be met by 2020 – including a cap on energy use, and targets for city air quality, carbon dioxide intensity, and reduction of soil and water contamination.

Targets are set to reduce China's water consumption by 23%, energy use by 15%, and carbon dioxide emissions by 18% per unit of GDP.

While improving the ecological environment and upgrading efficiency in resource utilization, China is also determined to achieve atmospheric haze control by 2020. The target is over 292 days of good air quality per year at prefecture level and above, as well as substantial cuts in obnoxious and deleterious PM2.5 concentrations.

China has contributed 58% of global energy conservation over the past couple of decades. China has also contributed about a quarter (24%-25%) of the global growth in renewable energy installed capacity. (10)

While sticking to the strictest environmental protection domestically, China remains strongly committed to global environmental conservation and duty-bound to "deeply participate in global climate governance".

A nationwide real-time online environmental monitoring system will be set up, and an air emission permit system will cover all companies with stationary pollution sources.

Forest protection will be upgraded, with the banning of commercial deforestation and the planned expansion of forested areas. While more land will be returned for agriculture, pasture protection will be improved. (11)

As for water conservation, the most stringent management will duly be implemented for the country's precious water resources, and a groundwater monitoring system will be established to check gross pollution and over-exploitation.   3,692 words o9.06.2017 20:28,

C (4) Opening up, Openness and Globalization

China's policy and strategy for greater openness and connectivity with the rest of the world has various objectives, including expanding overall trade (export/import) and two-way investment, promoting the internationalization of the *renminbi* (RMB), enhancing China's role in global economic governance, and expanding intra-regional as well as inter-regional development within the country such as the Beijing-Tianjin-Hubei (BTH), Yangtze Economic Belt (YEB) and Pearl River Delta (PRD) projects, and taking part in joint development with neighbouring countries and territories beyond through the **One Belt One Road (OBOR) Initiative** (also known as the **Belt and Road Initiative/BRI**) to harness international resources in win-win ventures to develop infrastructure, services and trade.

China has invested over US$30 billion in service industries in countries along the "Belt and Road" to strengthen international cooperation in key fields including technology, culture, finance, architecture, and service outsourcing through the OBOR/BRI Initiative. (12)

The opening up policy is expected to boost the share of services trade to 16% of China's total foreign trade by 2020.

Originated and launched by President Xi Jinping in 2013, the **OBOR/BRI development strategy** encompasses (1) the **Silk Road Economic Belt (SREB)** to expand and modernise the ancient overland trade route (the fabled conduit of China's 3,000-year-old sericulture) from China through Central Asia to Europe, and (2) the **21ˢᵗ Century Maritime Silk Road (21MSR**, which had its historical antecedents during the Song Dynasty 960-1279 AD), starting in Guangzhou in East China's Fujian province to the south, then crossing the Malacca Strait in Southeast Asia, traversing Kuala Lumpur at the core of the Malaysian mainland to Nairobi, the capital of Kenya in East Africa, by the Indian Ocean, the Horn of Africa, and through the Red Sea to the Mediterranean, and moving on to Venice, a port in NE Italy, once a great commercial and maritime power in the late 14ᵗʰ century.

Xi's **OBOR/BRI** represents a game- changing break from the historical walling up of the Middle Kingdom to the historic opening up of New China to the whole world, for closer international cooperation on a voluntary win-win basis for all participating countries. **OBOR/BRI** provides an open platform for global collaboration and cooperation, not collusion from within nor conflict without, and all for the common good. Come to think of it, it appears to be a smart move to thwart any attempt by another country to contain China!

According to the Asian Development Bank (ADB), the Asian region, home to 60% of the world's population, requires more than US$26 trillion worth of infrastructure development by 2030 to keep national economies growing. (13)

According to HSBC, about three billion people in today's emerging markets will join the middle classes by 2030, a social change that will pull the centre of gravity of human consumption towards Asia. (14)

The completion of needed new infrastructure will simplify supply chains, speed up physical trade, and lower the costs of doing business, according to HSBC. And, China anticipates its trade with OBOR/BRI partners to surpass US$2.5 trillion annually in the next decade.

Mukhtar Hussain, chief executive officer of HSBC Bank Malaysia Bhd, has described **OBOR (BRI)** as "ambitious and positive". He has said that by boosting investment," we can boost trade, because this in turn will boost gross domestic product." (15)

"China has not just the resources, which is key, but also the vision and desire and strategy to push its engagement outside its borders," Afghan ambassador to Beijing Janan Mosazai said on the eve of the "Belt and Road Forum", held at the Chinese capital and attended by leaders from 28 countries and others on 13-15 May 2017. (16)

A a news conference on 15 May 2017, President Xi said, "It is our hope that through the 'Belt and Road' development, we will unleash new forces for global economic growth..." (17)   4,370 words 11.06.2017 17:33

C (5) Comprehensive Development and Inclusive Growth

With its strong emphasis on inclusive growth to benefit all Chinese citizens, the **13th Five-Year Plan** has set specific targets to raise the people's standard of living, alleviate/eradicate poverty on the ground, improve/extend accessibility and affordability of healthcare, education and other essential public services, and further promote education for the complete modernization of New China.

With its 1ˢᵗ Five-Year Plan (1953-58), New China started its Long March of Modernization; the national grand objective aka the Chinese Dream is to complete China's modernization towards the end of the 19ᵗʰ Five-Year Plan (2046-2050).

To expand Chinese entrepreneurship and strengthen China's innovativeness and national innovation in science and technology, the **13ᵗʰ Plan** banks on mass entrepreneurship and innovation to leverage the nation's vast human resource of some 800 million employees and its extensive network of commercial and industrial bases for over 70 million small and medium-sized enterprises (SMEs) to create and grow new sources of economic growth and social development.

Prioritizing development of strategic emerging industries, smart manufacturing and modern services (production and consumption) and strengthening innovation in science and technology the **13FYP** will inevitably impact strongly on the future of the business community and the national economy.

Technological and business model innovations are nurturing waves of entrepreneurs and formidable competitors in China, according to a recent report by Dr Wendy Hong, Denise Cheung, and David Sit of Kowloon/Hong Kong-based Fung Business Intelligence Centre. (18)

"In particular, China is one of the leaders in business-model innovation. Many Chinese companies are changing the rules of traditional business with innovative models," Hong, Cheung and Sit have written.

But, fundamental to China's comprehensive, innovative and inclusive development is the country's well-being, prosperity and strength as well as the people's livelihood and wherewithal.

The cutting edge of **13FYP** development will hopefully excise and eradicate poverty by lifting the remaining 50 million indigent Chinese out of the poverty trap while building a moderately prosperous nation in all aspects by 2020.

"Without prosperity in rural China, particularly those impoverished areas, we can't complete building a moderately prosperous society in all aspects," said Xi Jinping in his first speech after being elected as the general secretary of the CPC on November 2012.

If fulfilled by 2020, it means that the transformative national goal of the world's largest developing country will be reached one human generation earlier than its original 2049 timeline which was to mark the centenary of New China on October 2049.

4,806 words 18 pages 11.06.2017 18:45

ADDENDUM

Industrial Internet (II) Development

According to the State Council's November 2017 guideline for integrating industry and the Internet in the development of China's "Industrial Internet" (II), the new II infrastructure will be complete to cover all regions and sectors by 2025. (19)

By 2035, China will lead the world in the key areas of the II, and by mid-century China should be among the top countries in terms of its overall strength in industrial internet.

The II guideline lists 11 major tasks and projects, such as increasing internet speed and reducing costs, setting industrial internet standards, establishing innovation centers, and improving network security.

Also, expanding equal market access, strengthening fiscal support, and stepping up direct financing.

The guideline also prioritizes development of advanced manufacturing that is smart and green. Of 260 pilot projects selected by the Ministry of Industry and Information Technology (MIIT), 28 are related to industrial internet innovation.

The bottom line: enhancing the international competitiveness (IC) of China's manufacturing sector, the world's largest, in line with **Made in China 2025 (MIC 2025)** development strategy.

According to the MIIT, China will also strive to build itself into a leading world cyber power by 2035, by advancing development of IT and Internet applications through a series of strategic projects to make breakthroughs in key technologies and accelerating the upgrading of the Internet. (20)

Since **MIC 2025** has worked up such a storm in a teacup although it remains largely a paper tiger until its successful completion, the enlightening comments by Lorand Laskai, a research associate in the Asia Studies Program at the Council on Foreign Relations, justify further consideration and contemplation (21):

"… Made in China 2025 is a blueprint for Beijing's plan to transform the economy into a high-tech powerhouse that dominates advanced industries like robotics, advanced information technology, aviation, and new energy vehicles. The ambition makes sense within the context of China's development strategy: countries typically aim to transition away from labor-intensive industries and climb the value-added chain as wages rise, lest they fall into the so-called "middle-income trap." Chinese policymakers have diligently studied the German concept "Industry 4.0," which shows how advanced technology like wireless sensors and robotics, when combined with the internet, can yield significant gains in productivity, efficiency, and precision…

"… Made in China 2025 calls for "self sufficiency" through technology substitution while becoming a "manufacturing superpower" that dominates the global market in critical high-tech industries. That could be a problem for countries that rely on exporting high-tech products or the global supply chain for high-tech components…

"Made in China 2025 lays out targets for achieving 70% "self-sufficiency" in core components and basic materials in industries like acrospace equipment and telecommunication equipment by 2025…"   11.01.2019 05:4

On 14 November 2018 the U.S.-China Economic and Security Review Commission stated in its Report to Congress (p. 444): "… The influential "Internet Plus" and "Made in China 2025" initiatives seek to capitalize on the rise of integrated digital economy and automation to transition China's economy to higher-value-added manufacturing and services and transform China into a technological powerhouse. Internet Plus seeks to leverage

China's huge online consumer market to build up the country's domestic mobile internet, cloud computing, big data, and the IoT, and create global competitors by assisting domestic firms' expansion abroad.

"Made in China reiterates China's long-held indigenous innovation and import substitution goals, but is larger in scope, resources, and intergovernmental coordination than previous plans…"   28.03.2019 17:01

Notes China's Five-Year Plan

1. Report by Tai Ming Cheung and co-authors, PLANNING FOR INNOVATION, prepared for the U.S.-China Economic and Security Review Commission, July 2016. **uscc.gov**

2. Xinhua/Beijing 2015-11-04 14-11-04
    Staff Research Report February 14, 2017 by Katherine Koleski, Research Director and Policy Analyst, Economics and Trade, U.S.-China Economic and Security Review Commission. **uscc.gov**

3. Zhang Honyin **People's Daily** 15:20 December 21, 2015

4. **english.cntv.cn** 14 November 2012

5. The attainment of middle-income status and "a moderately prosperous society" by 2020 is about three decades (one human generation) ahead of Deng Xiaoping's original target and timeline.

About two decades after Deng's formulation, two eminent Indian scientists APJ Abdul Kalam and Y.S. Rajan wrote in their book first published in 1998 and then in 2002 by Penguin **INDIA 2020**:

"The Chinese vision is to prepare the country into the ranks of mid-level developed nations by the middle of the twenty-first century. Acceleration of the nation's economic growth and social development by relying on advances in science and technology is pivotal in this…" (p. 33)

A top scientist and mastermind of India's satellite and missile technologies, Abdul Kalam (1931-2015) served as India's 11th President (2002-2007).

Scientific Secretary in the Office of the Principal Scientific Advisers to the Government of India, Rajan (born 1943) was a close associate of Kalam's.

"A developed India by 2020 or even earlier is not a dream," they wrote on 10 July 1998 (p. xv).

6. **People's Daily Online** 13:36 February 28, 2015

"If China is to flourish and rejuvenate, it must vigorously develop science and technology and strive to become the world's major scientific center and innovative highland," President Xi Jinping said on 28 May 2018 in a major speech at the 19th Academician Meeting of the Chinese Academy of Sciences (CAS) and the 14th Academician Meeting of the Chinese Academy of Engineering (CAE).

"Self-reliance is the basis for the struggle of the Chinese nation to stand on its own footing in the world," Xi stressed.   12.07.2018 22:09

7. Katherine Koleski, Staff Research Report Feb 14, 2017 re Note (2) above.

According to the Ministry of Human Resource and Social Security, 776.03 million Chinese were employed by the end of 2016. The primary sector (principally agriculture) accounted for 27.7% of total employment, secondary (mainly manufacturing) 28.8%, and tertiary (services etc) 43.5%. **Xinhua**/Beijing **People's Daily Online** 09:46 June 04, 2017.

As of Feb2016, there were over 2,500 business incubators, backed by a US$6.5 billion fund for business start-ups. **China Daily.com** 2016-02-26

8. New Materials to focus on specialty metals, high-performance structural materials, functional polymers, inorganic non-metals and advanced composites. To develop dual-use materials and to study disruptive materials. Also to prioritize smart materials and structures, high-temperature superconducting and highly efficient energy materials technologies.

9. ANNUAL REPORT TO CONGRESS CHINA 2016 by US Department of Defense April 2016 **freebeacon.com**

"… Technology will decide which country emerges as the world's dominant economic power in the long run. While about 20 percent of per-capita gross domestic product (GDP) growth is driven by labor and capital, the remaining 80 percent is determined by how rapidly an economy is developing and applying new technology to increase production," Ruchir Sharma, chief global strategist at Morgan Stanley Investment Management and contributing opinion writer, wrote June 28, 2018 in The Coming Tech Battle With China in **The New York Times (nytimes.com)**.

"China's ambition to catch up to Western living standards thus depends largely on how rapidly it can match or surpass Western technology…"   12.10.2018 23:04

Tom Holland, former staffer of **South China Morning Post (SCMP)**, wrote 2 July 2018 on China's ambition to leapfrog technologically and dominate burgeoning fields like AI and aerospace.

"Much of the international attention has focused on the old-fashioned import substitution elements of these plans, with Beijing typically aiming for Chinese companies to capture a three-quarter share of the domestic market over the next 10 years.

"But Beijing's plans go far beyond import substitution. In semiconductors for example, state planners want Chinese companies to command a third of the international market by 2030. And in artificial intelligence (AI), they are aiming at nothing less than global dominance…"

12.10.2018 23:27

10. NPC/CPCC report 2016-03-11 **china.org.cn**
11. **Xinhua** 2015-11-04 **xinhuanet.com**
12. Li Yan **People's Daily Online en.people.cn** 13:24 May 31, 2017
13. **AP**/Beijing report in **New Straits Times** May 13, 2017
14. **New Straits Times** May 11, 2017
15. **New Straits Times** May 11, 2017
16. **New Straits Times** May 13, 2017
17. **AP**/Beijing report in **New Straits Times** May 16, 2017

In a commentary in **Global Asia** June 26, 2018, policy analyst at RAND Corporation Ali Wyne noted that between 2000 and 2017, China's manufacturing increased from about a quarter of America's manufacturing output to more than that of the US and Japan combined.

China overtook Germany as the world's largest exporter in 2009, and displaced the US as the world's largest goods trader in 2013.

China accounted for some 34% of global economic growth between 2012 and 2016.   12.10.2018 22:50

18. China's Policy Think Piece November 2015 <u>China's 13th Five-Year Plan (2016-2020) Redefining China's development paradigm under the New Normal</u> **fbicgroup.com**

According to long-time futurist highly prolific website author (over 20,000 articles) Brian Wang, China should become a high income country by about 2023 as per the World Bank's criteria of a gross national income (GNI) per capita of US$12,236

(2016) as calculated by the Atlas method. **nextbigfuture.com** 24 October 2017

18(a) On his tour of Xuzhou Construction Machinery Group (XCMG), world's fifth largest construction machinery manufacturer, 12 Dec 2017, President Xi Jinping called for more innovation in the equipment manufacturing sector in order to accelerate China's drive towards becoming a manufacturing powerhouse, and to bolster the real economy,

Innovation is the source of business core competitiveness, Xi said after a briefing on XCMG's intelligent assembly lines and big data platform. He urged state-owned enterprises and others to "blaze a new trail (of modernisation) from high-speed growth to high-quality development", as well as to contribute more to China's two centennial goals (the 2021 goal of comprehensive moderate development, and the 2049 goal of a completely modernized and fully developed nation). **CCTV** Dec12, 2017 04.06.2017 17:51 1,780 words 05.06.2017 20:06 08.06.2017 19:52

Central China's Hunan Province has embarked on an ambitious 5-year plan to upgrade its heavy industries and migrate to intelligent manufacturing with advanced technologies like virtual design, simulation, AI, automation, etc.

According to **CCTV** report August 2, 2018, Hunan has made breakthroughs in equipment making, supercomputers, ultra-high-speed ground transportation, and China's first commercial science experiment satellite.

Hunan is now targeting 20 new industries in rail transportation and engineering machineries to build world-class industrial cluster of intelligent manufacturing.

Speaking at the Second World Intelligence Conference (WIC) in north China's Tianjin Municipality on 17 May 2018, Zhou Ji,

President of Chinese Academy of Engineering, said that smart manufacturing must be widely used across the nation by 2025, and intelligent manufacturing should feature as a leading force in China's manufacturing industries by 2035.   12.10.2018 22:32

Breakthroughs is the buzzword. The Pentagon report on 9 August 2018 for the establishment of the new US Space Force by 2020 highlights "Bold breakthroughs designed to obsolesce competitors" on top of its development priorities.   11.08.2018 18:28

18(b) "… China has developed a leading global economy faster than any country in modern history. This transformation began with the reform and opening up of China's economy under Deng Xiaoping in 1978 (with GNP of about $217 billion).

"By 2015, China's GDP was $11.4 trillion compared to the US at $18 trillion. However, in purchasing power parity (PPP), China is already (since 2013-2014) slightly larger than the U.S. This represents the first time the US has not been the largest economy since it overtook the U.K. in 1872," Michael Brown and Pavneet Singh have written in their February 2017 publication **China's Technology Transfer Strategy**… Brown is a White House Presidential Innovation Fellow working with DIUx where Singh is a consultant.

They have written: "Since the US economy is growing at 1-3% and China's is growing at 5-7%, the trajectory is clear in narrowing the GDP gap (some projections show China's GDP exceeding ours (the US) within the next decade).

"The time scale during which this growth occurred is stunning as China's economy has grown from 10% of the U.S. economy in the 1970s to the second largest global economy (with $6 trillion in 2010 to overtake Japan's) in just fifty years. Analogous growth in the U.S. economy to global leadership took a century to achieve.

"From this point forward (from 13 FYP 2016-2020), China plans to further transform its economy through a national focus on technology and indigenous innovation with a goal to reduce U.S. relevance and be double the size of the U.S. economy by 2050. (Pillsbury, The Hundred-Year Marathon)

"To accomplish this, China aims to displace the U.S. in key industries using its large market size to promote domestic champions which can become global leaders through state subsidies, access to low-cost capital and limiting China's domestic market access to foreign companies… (the basics of the SOP in emerging economies, the tried and tested practices of countries like Japan, South Korea, Taiwan, etc to catch up with the developed economies of the West)…"

18(c) "Practice repeatedly tells us, key core technology cannot be demanded, bought or begged," President Xi said on 28 May 2018, speaking on innovation.

"Only by firmly grasping key core technology in our hands can we fundamentally guarantee national economic security, national defense and other security."

(Michael Martina et al June 25, 2018 **reuters.com**)

In **South China Morning Post (scmp.com)**, Sidney Leng and Zheng Yangpeng reported 26 June 2018:

"… Made in China 2025, an ambitious plan to give the country a leading edge on several hi-tech fronts, has become a thorny issue between China and its trading partners, including the US (on the point of waging a trade war with China, Europe and much of the rest of the world, an economic offensive scheduled to start with an initial hit list of 25% tariffs on $50 billion worth in Chinese goods on July 6, 2018)) and the EU.*

"The plan aims to make China a tech superpower by calling for a dramatic increase in domestically made products in 10 sectors -- from robotics to biopharmaceuticals -- that the government hopes will accelerate an industrial upgrade as economic growth slows (in the process of economic maturation)…"

*"The destiny of the United States need not be written in Japan (which in 1990-1991 had a trade surplus of about $50 billion with the US)," Leon Anderson, an American businessman and director of a Pennsylvania-based consulting firm, wrote in his 1992 book **JAPANESE RAGE**.

Anderson added, pointedly: "America can recover its position of economic primacy in the world (by curing its own economic ills)…"

Trump should know that on paper China's **MIC25** is but a "paper tiger", to quote Mao. Nevertheless, it's a well-formulated blueprint of the country's legitimate and eminently notable pursuits of the highest goals in economic development, cutting-edge manufacturing capabilities and technological breakthroughs to further accelerate national modernization.   12-13.10.2018 00:27

As reported by **Bloomberg News** September 6, 2018, the goals listed in the Green Book published October 2015 and updated January 2018 by the National Strategy Advisory Committee, include an envisioned share of 56% of integrated circuits in the domestic market by Chinese companies by 2020 and 80% by 2030, and 90% Chinese control by 2025 of the domestic market for new-energy vehicles (NEVs) including hybrid and pure electric cars, domestic mobile communication equipment, key parts of industrial robots, new energy, renewable energy equipment, and energy storage equipment.

Bloomberg has commented: "China is not alone in supporting its industries. Industrial policy was central to Japan's rapid growth in the 1970s and 1980s and the Made in China 2025 plan itself draws heavily from Germany's "Industry 4.0 Plan" adopted in 2013. In the U.S. breakthroughs in semiconductors, nuclear power, imaging technology and others were all aided by industrial policy, said Stephen Roach, former chairman of Morgan Stanley Asia…"

19. **CGTN** Nov 27, 2017
20. **CGTN** Dec 26, 2017
21. **cfr.org** March 28, 2018

25pages 7,450 words 11.06.2017 13.06 12.12.2017 13:37 14.01.2018 05:27 12-13.07.2018 00:10 11.08.2018 19:12 19:23 08.09.2018 20:16 13.10.2018 00:33 **11.01.2019 06:06 06:21 28.03.2019 17:07**

NEW CHINA A(2)
ECONOMY

(A) Goal of Doubling 2010 GDP in 2020 is Achievable

"Since initiating market reforms in 1978, China has shifted from a centrally-planned to a market-based economy and has experienced rapid economic and social development. GDP growth has averaged nearly 10 percent a year – the fastest sustained expansion by a major economy in history – and has lifted more than 800 million people out of poverty.

"China reached all the Millennium Development Goals (MDGs) by 2015 and made a major contribution to the achievement of the MDGs globally. Although China's GDP growth has gradually slowed since 2012, it is still impressive by current global standards," the **World Bank** states in its overview of China (last updated March 28, 2017).

China's GDP of US$218.5 billion (slightly over one-fifth of one trillion dollars) with its per capita income of US$153 for a population of 956.17 million in 1978 grew to about US$11 trillion with a per capita GDP of around US$8,000 in 2015 for a population of over 1.37 billion in 2015.

Freedom from poverty for more than 800 million Chinese was equivalent to lifting virtually China's entire population in 1970 out of perennial poverty.

As the world's second largest economy since 2010 and also as the largest contributor (around 30%) to world growth since the global financial crisis of 2008, China is credited by the World Bank for its increasingly important and influential role in development and in the global economy.

To further quote the World Bank:

"Rapid economic ascendance has brought many challenges as well (in addition to the fact that China remains a developing country with 55 million poor in the rural areas in 2015), including high inequality; rapid urbanization; challenges to environmental sustainability; and external imbalances. China also faces demographic pressure related to an aging population (over 200 million above the age of 60 and expected 300 million by 2025) and the internal migration of labour (involving about 282 million rural migrants at the end of 2016).

"Significant policy adjustments are required in order for China's growth to be sustainable. Experience shows that transitioning from middle-income (which China attained by the early 2000s) to high-income-status can be more difficult than moving up from low to middle income.

"China's 12th Five-Year Plan (2011-2015) and the newly approved 13th Five-Year Plan (2016-2020) forcefully address these issues. They highlight the development of services and measures to address environmental and social imbalances, setting targets to reduce pollution, to increase energy efficiency, to improve access to education and healthcare, and to expand social protection.

"The annual growth rate target in the 12th Five-Year Plan was 7 percent and the growth target in the 13th Five-Year Plan is 6.5 percent, reflecting the rebalancing of the economy and the focus on the quality of growth while still maintaining the objective of achieving a "moderately prosperous" society by 2020 (doubling GDP for 2010-2020)."

In 2010 China's GDP of over US$6 trillion yielded its per capita of US$4,515 for a population of 1.337 billion.

In 2016, the first year of the 13th Plan, China's GDP grew by 6.7%, the slowest in 26 years. China's GDP came to 74.4 trillion yuan (US$10.82 trillion) for a population of 1.383 billion, including 792.98 million (57.35%) urban Chinese, and 776.03 million employed.

In 2017, Beijing's growth target is about 6.5%. It has come to 6.9%.

The International Monetary Fund (IMF) has forecast 6.7% growth in 2017, and expects China's growth to average 6.4% annually during 2018-2020. (1)

According to a **Xinhua** report published in **China Daily** 2017-03-15, China's GDP is forecast to exceed 90 trillion yuan (US$13 trillion) by 2020 for a population of about 1.42 billion. That will translate into a 2020 per capita GDP of slightly over US$9,200, prettily twice the amount of 2010.   620 words

(B) China's Developing Digital Economy

(1)What's Digital Economy & Its Importance

Based on digital computing technologies, the digital economy (DE) is also known as the Internet Economy, the New Economy, or Web Economy, fused and intertwined with the traditional economy. (2)

According to the Geneva-based World Economic Forum (WEC), the exponential growth in digitization and internet connectivity is the backbone of the Fourth Industrial Revolution. (3)

Digitization is transforming business models, the policy landscape and social norms.

Calling for, and promoting private-public collaboration in order to realize digital technology's potential to benefit humankind, the WEC has recently launched various initiatives including its 2015 Digital Transformation of Industries (DTI) project to change business models, and its 2016 project for a digital-ready trade policy to empower new forms of commerce in the increasingly digital-driven economy.

According to the European Commission (EC), the envisioned digital transformation of EU businesses and society presents enormous potential for Europe. (4)

European industry can build on its strengths in advanced digital technologies and its strong presence in traditional sectors to seize the range of opportunities that technologies such as the Internet of Things (IoT), big data, advanced manufacturing, robotics, 3D printing, blockchain technologies and artificial intelligence (AI) offer.

The EC also points out that digital transformation is characterised by a fusion of advanced technologies and the integration of physical and digital systems, the predominance of innovative business models and new processes, and the creation of smart products and services.

Currently, however, EU businesses for various factors and reasons are not taking full advantage of these advanced technologies or the innovative business models offered by the collaborative economy.

According to DIGITAL BIRMINGHAM in the UK, the digital economy is developing rapidly worldwide. (5)

As the single most important drive of innovation, competitiveness and growth, the digital economy holds huge potential for entrepreneurs and small and medium-sized enterprises (SMEs). How businesses adopt digital technologies will be a key determinant of their future growth.

According to DB, new digital trends such as cloud computing, mobile web services, smart grids, and social media, are radically changing the nature of work, the boundaries of enterprises, and the responsibilities of business leaders.

While these trends enable technological innovation, they also spur innovations in business models, business networking, and transfer of knowledge as well as access to international markets.

According to DB, however, only 2% of European enterprises are presently taking full advantage of new digital opportunities.

At the meeting of the Council for Strategic Development and Priority Projects on 5 July 2017 in Moscow, President Vladimir Putin instructed the government to finalise Russia's digital economy development programme (2017-20125). The authorities are to take into account key end-to-end digital technologies including artificial intelligence, robotics, quantum computing, development of computing, information and telecommunications infrastructure as well as financial incentives. (6)

(2) China's Digital Economy

According to the white paper recently issued by China Academy of Information and Communication Technology (CAICT), Ministry of Industry and Information Technology (MIIT), China's booming digital economy, a new major engine of growth, expanded by 18.9% in 2016 to 22.6 trillion yuan (about US$3.35 trillion), accounting for 30.3% of China's GDP. (7)

The central and local governments have been promoting digital economy as a "major development strategy" to upgrade socio-economic development.

On 12 July 2017, the State Council announced that the central government will formulate and issue a strategic plan for promoting the digital economy.

Of the world's 3.89 billion internet users in June 2017, 751 million are in China (over 800 million by mid-2018).

According to a March 2018 report by ChinaInfo100, a non-government information research platform, China's digital economy grew by 18.9% in 2016, as compared with US 6.1%, Japan's 17% and UK's 11.5%.

China had 592 AI firms (23.3% of global total) at end of June 2017.

According to McKinsey Global Institute (MGI) August 2017 Report on China's digital economy (**mckinsey.com**), China has one of the most active digital-investment and start-up ecosystems in the world, and "the potential to set the world's digital frontier in coming decades."

China is in the top 3 for venture-capital investments in key types of digital technology, including virtual reality (VR), autonomous vehicles, 3-D printing, robotics, drones, and artificial intelligence (AI).

China has become the world's largest e-commerce market with 42.4% of the global $1.9 trillion in 2016 (a huge surge from 0.4% of global $495 billion in 2005).

China has also become a major global force in mobile payments, to the tune of $790 billion in 2016 -- about 11 times the transaction value of the US ($74 billion).

As of mid-2016, one in three of the world's 262 unicorns (start-ups of over $1 billion) worth $883 billion is Chinese (34 unicorns with 43% of total valuations). The US has 47 unicorns with 45% of global value.

Together with the huge mass support base of 731 million Internet users in 2016 for rapid and large-scale commercialization of digital business models and the construction of a rich and resourceful digital ecosystem by Internet giants like Baidu, Alibaba and Tencent, and other digital innovators like Xiaomi and NetEase, the government has allowed space for all the various digital players to experment/innovate and grow before enacting regulations.

"Today, the government is playing an active role in building world-class infrastructure to support digitization as an investor, developer, and consumer," MGI has reported.

According to China Academy of Information and Communications Technology (CAICT), China's digital economy generated 27.2 trillion yuan (US$4.3 trillion) in 2017 (+20%) to contribute over 33% of GDP. Moreover, DE accounted for 22% of the country's total employment, with 171 million working in DE-related sectors.

According to e-Commerce Research Center (ECRC), China's e-commerce exports rose 14.5% to 6.3 trillion yuan (US$1 trillion) in 2017.

"The country's digital economy has stepped into a new phase, with the focus shifting from high-speed growth to both quantity and quality development," said Mr Lu Chuncong, Director of the Policy and Economic Research Institute at CAICT. (8)

According to Lu, China's technology innovation has helped to transform industry from a follower to a world leader, with information technology (IT) and telecommunications sectors contributing the most.

5G technology is expected to take off in 2019, with likely issuance of 5G licenses in 2019-2020 in China, among the first countries to do so.

However, as China lags behind in some core technologies, it has to accelerate core technology breakthroughs.

According to the Global Connecting Index (GCI) report by Huawei Technologies Inc released on 29 May 2018, China is ranked 27th in digital economy among 79 countries and regions assessed, very much behind the US in pole position.

"China lags behind the US in terms of industry integration and the research and development (R&D) of new technologies backing the digital economy," Gu Wenbin, an expert at CCID Consulting told **Global Times** 31 May 2018.

"It would take several decades for China to catch up with the US…"

According to the Huawei report, China is furthest behind the US in data center networks and big data analytics.

Chris Dong, global research director at technology advisory firm IDC China, told **Global Times** 21 June 2018 that China's fast growth is largely driven by the government's industry and innovation policies, and helped by a few giant IT firms which have developed leading-edge capabilities in big data and analytics, AI, and IoT (Internet of Things).

Digital transformation in China only began to pick up momentum in recent years, with its spending mostly in hardware and infrastructure.

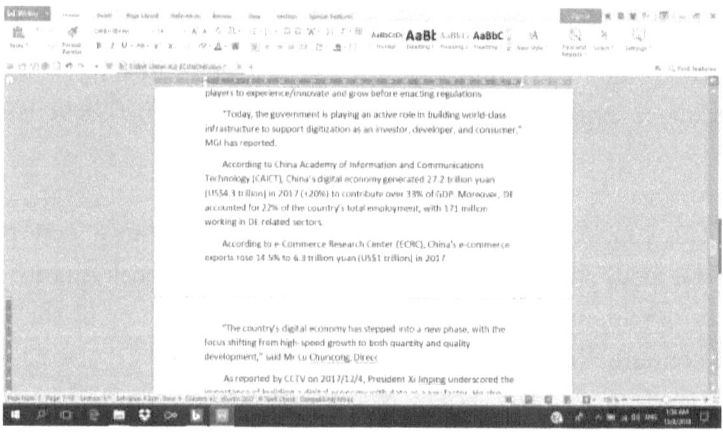

players to experience/innovate and grow before enacting regulations

"Today, the government is playing an active role in building world-class infrastructure to support digitization as an investor, developer, and consumer," MGI has reported.

According to China Academy of Information and Communications Technology (CAICT), China's digital economy generated 27.2 trillion yuan (US$4.3 trillion) in 2017 (+20%) to contribute over 33% of GDP. Moreover, DE accounted for 22% of the country's total employment, with 171 million working in DE-related sectors.

According to e-Commerce Research Center (ECRC), China's e-commerce exports rose 14.5% to 6.3 trillion yuan (US$1 trillion) in 2017

"The country's digital economy has stepped into a new phase, with the focus shifting from high-speed growth to both quantity and quality development," said Mr Lu Chuncong, Direc

As reported by CCTV on 2017/12/4, President Xi Jinping underscored the

In the US, major industries have long immersed in digital transformation and invested a lot in software, services and disruptive technologies.

According to Dong, China needs to accelerate building a self-sufficient innovation ecosystem, together with a more innovative-friendly open market.

"… Tencent Holdings and the Alibaba Group are ratcheting up their no-holds-barred contest to dominate the ways 770 million internet users (in China) communicate, shop, get around, entertain themselves and even invest their savings and visit the doctor," Raymond Zhong reported in **New York Times (nytimes.com)** May 3, 2018.

"Today, their fiercest fight is over digital money kept on smartphones.

"Mobile payments have transformed the Chinese economy…"

As reported by CCTV on 2017/12/4, President Xi Jinping underscored the importance of building a digital economy with data as a key factor. He also highlighted research on big data as well as its use, being indispensable in building a modern economy.

The Internet, big data and Artificial Intelligence (AI) should be interconnected. Industrialization and the use of information should be integrated in greater depth, Xi said. (9)   27.12.2017 17:37

According to Chen Zhaoxiong, vice-minister of industry and information technology, China will become the world's largest data producer to account for about one-fifth of global data by 2020, as the country ramps up its resources to integrate cutting-edge information technologies into the real economy.

"The country has already made significant progress in the big data industry, with big data platforms established in manufacturing, commerce, finance, transportation, and medical care," Chen said at the opening of the China International Big Data Industry Expo 2018 on 26 May 2018 in Guiyang, the capital of southwestern China's Guizhou Province. (10)

According to CAICT, China's digital economy is expected to deliver 32 trillion yuan (about US$4.5 trillion) and contribute 35% of GDP by 2020.

China's robust digital economy will account for over half of China's GDP by 2030. The Chinese economy is generally expected to become the world's largest before 2030.

Notes

1. **Reuters**/Beijing report published in **Sun** June 15, 2017.
2. **Wikipedia**
3. Formed in 1971, the World Economic Forum is a non-profit international organisation committed to improving the state of the world.
4. **ec.europe.eu**/growth/industry/digital last updated 21/07/2017
5. DIGITAL BIRMINGHAM are part of Birmingham City Council's Economy Directorate leading the region's digital and smart city development for a sustainable and inclusive economy for all sectors of city life.
   digitalbirmingham 7 September 2016 The importance of the digital economy

6. **tass.com TASS**/Moscow report July 19, 2017
7. **PEOPLE'S DAILY** 2017-07-20

According to **McKinsey & Company**, a global management consulting firm, following China's shift from investment-led to a productivity-led economic model, consumption will account for 47% of GDP by 2030, up from 34% in 2015, while investment will account for 38% of GDP in 2030, down from 49% in 2015.

China's population of some 700 million smartphone and internet users provides a large base to leverage digital consumption, particularly in tier-three and below cities.

In innovating for the future, China's R&D spending has grown from US$49 billion in 2007 and US$113 billion in 2012 to US$228 billion in 2015 (equivalent to China's GDP in 1978), and to projected US$404 billion by 2020. **Consumption.uk** 29 November 2016

7(a) While the US has 11 of the world's largest high-tech companies in 2018 (including the top 5 with Apple, Amazon, Microsoft, Google/Alphabet, and Facebook), according to the chart of the world's top 20 global Internet leaders prepared by Kleiner Perkins Canfield & Byers in partner Mary Meeker's annual report on internet trends,

China has 9 in Alibaba (6), Tencent (7), Ant Financial (9), Baidu (13), Xiaomi (14), Didi Chuxing (16), JD.com (17), Meituan-Dianping (19), and Tontiao (20), as ranked by market valuation on 5/29/18.

Report by Sally French May 31, 2018 **marketwatch.com 2018-05-31**

8. Report by Nicky Lung 28 May 2018 **China Daily/OPEN GOV (opengovasia.com)**
9. **Xinhua/Global Times** 2017/12/4 as reported by **CCTV**

In a congratulatory message to the inaugural Smart China Expo which opened on 23 Aug 2018 in Chongqing, President Xi stressed China's priority in innovation-driven development and accelerating data industrialization and industrial digitization for high-quality growth and high-quality of life. He said China will cooperate and collaborate with the international community in developing the digital economy and in creating new growth engines for the world economy. **CGTN** report Aug 23, 2018   24.08.2018 03:20

10. **Global Times/People's Daily Online en.people.cn** May28, 2018

According to Morgan Stanley, the China internet market will be worth $19 trillion by 2027.   13.07.2018 11:39

10 (a) Addressing the theme of the 2018 Smart China Expo, the first of its kind and attended by scholars, enterprises and organizations from the smart industry around the world, "Smart Technology: Empowering Economy, Enriching Life", President Xi said it reflects the trend of the world economy in the new round of technological revolution and industrial transformation as well as people's longing for a good life globally.

Report by **CGTN** August 23, 2018

(b) According to the report in **Economic Information Daily** September 20, 2018, National Development and Reform Commission (NDRC) and China Development Bank (CDB) have agreed to invest 100 billion yuan (US$14.63 billion) in the next five years to further develop China's digital economy, including creating and supporting key projects and facilitating construction of the "digital Silk Road".

According to the 2018 Global Digital Economy Development Index released on 18 September 2018, China ranks second in the world after the US.

With 772 million internet users by the end of 2017, China's e-commerce user penetration rate has risen to 50% in nine years, whereas the US took 14 years to do so.

According to Ren Zhiwu, NRDC Deputy Secretary General, China has constantly optimized its ecosystem for innovation and enhanced its capability to cultivate new drivers of growth.

According to various experts, the continuous upgrading of China's internet infrastructure, its fast-growing market, and the consistent improvement in new forms and new models of business as well as adoption of new technological development of new industries will continue to sustain the rapid evolution of China's digital economy.

People's Daily Online September 22, 2018

(c) According to **Made in China 2025 (MIC25)**, projected broadband penetration will reach 70% by 2020 to provide access to 400 million household in China, and 82% by 2025 for 480 million households.

11 pages 3069 words 02.07.2017 18:00 22.07.2017 06:41 28.11.2017 05:18 14.01.2018 05:33 24.08.2018 03:2 13.07.2018 11:41 13.08.2018 02:55 14.08.2018 16:48 13.10.2018 00:41 13.10.2018 01:42 18.11.2018 23:59

NEW CHINA A(3)
ROBOT REVOLUTION (UPDATED VERSION)

China's "Robot Revolution" Is Coming

The world's first industrial robot was created in the late 1950s at a small Connecticut machine shop in the north-eastern state of the US and animated by half a dozen ingenious young men, led by its patent holder and inventor George Devol and his new-found friend Joseph Engelberger, engineer and entrepreneur. They founded Unimation (Universal automation), and they originally called their handiwork Programmed Article Transfer (PAT) and then called it Robot (after Isaac Asimov's 1950 **I, Robot**).

They named their working prototype the UnimateA, and introduced it to the world in 1961 at a trade show in Chicago's Cow Palace.

The robot cut its teeth in the auto industry in 1961when put to the test at GM's die casting plant in Trenton, New Jersey.

"In wild anticipation, we readied Serial Number 001 for shipment," recalled George Munson, one of the pioneers. (1) Eventually some 450 Unimate robots were employed in die casting.

In Japan Professor Ichiro Kato of Waseda University initiated in 1967 the WABOT project on humanoid robot, and he delivered the world's first full scale humanoid robot in 1972. The world's original android, WABOT-1 had two arms, walked on two legs, and saw with two camera eyes. (2)

In 1969 Kawasaki Heavy Industries (KHI) was licensed to manufacture and market Unimate robots in the Asian market. By 1983 KHI had shipped over 2,400 of them.

Following indigenous R&D and transfer of American technology in industrial robots, Japan has since the 1970s been leading the world of robotics.

288 words 03-04.07.2017 01:55

"Japan leads the world in the field of robotics with highly innovative research, development and applied technologies. Since the 1970s, Japan has been at the world's cutting edge of industrial robotics," The University of Tokyo declares on its website **u-tokyo.ac.jp**.

"Robots are now working on the front lines in a diverse array of areas, including aeronautics, medicine/welfare, disaster mitigation, disaster investigation and rescue...

"The technological and creative prowess developed by the "robot nation" of Japan, which has been a driving force in the field of robotics, will no doubt help Japan continue to lead the world in this area for years to come."

On 15 May 2015 Prime Minister Shinzo Abe called for a "robot revolution" in Japan, after President Xi Jinping had in 2014 called for one in China. According to Abe, advances in robotic computing power, voice and image recognition, and machine learning could help Japan overcome constraints of a fast-aging population and declining workforce (the same problems in China). And Abe has urged Japanese companies to "spread the use of robotics from large-scale factories to every corner of our economy and society." (3)

Backed by some 200 companies and universities, the government-led five-year drive aims to deepen the use of intelligent machines in manufacturing, supply chains, construction, and health care, while expanding robotic sales from 600 billion yen (US$6.4 billion) annually to 2.4 trillion yen (US$25.6 billion).

According to the Ministry of Economy, Trade and Industry (METI), Japanese companies including Fanuc, Yaskawa Electric and

Kawasaki Heavy Industries (KHI) command 50% of the global market in factory robots, and 90% share in parts such as precision gears, servo motors, and specialized sensors.

Of course, Japan wants to maintain its long-standing premier position in global robotics. But, for how long more? For across Sea of Japan and East China Sea, the rapid rise of China's robotic industry prefigures a sea change in very near future. In 2013, China displaced Japan as the world's top market for industrial robots.

"Not only do we need to upgrade our robots, we also need to capture markets in many places," President Xi Jinping said in a speech before the Chinese Academy of Sciences in 2014 when he called for a "robot revolution" in China.

Xi wants Chinese makers of industrial robotics like E-Dodar Robot Equipment, Anhui Efort Intelligent Equipment and Siasun Robot & Automation to take on major foreign players like Japan's Fanuc and California-based Adept Technology for leadership in the global market.

In 2015 Chinese manufacturers bought 66,000 industrial robots out of the 240,000 sold worldwide.

In 2016 China bought 85,000 and installed 90,000 new robots, one-third of the world's total.

In 2017 China purchased 141,000 industrial robots, of which 37,825 (29.8%) were manufactured domestically. According to the International Federation of Robotics (IFR), 387,000 industrial robots were installed worldwide in 2017.

China has been the world's largest market for industrial robots since 2013.

According to Li Yan in his article on the need to upgrade robotics in China published in **People's Daily Online** May 09, 2017, the domestic market is over 60% foreign supplied, with 90% of imported robots (quoting Qu Daokui, president of a robotics company in Shenyang) employed in the high-end auto industry.

According to Zuo Shiquan, an expert at Beijing-based CCID Institute, there's a huge demand for mid-range and low-end industrial robots.

Chinese manufacturers have to master the core technologies. R&D must be stepped up in welding, sensing, controlling, and human-computer interaction (for collaborative robots).

Li Yan has reported that China is expected to have over 800,000 industrial robots by 2020 with annual sales of close to 300 billion RMB (US$72 billion). According to his report, China has over 800 robot manufacturers and 3,400 related enterprises.

According to technology research firm IDC, China will spend US$59.4 billion on robotics in 2020 (from US$24.6 billion in 2016), about half of Asia-Pacific's forecast robotic spending of US$133 billion in 2020. (4)

Of China's projected robotic spending, over US$30 billion (over 50%) is for so-called discrete manufacturing (assembly-line production of cars and smartphones) and so-called process manufacturing (bulk production of goods like food, beverages, and semiconductors). Over US$15.8 billion in 2020 on services-related robotics spending, such as application management, education and training, hardware development, systems integration and consulting across various domestic industries.

According to International Federation of Robotics (IFR), robotics promotes productivity and competitiveness. Used effectively and efficiently, robots enable companies to become or stay competitive, particularly small and medium-sized enterprises (SMEs) which form the backbone of the developed and developing economies. IFR estimates that over 2.5 million industrial robots will be at work in 2019 (about one-third of them in China). (5)

Robots improve productivity when they are applied to tasks that they perform more efficiently and to a higher and more consistent level of quality than humans.

A recent study of 17 countries between 1993 and 2007 found that robot densification increased annual GDP growth by about 0.37% and labour productivity by 0.36%, representing 10% of total GDP growth over the 15-year period. (6)

In terms of robot density, China had only 36 robots per 10,000 manufacturing workers in 2015 (ranking 28th in the world) as compared with Germany 292, Japan 314, South Korea 478. (7)

According to IFR, China's robot density grew to 68 in 2016, as compared with US 189 and South Korea's 631. Asia's regionally averaged 63, as compared with the average robot density of 99 units in Europe and 84 in the Americas.

Robot density in China rose to 101 robots per 10,000 persons in the manufacturing industry in 2017.

According to IFR, China will have to install around 650,000 new industrial robots from 2016 to 2020, two and a half times the total installed globally in 2015, for the country to achieve its robot density target of 150 units per 10,000 workers.

According to the MIC25 industrial master plan, China will operate 1.8 million industrial robots by 2025 (70% of the total in use in China), 10 times more than in 2018 (30% of the total).

"The country aims to become a leader in automation globally," Joe Gamma, IFR president said in February 2017. (8)

According to a 2016 report by the Ministry of Industry and Information Technology (MIIT), there are over 1,000 robot firms in China and a new robotics association known as the Chinese Robotics Industry Alliance (CRIA) has emerged on the scene, following the launching of the "Made in China 2025" programme and the 5-year robot plan (2016-2020).

Their focus is on automating the key sectors of the national economy, including manufacturing, electronics, home appliances, logistics, and food production.

According to the Ministry, the robotics industry was virtually non-existent a decade ago. Now the government wants production of Chinese robots to exceed 50% of national demand by 2020, from 31% in 2016.

China has set goals to make 150,000 industrial robots in 2020, 260,000 in 2025 (equivalent to world output/sales in 2015), and 400,000 by 2030. (9)

According to a late October 2016 report prepared for the U.S.-China Economic and Security Review Commission, China's military and commercial robotics are growing rapidly in quality and quantity to strengthen the country's military capabilities and the competitiveness of its manufacturing industry. Ever more capable and numerous unmanned systems are being deployed in the air, on land, and sea. (10)

"Simply said, China has three drivers helping them move toward country-wide adoption of robotics: scale, growth momentum, and money. Startup companies achieve scale quickly because the domestic market is so large. Further, companies are under pressure to automate thereby causing double-digit demand for industrial robots (according to International Federation of Robotics). Third, the government is strongly behind the move," Frank Tobe posted his illuminating piece on China's strategic plan for a robotic future. (11)

Robot makers and companies that automate have access to subsidies, low-interest loans, tax relief, rent-free land, and other incentives.

In "The Rise of Chinese Robotics", **China Daily** Columnist Dan Steinbock has written:

"Until recently, Chinese industrial robots were still relatively simple.

"Today, China is rebalancing from a low-cost "world factory" to a world-class advanced-manufacturing power, which is precipitated by new technology-related initiatives, including Strategic Emerging Industries, Sci-Tech Innovation 2030, Internet Plus, and Made in China 2025. At the same time, Chinese industry leaders are moving from low prices to world-class innovation.

"But market leadership will not come without competitive friction. And as global robotics are consolidating, rivalries are about to become tougher (among the leading players including the US, Japan, South Korea, Europe, and China)...

"Nevertheless, as the largest growth market, China is moving toward production leadership... Indeed, the fundamentals of the emerging industry and economic realities are supporting the rise of Chinese robotics in a way that is no longer possible for other major industry players." (12)

"The mantle of leadership is wide open," said Justin Rosc, a partner and manufacturing expert with Boston Consulting Group in Chicago. (13)

"China has the ability to rise to prominence."

In the13[th] Five-Year Plan (2016-2020), the technological thrust in robotics is "to develop new products, promote standardization, modular development, and expand market applications in automobile, mechanical, electronics, hazardous materials, national defense, chemical, light, healthcare, and domestic services..." (14)

As stated in the MIC 2025 initiative and the 5-year robot plan (2016-2020), China's goal is to overtake Germany, Japan, and the US in terms of manufacturing sophistication and quality by 2049, the centenary of the founding of New China. (15)

Notes

1. Book by George E. Munson, **Pity the Pioneer: The Rise and Fall of Unimation, Inc.**, condensed and edited by Leslie Ballard in **ROBOT botmag.com** Dec 2, 2010
2. **Wikipedia**
3. Report by Brian Bremner, **The Sydney Morning Herald smh. com.au** May 29, 2015
4. Report by Bien Perez **South China Morning Post scmp.com** 5 April 2017
5. Positioning paper April 2017 by International Federation of Robotics (IFR) **ifr.org**
6. **Ibid.** 2015 study by Georg Graetz and Guy Michaels for the Centre for Economic Performance at the London School of Economy. IFR reported on 27 Sept 2017 that robotics turnover came to $40 billion in 2016.
7. Report by Ben Bland **FINANCIAL TIMES** JUNE 6, 2016
8. **Ibid.**
9. **therobotreport.com** posted by Frank Tobe 06/02/17

According to IFR World Robotics 2017, the demand for industrial robots has accelerated considerably since 2010 due to ongoing trend toward automation and continued innovation technical improvements in industrial robots.

China has significantly expanded its leading position as the world's biggest market, with sales of about 87,000 industrial robots (31% of global sales) in 2016 (+27%) -- nearly as many sold in Europe and the Americas (97,300).

According to IFR (**ifr.org**) May 30, 2018, more than 3 million industrial robots will be at work in factories around the world by 2020 -- from 1.47 million in 2014, and slightly over 1 million in 2008.

Of 1.9 million units in Asian factories in 2020 (from slightly over 1 million in 2016, 950,000 industrial robots will be employed in China.

10. Report prepared by Defense Group Inc. And released 25 October 2016.

11. **therobotreport.com** 06/02/17
    Frank Tobe is owner and publisher of **The Robot Report** and founder of **ROBO Global**.

12. **straitstimes.com** March 24, 2017

13. **Bloomberg News** Report on CHINA'S PLAN FOR ROBOT INDUSTRY with assistance of Dexter Roberts and Rachel Chang 25 April 2017

14. **PLANNING FOR INNOVATION** A July 2016 report prepared by Tai Ming Cheung et al for the U.S.-China Economic and Social Security Review Commission **uscc.gov**

15. **therobotreport.cor** posted by Frank Tobe 06/02/17 China's strategic plan for a robotic future is working.

15(a) "… In sharp contrast to industrial robotics, China is the world's undisputed leader in commercial drones, with the Chinese firm Dajiang Innovation (DJI) accounting for around 70 percent of the global commercial drone industry in 2015.

"DJI outcompetes its rivals based on its technological superiority, price, ability to use powerful commercial software applications, and customization," the U.S.-China Economic and Security Review Commission reported to Congress on November 2017.

"U.S. commercial drone manufacturer 3D Robotics, formerly the world's second-largest commercial drone manufacturer, struggled to compete against DJI, and in August 2017, formed a partnership with DJI to supply their software to DJI's drones…"

15(b) According to the report released on 11 May 2018 at the 5th China Robot Summit, about 1,686 robotics companies were established in China in 2017 pushing the grand total to over 6,500 in the country, mainly located in the three main regional development belts of the Beijing-Tianjin-Hebei (BTH) region, the Yangtze River Delta (YRD), and the Pearl River Delta (PRD).

15©. China produced over 130,000 industrial robots in 2017.

Having grown at nearly 30% annually over the past five years, China's robot industry had a revenue of almost $7 billion in 2017, out of the global $25 billion (according to IFR).

According to Miao Wei, Minister of Industry and Information Technology, China is paying close attention to the development of the robot industry with its crucial role in the latest technological revolution and industrial transformation as well as in building national manufacturing power.

Still facing many challenges, China will further advance its robot industry by deepening supply-side structural reform, enhancing innovation capabilities, strengthening talent cultivation, and extending global cooperation in areas like policy formulation, R&D, market promotion and training, to attain high quality and sustainable development.

"China welcomes companies from all over the world to share opportunities and shoulder the burden of development with us," Miao said at the World Robot Conference 2018 in Beijing on 15 August 2018. 19.08.2018 10:01

According to I-Ting Shelly Lin's report as posted on May 14, 2018 by **China Briefing** (produced by Dezan Shira & Associates), China has been operating the most industrial robots globally since 2016.

By 2020 China expects to operate 950,300 industrial robots and produce 150,000. A national robotics innovation center will be built, according to the Ministry of Industry and Information Technology.

Robotics development focuses primarily on servo control, motor, and reducer, human-machine interaction, robot vision and intelligent speech, and underwater robots.

In addition to the regional clusters mainly in the Yangtze River Delta, Pearl River Delta, and the Beijing-Tianjin-Hebei (Jing-Jin-Ji) region, there over 40 robotics-focused industrial parks in China.

Industrial robots in automobile manufacturing (50% of industrial robots, of which over half are welding robots), electrical and electronics, rubber plastics, metallurgy, food, chemical engineering, medicine, and cosmetics.

Service robots: healthcare/medical devices, finance, warehousing/logistics, customer services/catering, entertainment robots, and education robots.

Specialized service robots for military applications, extreme operations, and emergency rescue.

9 pages 2,781 words 03-04.07.2017 08:25 18.07.2017 06:03 28.07.2017 04:44
14.01.2018 05:37
19.08.2018 10:10 14.10.2018 02:37 18.10.2018 18:29 14-15.12.2018 00:37

Entering the New Era of Robot.2

15 (d) With more than 200 Chinese and international exhibitors, the July 2019 China International Robot Show in Shanghai displayed revolutionary breakthroughs in the robotic industry.

As reported by **CCTV** 2019-07-14, the new revolutionary robots are developed by integrating robotics technology with digital technology, networking, AI, virtual technology, speech perception and others in the plenitude of cutting-edge software and automation technologies.

The 2019 Shanghai Robot Show also highlighted performances through multi-robot collaboration rather a solitary robot's solo.

According to Qu Daokui, president of China Robot Industry Alliance, a non-profit research organization in robot manufacturing and application, technological advances in the robotics industry are ushering in the new **robot.2** era.

11 pages 2901 words 15.07.2019 15:39

NEW CHINA A(4)
ARTIFICIAL INTELLIGENCE (AI)

China is Competing for Global AI Leadership

"The tech world is shifting from a 'mobile' to an 'artificial intelligence' (AI) era, driven by deep learning, big data, and graphics processing units (GPUs), all of which accelerate the ability to compute," Rex Wu, an equity analyst at Jeffries Hong Kong, was reported to have said in March 2017. (1)

In his keynote address Google chief executive Sundar Pichai said the same thing at the tech giant's Google annual developer conference on 17 May 2017, when he said the world has shifted from being "mobile-first" to "AI-first" as computing continues to evolve. (2)

"In a AI-first world, we are rethinking all our products and applying machine learning and AI to solve user problems," Pichai said. "And we are doing this across every one of our products..."

According to a press release by International Data Corporation (IDC) on 26 October 2016, the market for cognitive systems and AI solutions will grow at a compound annual growth rate (CAGR) of 55.1% from 2016 to 2020, from $8 billion in 2016 to over $47 billion in 2020.

Fastest growth will be in public safety and emergency response, pharmaceutical research and discovery, diagnosis and treatment systems, supply and logistics, quality management investigation and recommendation systems, and fleet management.

Forecast growth champions are healthcare (+69.3%) and discrete manufacturing (+61.4%). Education and process manufacturing will also grow significantly. (3)

18.07.2017 06:15

According to the press release issued on 28 September 2016 by New York-based Accenture, a leading global professional services company, AI could double annual economic growth in developed economies by 2035, by changing the nature of work and spawning a new relationship (of collaboration) between man and machine. (4)

The impact of AI technologies on business is projected to boost labour productivity by up to 40% by fundamentally changing the way work is done and reinforcing the role of people to drive growth in business.

"AI is poised to transform business in ways we've not seen since the impact of computer technology in the late 20th century," said Paul Daugherty, chief technology officer, Accenture.

"The combinational effect of AI, cloud, sophisticated analytics and other technologies is already starting to change how work is done by humans and computers, and how organizations interact with consumers in startling ways.

"Our research demonstrates that as AI matures, it can propel economic growth and potentially serve as a powerful remedy for stagnant productivity and labour shortages of recent decades."

Of 12 developed economies under study by IDC, AI was found to produce the highest economic benefits for the US, increasing its annual growth rate from 2.6% to 4.6% by 2035, and yielding additional US$8.3 trillion in gross value added (GVA).

According to a report released by Accenture Plc and Frontier Economics on 26 June 2017, the impact of AI on China will be huge. AI could increase China's annual growth rate by 1.6% to 7.9% by 2035, to add US$$7 trillion to its gross value added (GVA), a close proxy for GDP. (5)

The Chinese government is prioritizing AI development. Of the19 national engineering labs recently approved by the National Development and Reform Commission (NDRC), 3 are completely dedicated to AI research and application. To cover technologies based on deep learning, virtual reality (VA), augmented reality (AR), and brain-like intelligence.

According to the Key Area Technology Roadmap of "Made in China 2025" programme, autonomous industrial software will be indigenised and localised to over 50% by 2025.

The 13th Five-Year Plan (2016-2020) articulates strong government support for AI to "facilitate commercial application of artificial intelligence technologies in all sectors" of the national economy.

With the strong support of government, Chinese firms such as Baidu, Alibaba, and Tencent are becoming the world leaders in commercial AI.

On December 2015 Baidu reportedly made cutting-edge breakthroughs in English and Mandarin speech recognition. In early March 2017 Baidu developed its rapid synthetic speech system known as Deep Voice, capable of converting text into an almost human-quality voice reportedly over 400 times faster than Google's Deep Mind, the world's previous leader. Such achievements position Baidu in direct competition with leading US AI companies like Google, Microsoft, IBM, and Facebook.

According to Liu Guifeng, president of Shenzhen-based company iFLYTEK, its speech recognition software has 95% accuracy, and it has won multiple championships at global speech synthesizer competitions, and it's being used in BMW, Mercedes Benz, and Audi vehicles worldwide. (6)

"I believe that human-computer interaction platforms will be mainly controlled by vocals within the next 10 years, with assistive touch on screens or keypads," Liu said.

"AI will enter everyday life as an essential along the lines of water and electricity."

Zheng Nanning, an academician with the Chinese Academy of Engineering Sciences, told Jiang Je of **People's Daily**: "China holds a great advantage in its number of data firms and user population, which can contribute greatly to AI development."

AI is crucial, he said, to China's ambition to become an innovative power by 2020, and a major science power by 2030.

On the militarisation of AI, Elsa Kania, an analyst at the Long Term Strategy Group, has written that China may soon surpass America on the Artificial Intelligence Battlefield. (7)

"Evidently, the PLA recognizes the disruptive potential of the varied military applications of artificial intelligence, from unmanned weapons systems to command and control," Kania has written.

"Looking forward, the PLA anticipates that the advent of artificial intelligence will fundamentally change the character of warfare, ultimately resulting in a transformation from today's "informationized" ways of warfare to future "intelligentized" warfare.

"The Chinese leadership has prioritized artificial intelligence at the highest levels, recognizing its expansive applications (such as development of swarm intelligence for UAVs and "intelligentization" of cruise missiles) and strategic implications...

"China's rise as a major power in artificial intelligence could thus become a critical force multiplier for the PLA's future capabilities..."

According to the national AI development plan July 2017, China aims to make AI a major growth driver and to develop its AI industry to over 150 billion yuan in 2020, 400 billion yuan and global leadership by 2025. AI will become a trillion-yuan (US$147.9 billion) industry in China by 2030.

According to experts and business leaders at the October 2016 AI expo in Beijing, AI technology has been developing rapidly in China, and these authorities acknowledge that China has become a major AI power in the world. (8)

"AI is a vital driving force for a new round of technological revolution and industrial transformation, and accelerating AI development is a strategic issue to decide whether we can grasp (arising) opportunities," President Xi said on 31 Oct 2018.. He stressed the importance of China occupying "the high ground of AI technology" and firmly holding the technology by leveraging China's massive data and huge market potential. (9)   18.11.2018 23:16

According to a report by Price Waterhouse Coopers (**People's Daily Online** July 07, 2017), AI could help the global economy grow by as much as 14% by 2030, the equivalent of an additional $15.7 trillion on the back of productivity gains and increased consumer demand. China stands to gain the most, as AI will likely boost its economy by 26% in 2030. (10)   08.07.2017 08:29 25.07.2017 10:10

Notes NEW CHINA A(4) ARTIFICIAL INTELLIGENCE (AI)

1. **TrendinTech trendintech.com** Linda Johnson March 21, 2017
2. **StraitsTimes.com** May 18, 2017 Lester Hio Mountain View, California
3. IDC is premier global provider of market intelligence and advisory services for IT, telecommunications and consumer technology markets. **Idc.com**
4. **newsroom. accenture.com**
5. **Bloomberg**/Dalian (China) report in **New Straits Times** June 30, 2017
6. Report by Jiang Je **People's Daily Online** October 19, 2016
7. **THE NATIONAL INTEREST nationalinterest.org** February 21, 2017

A graduate of Harvard College (summa cum laude, Phi Beta Kappa), Elsa Kania was a 2014-2015 Boren Scholar in Beijing.

7(a) "… AI research is underway in the fields of intelligence collection and analysis, logistics, cyberspace operations, command and control, and a variety of military autonomous vehicles. AI applications are already playing a role in operations in Iraq and Syria, with algorithms designed to speed up the target identification process," Congressional Research Service

(CRS) submitted on 26 April 2018 in its report to Congress on Artificial Intelligence and National Security.

"International rivals in the AI market are creating pressure for the United States to compete for innovative military AI applications.

"China is a leading competitor in this regard, releasing a plan in 2017 to capture the global lead in AI development by 2030.

"Currently, China is primarily focused on using AI to make faster and more well-informed decisions, as well as developing multiple types of autonomous military vehicles…

"While a small number of analysts believe that the technology will have minimal impact, a larger number of experts believe that AI will have at least an evolutionary if not revolutionary effect…"

8. Report by Jiang Je, **People's DailyOnline en.people.cn** 14:41Oct 19, 2016

According to the new plan for artificial intelligence (AI) issued by the State Council on July 2017, China aims to keep pace with the leading countries in AI technology and applications in general by 2020.

The AI industry will serve as a new major engine of economic growth and help improve people's lives by 2020.

China will then seek major breakthroughs in AI research as well as progress in intelligent society building by 2025.

And, China's target is to become a major centre for AI innovation as well as to lead the world in AI technology and applications by 2030.

Specific goals for AI development include creating an open and coordinated system for AI sci-tech (science & technology/S&T) innovation, fostering a high-end intelligent economy, building a safe and convenient society, and upgrading infrastructure for internet, big data, and computers.

8(a) According to Ministry of Industry and Information Technology (MIIT), China had over 2,000 companies in AI-related industries by the end of 2017. **Xinhua/People's Daily** May 17, 2018

On November 2017 the government announced its plan to build four national AI open innovation platforms, working with Alibaba Group Holdings Ltd in smartcity technologies, Baidu Inc in selfdriving technologies, Tencent Holdings in AI-enabled medical treatment, and iFlytek Co Ltd in voice-recognition technology.

According to Li Zhengmao, vice general manager of China Mobile, the country's largest mobile telecom carrier by subscribers, CM is building a large-scale internet of things (IoI) network to provide a sound foundation for the era of AI. **China Daily/People's Daily Online** May 18, 2018

8(b) At the opening ceremony of the Second World Intelligence Congress (WIC) in north China's Tianjin Municipality on 17 May 2018, Wang Gang, Chairman of China Association for Science and Technology, described AI as a strategic technology with a leading role in future development. As the core driving force of industrial revolution, AI will promote emergence of new technologies, products, industries, and economic growth patterns.

Chinese companies are world leaders in image recognition, voice translation, and behavioral analysis, he said.

"Remarkable achievements have been made in intelligent robotics, unmanned shops, machine translation, shared and driverless vehicles. There are wide applications in the fields of city planning, smart transport, social governance, health, agriculture and national security," Wang said.

"China has advantages in the speed of AI development and its wide applications, but our weak points are the depth of basic research and originality…"

He called for strengthening basic research and more input in developing core technology.

Experts and entrepreneurs at the meet called for more education from middle and elementary schools in China to nurture the next generation talent.

9. "… The future of AI will likely have <u>socialist characteristics</u>, since by the time AI matures, China will be the leader. All that Alibaba, Tencent, Baidu, Huawei, Xiaomi and others do, will essentially be to service that future.

"The companies that arise in China's tech dynasty will grow faster and grow larger than any other global equivalents for various reasons including state-sponsored support and funding," Michael K. Spencer, a tech futurist, wrote in **Medium** June 7, 2018.

"If China can figure out how to onboard global talent, it will be unstoppable by as early as 2030 as the definite leader in technology, innovation and the future of AI."   13.07.2018 14:365 pages 1,393 words 06.07.2017 11:00 08.07.2017 08:30 22.07.2017 07:09 25.07.2017 10:10

Former US Deputy Defense Secretary Bob Work told Colin Clark that the Chinese have estimated that they can boost economic growth with AI by 26% by 2030. "it's quite astounding," Wok said.

(Report by Colin Clark Nov 12, 2014 **BREAKING DEFENSE**, Raytheon)   09.09.2018 19:29

ARTIFICIAL INTELLIGENCE (AI): Additional Notes.

According to a new report released on 29 November 2017 by the Department of Defense (DOD) on **ARTIFICIAL INTELLIGENCE, BIG DATA AND CLOUD TAXONOMY**, the US military must decide now if it wants to "lead the coming revolution, or fall victim to it" amid emerging challenges from China and Russia.

"This stark choice will be determined by the degree to which the Department of Defense (DoD) recognizes the revolutionary military potential of AI and advanced automated systems," said the report, which was prepared by DoD and Govini, a big data and analytics firm in Arlington, Virginia.

Specifically, the White House and Pentagon must determine to what extent the US will ramp up its R&D in technologies associated with AI – including advanced computing, artificial neural networks, big data, machine learning, unmanned systems and robotics. (Report by Zachary Cohen, **CNN** November 29, 2017)

According to President Vladimir Putin, the country that takes the lead in the sphere of computer-based artificial intelligence (AI) will rule the world.

"Artificial intelligence is the future not only of Russia but of all mankind," Putin said to students in a national "open lesson" on September 2017.

According to a recent study by Greg Allen of Harvard's Belfer Center for Science and International Studies, AI has "the potential to be a transformative national security technology, on a par with nuclear weapons, aircraft, computers, and biotech..."

AI has alpha status in China's future development.

"Artificial intelligence has become the new form of international competitiveness. Artificial intelligence is the strategic technology that leads the future," the Chinese government has stated in its publication **New Generation Artificial Intelligence Development Plan**, released on 8 July 2017.

"The major developed countries in the world regard the development of artificial intelligence as a major strategy to enhance their national competitiveness and safeguard their national security..."

"By 2020, they (the Chinese) will have caught up," Eric Schmidt, former Google chairman, said at the 2017 AI summit. "By 2025, they will be better than us (US). And by 2030, they will dominate the industries of AI..."

--- As quoted by Adam Segal in a commentary When China Rules the Web, published in **FOREIGN AFFAIRS foreignaffairs.com** September/October 2018 Issue   08.09.2018 20:32

According to the new plan on new generation AI, released by the State Council in July 2017, AI industry should be a major new growth engine and improve people's lives by 2020. China's target is to become a major center and world leader for AI innovation by 2030.

Xinhua/People's Daily May 17, 2918   14.10.2018 03:12

According to the April 2007 report by McKinsey Global Institute (MGI) on China's AI, China is becoming a hub for global AI development.

As its capacity for innovation deepens, China has become one of the leading global hubs for AI development. Recognizing that the country's vast population and diverse industry mix can generate a huge volume of data as well as provide an enormous market within, leading Chinese tech companies are investing significantly in AI R&D.

Automating workplaces with AI could add 0.8-1.4% to annual GDP growth, depending on the rate of adoption across the board including high-tech and traditional industries.

MGI estimates that half of all work activities in China could be automated, making it the nation with the world's largest automation potential.

MGI states that China has the capability and opportunity to lead international collaboration on AI development and governance, to ensure that breakthrough technologies to improve health care, environment, security, and education, contribute positively to global growth and human welfare.

Artificial Intelligence: Implications for China, McKinsey Global Institute (MGI) Report, April 2017, by Dominic Barton, McKinsey's global managing partner, Jonathan Woetzel, MGI director, Jeongmin Seong, senior fellow, and Qinzheng Tian, a consultant in McKinsey's Beijing office.   14.10.2018 03:53

According to August 2018 Report of the US Department of Defense (p. 122), China's AI 2.0 project moves beyond its focus with AI 1.0, which centered solely on discovering AI, to focus on the networking and intelligentization of the entire industry chain.

In July 2017, China published a national AI blueprint that lays out its R&D trajectory to achieve major breakthroughs in the AI field and become the world's primary AI innovation center by 2030.   14.10.2018 04:03

The Chinese government has appointed four of its biggest companies, the quartet of Baidu, Alibaba Group Holding, Tencent Holdings, and iFlytek, as "national champions" to lead the development of AI innovation platforms in self-driving cars, smart cities, computer vision for medical diagnosis, and voice intelligence respectively.

Subsequently, the Hong Kong start-up Sense Time, which specializes in face- and image-recognition technology, has also been enlisted to establish an AI innovation platform for intelligent vision.

According to Kai-fu Lee, former head of Google China and founder of technology-focused venture capital firm Sinovation Ventures, China's access to massive amounts of consumer data provides the lifeblood of AI development.

"In the age of AI," Lee said, "data is the new oil, and China is going to be the new Saudi Arabia…" (10)

According to the March 2018 report by the Future of Humanity Institute of Oxford University, China remains far behind the US in the three core areas of AI development: hardware, research and algorithm development, and commercialization of the industry.

But, Lee Kai-fu takes a more pragmatic view, writing in his new book **AI Superpowers: China, Silicon Valley and the New World Order**: "I believe that China will soon match or even overtake the US in developing and deploying AI…"

Lee's rationale is that China's entrepreneurs are using AI to solve real-world problems just like the 19th century entrepreneurs who had applied the invention of electricity to cooking, lighting, and powering industrial equipment in IR 2.0. (11)

10. Report by Rodger Sadler, Chuan Shen 22 Oct 2018 **SCMP**
11. Report by Sarah Dai, Alice Shen 02 Oct 2018 **SCMP**

11 pages 3,232 words 27.12.2017 18:52 14.01.2018 05:41 13.07.2018 14:51 14.08.2018 18:09
09.09.2018 21:33 14.10.2018 04:10 18.11.2018 01:15 23:41

NEW CHINA A(5)
CHINA'S NUCLEAR RISE (UPDATED COPY)

China's Rise to Global Nuclear Power Leadership by mid-2020s

"Nuclear power is a significant element of a country's geopolitical influence. There are long timeframes and deep relationships that are developed in the course of building and operating a nuclear plant and through the exchange of technologies," states the April 2017 report of Global Nexus Initiative (GNI) on Nuclear Power for the Next Generation. (1)

"The control of market share translates into the power to create nuclear governance rules and prevent commercial competition from eroding vital safety, security, and non-proliferation standards..."

Richard Meserve, former chairman of the US Nuclear Regulatory Commission and member of GNI working group, said at a GNI-held press conference on 2 May 2017: "The nuclear rules are shaped by the countries with the largest market share, and traditional leaders like the US will soon be overtaken by China and Russia. There is a danger that the US will lose the capacity to influence the global norms for safety, security and non-proliferation. There are thus national security issues at stake.

As of 1 July 2018 (according to 2018 World Nuclear Industry Status Report **worldnuclearreport.org**), there are 413 nuclear reactors operating in 31 countries with gross capacity of 363.4 GW (363,400 MW).

Of 5 new reactors connected to the grid, 3 were in China including the world's first two third-generation units premiered by a Framatome-Siemens designed European Pressurized Water Reactor (EPR) Taishan-1 and a Westinghouse AP1000 Sanmen-1. Russia fielded 2 new units.

In the US 99 commercial reactors (packing 99.9 GW) produced 805 TWh in 2017 (below the 2010 record high of 807.1 TWh).

The US reactor fleet averages 38.1 years (close to standard operational lifespan of 40 years). 86 reactors have received a 20-year license extension, 44 of which have operated over 40 years. Only two new nukes are being built.

In France 57 operating reactors generated 381.85 TWh in 2017.

In China nuclear generated 233 TWh (wind power 286 TWh) in 2017 (+18%). China's 41 reactors have a total installed capacity of 38 GW (38,000 MW). The Chinese reactor fleet is very young, averaging 7.1 years, including 3 comparative seniors of 21-30 years.   15.10.2018 00:33

Of 50 reactors under construction as of 1 July 2018, 16 are in China with a combined capacity of 15,450 MW for grid connection in 2018-2023.

In an article published on 3 May 2017 in **THE NATIONAL INTEREST**, Andrew Follet wrote: "China is set to triple the amount of nuclear power it generates by 2026, overtaking the US as the country with the most nuclear power. China plans to spend $570 billion building more than 60 nuclear power plants over the next decade..." (2)

China's current generation of nuclear electricity of about 38-5 gigawatts with 41 operable reactors om August 2018 will surge to 80-90 gigawatts in the mid-2020s at the end of the 14th Five-Year Plan (2021-2025). The US has maintained its nuclear generation level of 80 GWe since 2012 with its fleet of 99 nuclear reactors.

Global leadership will crown China's nuclear power development over seven decades from the launching of its First Five-Year Plan (1953-1958).

China's rise to ascendancy has only recently accelerated, from the time of its audacious and game-changing initiative to ignite a nuclear renaissance shortly after the 2011 Fukushima meltdown in Japan.

According to a report in **DAILY CALLER** 2016/09/20 (citing World Nuclear Association), China was operating 36 reactors and building 21. China plans to generate 58 gigawatts of nuclear power by 2020 (with new plants 30 GWe capacity under construction), 150 gigawatts by 2030 (about 10% of the country's total electricity supply), and over 350 gigawatts by 2050, on the eve of New China's centenary.

In the 13th Five-Year Plan (2016-2020), main development projects include:

1. Construction and completion of the first four AP 1000 units at Sanmen in Zhejiang province and at Haiyang in Shandong province.

   Work on Sanmen 1 started in April 2009, the world's first AP 1000 reactor, and construction of Sanmen 2 started on December 2009. Several months after its completion, Unit 1 of Sanmen nuclear power plant was commissioned and it reached full power for the first time at 2.10 pm on 14 August 2018. A total of 8 Generation III units are envisaged.

   Of 6-8 Generation III plants at Haiyang, the first two are AP 1000, of which construction of Haiyang 1 commenced on September 2009 and of Haiyang 2 on June 2010.

   Sanmen 2 and Haiyang 1 are expected to start operating by end of 2018, and Haiyang 2 to start up in 2019.

2. Construction of demonstration Hualong One HPR 1000 reactors: construction of units 5 and 6 started in May and December 2015 at Fuqing in Fujian province, and also 2 units of HPR 1000 at Fangchenggang in Guangxi province.

   Fangchenggang 3 & 4 will serve as the reference plant for UK's Bradwell B Nuclear Power Station.

   Construction of unit 3 started in December 2015. And HPR 1000 (third generation technology) is destined for the international market.

3. Construction of the first two demonstration CAP 1400 reactors at Rongcheng, Shidaowan in Shandong province.

   CAP 1400 reactors will also be installed at Igneada in Turkey and Thyspuntin in South Africa.

4. In Phase III of Tianwan, Jiangsu province, construction of unit 5 started in December 2015 and unit 6 in September 2016. They are the last ACPR 1000 units to be built.

   In Phase IV development, units 7 & 8 will be Russian nuclear reactors.

The 13th Plan will start building a new coastal power plant, prepare work for construction of inland nuclear power plants, accelerate building demonstration and large commercial reprocessing plants.

The fuel security system will be further strengthened.

As reported by Ma Danning in **People's Daily Online** July 12, 2017, China plans to build a world-class nuclear energy innovation hub within five years in Shanghai, the birthplace of China's nuclear power, the site of the nation's first domestically designed and developed 300 MWe Qinshan Nuclear Power Plant, and for long a hotbed of indigenous nuclear innovations.

Initiated by the Shanghai-based State Nuclear Power Technology Corporation (SNPTC), the groundbreaking project seeks to make major breakthroughs conducive to a full industrial upgrading.

It will include R&D, manufacturing of fourth-generation reactors and new types of pressurized water reactors (PWRs); small reactors, marine nuclear power platforms, special nuclear materials; construction of high quality test benches and manufacturing chains. New innovative bodies will be established in Shanghai, including an industry cloud and big data center, an advanced manufacturing center, and a basic science innovation center, to further establish China as a nuclear tech leader, high-end facility manufacturer and exporter.   30.07.2017 14:50

Of China's total installed generating capacity of 1645 GWe at the end of 2016 (having increased by nearly 10% annually since 2010), fossil-fuelled capacity (mostly coal) topped 1054 GWe, hydro 332 GEw (+13 GWe in 2016), wind 149 GWe, solar PV 77 GWe, and nuclear 33.6 GWe.

The 13FYP for power production, as announced by the NEA on November 2016, limits coal capacity to 1100 GWe, and prescribes gas 110 GWe, hydro 340 GWe, wind 210 GWe, solar 110 GWe, and nuclear 58 Gwe. Non-fossil 770 GWe will generate 15% of China's electricity

The 13th Plan will invest $368 billion on smart grids and the ultra-high voltage/UHV (1000 kv AC and800 kv DC) transmission network which is expected to reach some 300 GW by 2020 and operate as the backbone of the country's power transmission and distribution system, connecting six regional clusters.   15.08.2018 22:15

Notes. NEW CHINA A(5) CHINA'S NUCLEAR RISE

1. Nuclear Power for the Next Generation:
     Addressing Energy, Climate, and Security Challenges
     Findings and Recommendations

1. Nuclear Power is Necessary to Address Climate Challenges
2. Nuclear Governance Needs Significant Strengthening

3. Evolving Nuclear Supplies Impact Geopolitics
4. Innovative Nuclear Policy Requires Partnerships posted by michelle 27 April 2017

Formed in 2015 and co-sponsored by Partnership for Global Security and Nuclear Energy Institute, GNI assembles leading experts from nuclear industry, nuclear security and environmental communities in the US to examine the complex challenges posed by climate change, energy demand and global security.

In Beijing the National Development and Reform Commission (NDRC) and the National Energy Administration (NEA) announced on January 2017 the 13th Five-Year Plan (2016-2020) for Energy Development and Energy Industry Reform, as a guideline for promoting and deepening an "energy revolution" in China.

Its salient points include:

1. Structural adjustments to support oil and gas in place of coal, and renewable energy to gradually replace fossil fuels.
Total energy consumption to within 5 billion tons of coal equivalent, at an annual growth rate of 2.5%, being 1.1% lower than in the 12th Plan (2010-2025).

2. Development through innovation in science and technology (S&T) to promote clean and intelligent energy, spurring new industries and businesses.

Following gradual shift from traditional high energy-consuming industries to service industries and household consumption, energy consumption growth will focus on modern manufacturing, big data centres, and new energy, offering opportunities to companies with expertise in energy efficiency.

3. Diversification of energy sources, development and commercialisation of geothermal energy, predominantly to fuel growth in towns and rural areas.
4. Cooperation with other countries in energy technology, equipment, engineering services, and capacity development in foreign electricity projects.

    China will also invest, construct, and operate overseas power grids and new energy projects.

5. Fiscally supportive policies and projects to further Chinese energy reform, including pilot projects in drilling and developing non-traditional oil and gas, deep-water oil and gas, and natural uranium resources.

Regarding Nuclear Industry Development:

Improve nuclear safety and emergency systems, increase security capacities, ensure uranium and nuclear fuel supplies and radioactive waste management.

R&D in floating nuclear power plants.

From report by David Solomon, Josie Cai, and Owenttaacke, China Business Review, US-CHINA BUSINESS COUNCIL May 17, 2017 **chinabusinessreview.com**

In a highly detailed backgrounder on Nuclear Power in China, updated June 2017, the World Nuclear Association (WNA) states clearly:

China's policy is to have a closed nuclear fuel cycle.

China has become largely self-sufficient in reactor design and construction as well as other aspects of the fuel cycle, but is making full use of western technology (from France, Canada, Russia, and more recently from the US via Toshiba-owned Westinghouse) while adapting and improving it.

Relative to the rest of the world, a major strength is the nuclear supply chain.

China's policy is to 'go global', with exporting nuclear technology including heavy components in the supply chain.

world-nuclear.org

2. According to China's new nuclear power plan released on 20 September 2016, the number of 60 reactors includes 21 under construction (to raise installed nuclear power capacity to 880 million kW by end of 2020 vis-a-vis US installed capacity of 99 GWe/99,000 MW in 99 reactors) and 38 planned for construction in the early 2020s. A total of 174 reactors has also been proposed.

As of August 2017, China is operating 37 nuclear reactors and building 20 more. China's aim is to have 58 million kilowatts (58,000 MW) of nuclear power capacity in operation by the end of 2020, and more than 30 million kilowatts (30,000 MW) under construction. **Xinhua/PEOPLE'S DAILY** 2017

2018 **operable reactors under construction reactors planned & proposed**

	operable reactors	under construction	reactors planned	& proposed
China	41 (38,419 MW)	17 (17,178MW)	43 (50,900MW)	136 (154,000 MW)
Russia	37 (28,961 MW)	6 (4,889 MW)	25 (27,135MW)	22 (21,000 MW)
US	99 (99,829 MW)	2 (2,500 MW)	4 (4,800 MW)	6 (7,100 MW)

WORLD NUCLEAR ASSOCIATION world-nuclear.org
August 2018   15.08.2018 22:45

6 pages 1,438 words 08.07.2017 06:15 18.07.2017 06:19 30.07.2017 14:52 16.10.2017 04:39

APPENDIX:

Is the US nuclear power industry in its twilight years?
Will China take over the lead as early as by the mid-2020s?

In the foreword to the 2017 **World Nuclear Industry Status Report (WNUSR)**, former Tennessee Valley Authority (TVA) Chairman S. David Freeman notes:

"...China is building 20 reactors, compared to a half dozen in Western Europe and four in the United States. South Korea is building 5 as well as a 4-unit plant in United Arab Emirates.

"In the US nuclear operators in competitive electric markets are losing ground to cheap natural gas. To keep their reactors online, many are seeking state subsidies as a largely carbon-free source. The only US reactor to join the grid in 2016, at Tennessee's Watts Bar nuclear plant, came into service 43 years after the project was launched.

"The first new American reactors being built in decades – two each in plants in Georgia and South Carolina – are years behind schedule and billions over budget. Those overruns drove their builder, Westinghouse, into bankruptcy in March (2017), but the utilities behind those projects expressed confidence they'll be finished no matter what happens in bankruptcy court.

"Westinghouse is also building four reactors of the same design in China...

"China is now deploying its third generation of reactors... Beijing froze its building for four years after the massive Japanese earthquake in (March) 2011, which led to catastrophic meltdowns in three reactors at the Fukushima Daiichi nuclear power plant – the industry's worst disaster since Chernobyl (April 1986)..." **worldnuclearreport** May 8, 2017

In 2016 China started up 3 new reactors and South Korea 1.

According to Ed Kee, CEO of Nuclear Economics Consulting Group, China's new designs are safer and easier to operate than American reactors, which were conceived in the 1970s and 1980s. Their current designs "are comparable to the best the Russians, the French or the US could offer..."

In **Bloomberg Businessweek**, Jim Polson reported on July 14, 2017: "... A decade ago, nuclear power plants in the U.S. were cash cows. Now more than half of them are bleeding cash, knocked from profitability by the shale-gas glut that's tanked electricity prices. Five nuclear plants were closed prematurely in the past five years, and more are on the chopping block.

"Without state intervention (annual subsidies), plants have closed or are scheduled to close prematurely in California, Massachusetts, Michigan, Nebraska, New Jersey, Pennsylvania, Vermont and Wisconsin..."

Natural gas power plants are cheaper to build and in less time than their nuclear counterparts.

According to a report by Samuel Brinton and Josh Freed in **Third Way** August 21, 2015, if aging reactors are closed down after their 40-year operational lifetime, the US will have only about 40 reactors with about 38.6 GW/38,600 MW capacity in 2025, and then only a handful of 5.7GW/5,700 MW by 2025.

China's operational nuclear power capacity came to 35GW/35,000 MW at the end of March 2017.

China plans to operate 58GW/58,000 MW of nuclear power by the end of 2020.

According to the International Atomic Energy Agency (IAEA), China has 40 operational reactors as of June 2018, the fourth most worldwide. China is constructing 17 nukes followed by India 7, Russia 6, South Korea 4, Japan and US 2 each, and France 1.

China is expected to operate over 100 reactors by 2030.

April 25, 2018 marked the start of fuelling for trial run of the 1250 MW No 1 unit AP (Advanced Passive) 1000 third-generation (3G) nuclear reactor, the world's first, at the Sanmen Nuclear Power Station (NPS) in east China's Zhejiang Province.(3)

Sanmen will have six 1250 MW reactors with a total installed capacity of 7.5 GW (7,500 MW), among the world's largest NPSs

The AP 1000 is reportedly the world's safest reactor technology for commercial nuclear generation, designed to passively cool itself during an accidental shutdown.

With some 20,000 scientists and technicians working over ten years, China has developed CAP (China Advanced Passive) 1400 nuclear model of 1400 MW capacity with an even more stable and safer design.

China Nuclear Power Group (CNPG) is constructing two Hualong One (homegrown 3G design) nuclear power stations in Karachi, Pakistan. (3)

On 29 June 2018, the first of the quartet of 1,750 MW European Pressurized Reactors (EPRs) at the Taishan Nuclear Power Plant (NPP) in Guangdong Province was connected to the grid -- "the first of its kind to be put into service in the world" (to quote Xavier Ursat, an executive with the French EDF, a partner of CGN). Sanmen-1 AP1000 joined the grid on 30 June 2018.

Fuqing-4 and Yangjiang-4 CPR-1000 units went into commercial operation on 17 September 2017 and 15 March 2017 respectively.

In October 2017, Terra Power, a nuclear reactor design company headed by Microsoft founder Bill Gates, reached an agreement with CNNC to form a joint venture for studying a "fourth generation" (4G) technology for travelling wave reactors (TWRs) which will be fueled by depleted (recycled) uranium.

A prototype 600 MWe TWR-P unit will reportedly be built at Xiapu in Fujian province over 2018-2025. A commercial reactor TWR-C 1150 MWe will follow in the late 2020s.   15.08.2018 23:12

Premier Li Keqiang has described the joint venture as a leading-edge program for US-China cooperation in the field of high technologies."

Going by electricity output projections, China appears destined to become a nuclear energy superpower.

According to the IAEA, worldwide nuclear power generation is forecast to expand from 2,611 terawatt-hours in 2016 to 3,844 terawatt-hours in 2040.

China's nuclear power output is projected to soar from 213 terawatt-hours (213 billion kWh) in 2016 to 1,102 terawatt-hours (1.1 trillion kWh) -- nearly 30% of the world's nuclear electricity in 2040.

"The Chinese are now in a premium position to be able to make changes and make innovation in this technology of an evolutionary nature," said Mark Hibbs, senior fellow of Nuclear Policy Program at Carnegie Endowment for International Peace. "China's quest is not only about improving safety and enhancing efficiency. They are doing this also to establish (their own) intellectual property in this area. Depending on how successful they are, (they) could have a profound impact on the future of nuclear power..." (4)

The 13th Five-Year Plan (2016-2020) envisions the commissioning and grid connection of the 200 MW high-temperature gas-cooled reactor nuclear power plant demonstration project in 2017, and completion of the advanced pressurized water reactor CAP 1400 demonstration project in 2020.

The 13FYP agenda includes forming international advanced nuclear power technology R&D, test verification, key equipment design and manufacturing, standards and independent intellectual property (IP) rights system, to "create an internationally competitive nuclear power design, construction and service industry chain."   18.10.2018 18:57

China's CFR600 demonstration fast reactor (CDFR) is expected to start operating from about 2023 at Xiapu in Fujian province, where CGNPC and Bill Gates's Terrapower will build a demonstration prototype 600 MW travelling wave reactor (TWR) over 2018-2025. A commercial reactor TWR-C 1150 MW will follow in the late 2020s.

In China Generation IV PWRs are expected and level off at 200 GWe around 2040 while fast neutron breeder reactors will debut from 2020 to progress to 200 GWe by 2050, and then on to 1400 GWe by 2100.   18.10.2018 19:23

Notes.

3.Report by Ma Danning 11:18 April 27, 2018 **People's Daily**

4. Report by Yasno Takeuchi and Tallulah Lutkin, **NIKKEI ASIAN REVIEW** July 03, 2018 **asia.nikkei. com 12 pages 3267 words**   27.11.2018 17:33

13 pages 3269 words 16.10.2017 05:55 14.01.2018 05:45 14.07.2018 12:23 15.08.2018 22:57
15.08.2018 23:23 19.08.2018 20:10 15.10.2018 00:57 18.10.2018 19:27

NEW CHINA A(6)
ASCENDING HIGH GROUND

Ascending the "ultimate high ground": China's manned spaceflight, lunar and deep-space exploration

Werner von Broun (1912-77), the eminent German-born American rocket scientist, was attributed as having said on space travel and exploration: "It will free man from his remaining chains, the chains of gravity which still tie him to this planet. It will open to him the gates of heaven..." (1)

When American astronaut Neil A. Armstrong (1930-2012) stepped onto the Moon at 10:56 (GMT) on Monday 21 July 1969 (8th day of the 6th lunar month in the year of the Rooster), the first human to do so, he said: "That's one small step for (a) man, one giant leap for mankind..." (2) An intrepid human being reached the first of the six, seven, or more heavens, according to certain religious beliefs and mythologies.

With the revving up of the Space Race after the first spacewalk by Alexi Leonov who spent 12 minutes of weightlessness in microgravity outside the Voskhod 2 spacecraft on 18 March 1965, and the first American spacewalk by Edward H. White in the second manned Gemini (4) flight on 3 June 1965, Mao Zedong and Zhou Enlai decided on 14 July 1967 that their country should not be left behind.

They started China's own crewed space program with the Shuguang-1 manned spacecraft. 19 astronauts were selected on 15 March 1971 for the first mission to send two of them into space by 1973. On 13 May 1972, however, the manned space project was officially shelved for economic reasons amidst the political turmoil of the Cultural Revolution (1966-76).

A more ambitious crewed space program was proposed in March 1986, known as Astronautics plan 863-2. Although it failed to carry out its project to ferry astronauts to a space station, it ultimately evolved into the 1992 Project 921. (3)

When China succeeded in sending its first astronaut Yang Liwei into space aboard the Shenzhou 5 spacecraft on 15 October 2003, the PRC became the third country to have a successful crewed space program after the Soviet Union (1961) and the United States (1962).

In 2000 China published its first quinquennial White Paper on China's Space Activities, followed by its successors in 2006, 2011, and 2016 articulating the national aim to become a space power.

As stated in the 2011 White Paper as well as in the previous two, the purposes of China's space program are "to explore outer space and to enhance understanding of the Earth and the cosmos; to utilize outer space for peaceful purposes, promote human civilization and social progress, and to benefit the whole of mankind; to meet the demands of economic development, scientific and technological development, national security and social progress; and to improve the scientific and cultural knowledge of the Chinese people, protect China's national rights and interests, and build up its national As spelt out in the 2016 White Paper, the envisioned objectives and principles of China's space program:

"To build China into a space power in all respects, with the capabilities to make innovations independently, to make scientific discovery and research at the cutting edge, to promote strong and sustained economic and social development, to effectively and reliably guarantee national security, to exercise sound and effective governance, and to carry out mutually beneficial international exchanges and cooperation; to have an advanced and open space science and technology industry, stable and reliable space infrastructure, pioneering and innovative professionals, and a rich and profound **space spirit**; to provide strong support for the realization of the Chinese Dream of the renewal of the Chinese nation, and make positive contributions to human civilization and progress..." (5)   30.07.2017 14:00

As of mid-September 2018, the Long March rocket series have been launched 284 times, sending more than 400 spacecraft into space, according to **Xinhua/People's Daily** September 19, 2018.

Timeline in China's Space Activities

24 April 1970	Highly successful debut of the CZ-1 satellite known as the Dong Fang Hong (The East is Red) aka Mao-1. The 173kg CZ-1 was the heaviest maiden satellite launched into orbit.
20 November 1999	Shenzhou-1 space capsule launched to mark the 50th Anniversary (Golden Jubilee) of the founding of the People's Republic of China (PRC)
October 2000	First BeiDou Navigation Experimental satellite launched.
09 January 2001	Shenzhou-2
25 March 2002	Shenzhou-3
29 December 2002	Shenzhou—4
15 October 2003	Shenzhou-5 with Yang Liwei to make China the third country to orbit a spaceman, after the Soviet Union (Yuri Gagarin 12 April 1961) and the US (Alan Shepard 5 May 1961)
12 October 2005	Shenzhou-6 with Fei Junlong and Nie Haisheng
24 October 2007	Chang'e-1 spacecraft, China's first to orbit Moon
26 November 2007	China releases the first image of the moon's surface, exactly 22 years after successful launch of its first recoverable satellite.

25 September 2008	Shenzhou-7 with Zhai Zhigang, Liu Boming, and Jing Hai
27 September 2008	China's first spacewalk with mission commander Zhai Zhigang floating in orbit 215 miles above Earth
October 2010	Chang'e-2
29 September 2011	Tiangong-1 space lab
31 October 2011	Shenzhou-8 unmanned mission to dock twice with Tiangong-1
February 2012	Publication of moon map and moon images with a resolution of 7 meters captured by China's second moon orbiter Chang'e-2
16 June 2012	Shenzhou-9 with Jing Haiping, Liu Wang, and woman cosmonaut Liu Yang
18 June 2012	First manned docking with Tiangong-1
December 2012	Chang'e-2 lunar probe made a successful observation trip over asteroid 4179 (Toutalis)
11 June 2013	Shenzhou-10 with Nie Haisheng, Zhang Xiaoguang and Wang Yaping, second Chinese woman in space Second manned docking with Tiangong-1
14 December 2013	Chang'e-3 makes first soft landing on the Moon to explore lunar surface with China's first lunar rover, Yutu in service For 972 days up to August 2016
November 2014	China's success in the re-entry and return flight
December 2015	Dark matter detection satellite Wukong (Monkey King) launched.
15 September 2016	Tiangong-2 spacelab. TG-2 brings on board equipment for scientific research including quantum and laser communications, and the world's first-in-space cold atomic fountain clock.
April 2016	Shijian-10, China's first microgravity satellite

10 October 2016	Shenzhou-11 with Jing Haipeng, Chen Dong
17 October 2016	First manned docking with Tiangong-2
January 2017	Mozi, world's first quantum communications satellite
January 2017	Gaofeng-3, a high-resolution observation satellite, begins its 24-hour all-weather imaging of Earth
20 April 2017	Tianzhou-1 cargo spacecraft, essential for construction of China's multi –modular space station by 2022 (the third after the Soviet-Russian Mir (1986-2011) and International Space Station (ISS 1998-) and manned lunar exploration program.
April 2017	Docking of Tiangong-2 and Tianzhou-1
June 2017	Insight, China's first X-ray space telescope launched.
Nov 2017	Mar 2018 8 BeiDou-3 satellites launched. Future Shenzhou missions (as reported): SZ-12 in 2018, SZ-13 in 2019, SZ-14 in 2020, SZ-15 in 2021, and SZ-16 in 2022.　　06.08.2017 12:29

Manned spaceflight

After half a dozen successful manned expeditions, China has chalked up discernible progress in its relatively belated but robust participation in space exploration.

To quote the 2016 White Paper, China has mastered major space technologies for manned space transportation, space extravehicular activity (like operating outside space capsule), space docking, operating in assembly and astronaut's mid-term stay in orbit(of over a month in space).

The object of docking the Tianzhou-1 cargo spacecraft with Earth-orbiting Tiangong-2 space lab, successfully carried out in April 2017, is to master key technologies for cargo transport and replenishment prior to building and operating a space station.

By 2020 or so, the goal is to complete R&D on space station modules, and to start assembly and operation of China's first-ever space station, Also, to raise manned flight capacity, laying a foundation for exploring and developing cislunar (Earth-Moon) space.

According to Wang Zhaoyao, director of China Manned Space Agency (CMSA, China will begin constructing its space station in 2019. A core module, Tianhe-1, will be launched in 2019 to begin assembly of space station. (6)

Two support sections will follow by 2022 to complete its construction and to commission and operate the new space station. Three-person crews will be on station for 3-6 months.

The space station will be about 60 tonnes, about one-seventh that of International Space Station, but comparable to NASA's Skylab, America's first space station launched mid-May 1973.

According to Yang Liwei, deputy director of CMSA, China's space outpost will begin operation by 2022 and operate in orbit for at least ten years. Its three modules will be equipped with advanced multipurpose facilities for scientific experiments in many fields, including space life science and biotechnology, microgravity fluid physics and combustion, etc. (7)

With the scheduled retirement of International Space Station in 2024, China will be the only country with a permanent space station 340-450 km above Earth.

China Academy for Space Technology (CAST) has plans for tapping solar power in Earth-Moon space. According to its roadmap, the first 100 MW Solar Power Station (SPS) will generate electricity at low Earth orbit (LEO) in 2025, and the first commercial scale 1GW (1000 MW) SPS system will start operating at geostationary orbit (GEO) in 2050. (8)

Deep space exploration

With the successful re-entry and return flight of Chang'e-3 lunar probe on November 2014 in the third phase lunar exploration engineering, the 2017 White Paper states that its success has indicated that "China has mastered the key technology of spacecraft re-entry and return flight in a speed close to second cosmic velocity" (or escape velocity).

According to the 2016 White Paper, the Lunar Exploration Program delivered a high-resolution map of the Moon and a high-definition image of *Sinus Iridium* (a lava-filled crater), and conducted research of lunar surface morphology, lunar crust structure, elemental composition of the lunar surface, lunar surface environment, and **moon-based astronomical observation.**

Chang'e-5 lunar probe will be launched in 2019 for soft landing, sampling and returning.

Chang'e-4 will be launched in late 2018 for the world's first-ever soft landing on the far side of the Moon. (To update, Chang'e 4 landed on 3 Jan 2019 in the South Pole-Aitken. Among its tasks, the lander will conduct the first lunar low-frequency radio astronomy, and explore for water and other resources.

According to a report in **Space Daily** April 26, 2017, experts in Beijing predict that China could realise the dream of putting astronauts on the Moon within 10 years. According to Yang Liwei, Chinese astronauts will land on the Moon around 2030. China also has in mind a moon village and a lunar research base.

The US became the first to set foot in the lunar world when on 20 July 1969 Neil Armstrong and "Buzz" Aldrin became the first men to land on the Moon.

The first Mars probe will be launched in 2020 to carry out orbiting and roving exploration, then a probe in 2028 to bring back samples from Mars by 2030.

Subsequently, asteroid exploration around 2022, exploration of the Jupiter system around 2029 and planet fly-by exploration. China plans to send probes to Jupiter in 2036 and to Uranus in 2046.

Research into origin and evolution of solar system, search for extraterrestrial life (ET), and other major scientific issues.

International Cooperation

According to the December 2016 White Paper, China has since 2011 signed 43 cooperation agreements or memoranda of understanding (MOUs) with 29 countries, space agencies and international organisations. China has taken part in relevant activities sponsored by the UN and other international organisations, and supported commercial cooperation in space.

"China will promote the lofty cause of peace and development together with other countries," the White Paper concludes.

Calling on the US National Space Council "to recognize China's impressive space exploration agenda", Buzz Aldrin reiterated his 30-year call for the international community to establish a permanent human settlement on Mars. "Striving to do so, I strongly believe, summons the very best of humankind to transform this lofty ambition into reality," Aldrin wrote persuasively in an Opinion piece published in **THE HILL** on August 01, 2017

His plan is to put people on Mars by 2039. He believes passionately that it's "our rendezvous with destiny."

Apollo 11 moonwalker who set foot on the Moon at 03:15:16 on 21 July 1969, following mission commander Neil Armstrong (9), 87-year-old Buzz Aldrin is an American engineer, author and an international advocate of space science and planetary exploration.

"To occupy Mars is a task like no other," Aldrin wrote.

"This enterprise can unite the great nations of the world in a cooperative way. Setting sail to Mars, putting in place a thriving civilization on that far-off world, is a peaceful pursuit that's unparalleled in history. It is time to place spacefaring nations on that trajectory..."

Like-minded China's response is likely to be highly positive.

"China's ambitions in space are as strategic as the Vostok and Apollo programs of the 1960s," Marina Koren commented in **The Atlantic** January 23, 2017. (10)

"China's space program continues to mature rapidly," the Pentagon stated in its annual report to Congress on May 2017.

"Our overall goal is that, by around 2030, China will be among the major space powers of the world," said Wu Yanhua, deputy chief of the China National Space Administration (CNSA), in Beijing on 5 January 2017.

China's Road Map (2017-45) To Space Leadership

On 17 November 2017 Tian He reported in the **Global Times** the gist of the remarkable document on China's space transportation system development programme in the coming three decades to attain leadership in the domain of space.

The space development report was issued by Beijing-based China Academy of Launch Vehicle Technology (CALT), the premier space launch vehicle manufacturer in China, and a major subordinate entity of China Aerospace Science and Technology Corporation (CASC), the main contractor for China's space projects.

2020   To launch Long March-8 carrier rocket, a medium-size launch vehicle which will deliver satellites to low-medium orbits for suborbital space travel, and to inaugurate commercial launch services.

According to **Xinhua**/Beijing report Nov 02, 2017, China plans to launch its reusable spacecraft in 2020. (11)

China plans a probe to Mars in July 2020, which will land on the Red Planet in 2021.

China's manned space station is planned for completion around 2022 and will stay in orbit for over 10 years to conduct various space experiments and R&D projects from space astronomy to space life science, fundamental physics, and space materials.

2025   To produce reusable suborbital carriers, and to operate suborbital spaceflights at 20-100 km altitudes.

2028   To launch 90-m heavy-lift carrier rocket Long March-9, capable of carrying a payload of 140 tonnes into low-Earth orbit (LEO), five times more than LM-5.

2030   To launch 100-ton heavy-lift carrier Long March-9 rockets capable of carrying up to 100 tons (currently 20 tons), and to provide support to manned lunar landing missions and sampling missions in Mars probes.

China's first super-heavy-lift rocket, Long March-9 will be used in launching crewed missions to the Moon and unmanned trips for sampling tasks to Mars.

According to Lu Yu, a senior rocket engineer with CASC, China will by then join the ranks of world-leading countries in space transport capabilities.

2035   Carrier rockets to be completely reusable.

The future generation of intelligent carrier rockets with advanced power will be widely used by 2035.

2040   Nuclear-powered space shuttle will be built, and deployed in interstellar missions including large-scale resource exploration in space, mining of asteroids, and building of space solar power stations (SSPSs).

To develop hybrid power reusable carriers, and to deploy the future generation of carrier rockets in longer-term and multiple space trips.

"Nuclear-powered space shuttles are mainly used for long-distance space travel and deep space exploration. They are the cornerstone for the Mars space stations," Jiao Wexin, a space science professor in Peking University, told the **Global Times**.

According to China Aerospace Science and Technology Corporation (CASTC), future generation carrier rockets will be put into service around 2040, and hybrid power reusable carriers will be developed.

By 2045, regular exploration of the solar system will be conducted on a large scale, with coordination between humans and machines.   15.10.2018 02:23

2045   To build space ladder, Earth station and space post. Radical developments in space transportation will enable regular and large-scale exploration of the solar system. Through its revolution in space transportation by 2045, China will become an all-round world-leading country in space equipment and technology as well as a world leader in space exploration.

According to Lu Yu of CASC, space exploration will enter a stage of rapid development with advanced space transport facilities.

Reporting in **South China Morning Post** 18 November 2017, Stephen Chen has highlighted several salient points in the CALT report:

China will catch up with the US on conventional rocket technology by 2020.

In 2025 China is expected to launch a reusable suborbital carrier and start suborbital space tourism. (11)

By 2030, China will land astronauts on the Moon and bring samples back from Mars.

In the 2040s, a nuclear-powered fleet will be ready to carry out mining operations on asteroids and planets.

"By 2045, China will have the best transport system in space," Li Hong, CALT director, posted on the academy's website on 16 November 2017.

By completing its revolution in space transportation by 2045, China will emerge as a world leader in space exploration.

Notes CHINA A(6) ASCENDING HIGH GROUND

1. **Oxford Dictionary of Scientific Quotations,** OUP, 2005, p. 86
2. Ibid. p. 23
3. **wikipedia.org**
4. Information Office of the State Council, **China's Space Activities in 2011**, December 2011, pp. 2-3
   As quoted in **China Dream, Space Dream**. A report prepared for the U.S.-China Economic and Security Review Commission, by Kevin Pollpeter with Eric Anderson, Jordon Wilson, Fan Yang. 03/02/2015 **uscc.gov**

5. **Xinhua People's Daily Online** Dec 27, 2016   673 words
   30.07.2017 13:57
6. Wang Zhaoyao spoke at a press conference on China's Space Day, 28 April 2017. Report by Stephen Clark **spaceflightnow. com** April 29, 2017

   According to the December 2016 White Paper issued by the China National Space Administration (CNSA) **cnsa.gov.cn** 2016-12-27, "to advance China's space spirit and stimulate enthusiasm for innovation", the Chinese government set as April 24 as the country's Space Day in 2016.

   China's Space Day commemorates the successful debut of the CZ-1 satellite launched on April 24, 1970. Known as the Dong Fang Hong (the East is Red), or Mao-1, the 173-kg cZ-1 was the heaviest maiden satellite placed into orbit by a nation. **wikipedia.org** Nov 2017   08.09.2018 20:59

7. **Xinhua/SPACE DAILY** June 08, 2017
8. **Wikipedia**
9. **Wikipedia**

According to the **CNN** report Apr 4, 2019 by Michelle Lou and Brandon Griggs, NASA administrator Jim Bridenstine, a former Republican congressman, is following President Donald Trump's orders to accelerate the return of American astronauts to the moon by 2024 (originally scheduled as 2028 following their last lunar landing in 1972), and then to land astronauts on Mars by 2033, over 33 million miles away in a round-trip voyage of over a couple of years.   04,04.2019 22:00

10. **theatlantic.com**
11. China plans to master rocket recycling technology by 2020.

At an aerospace industry seminar on 24 April 2018, leading Chinese carrier rocket designer Long Lehao said China expects to realize vertical recycling -- similar to the technology employed by the US-based firm SpaceX -- by 2020.

According to SpaceX, a reusable rocket needs only refueling and a few replacement parts to reduce launch costs by as much as 30%.

--- Report by Chu Daye, **Global Times** 2018/4/26 08.09.2018 21:09

13 pages 3, 379 words 07.08.2017 15:45 03.10.2017 17:11 28.11.2017 04:37 27.12.2017 19:17
14.01.2018 05:57 08.09.2018 21:09
15.10.2018 02:32 22.11.2018 02:27
29.03.2019 15:15 04.04.2019 22:00

NEW CHINA A(7)
CHINA'S SPACE ASSETS (UPDATED COPY)

China's Space Assets for National Development and Securt

"... Outer space has become a commanding height in international strategic competition. Countries concerned are developing their space forces and instruments, and the first signs of weaponization of outer space have appeared. China has all along advocated the peaceful use of outer space, opposed the weaponization of and arms race in outer space, and taken an active part in international space cooperation," the Beijing government has stated in its May 2015 White Paper on **China's Military Strategy**. (1)

"China will keep abreast of the dynamics of outer space, deal with security threats and challenges in that domain, and **secure its space assets to serve its national economic and social development, and maintain outer space security**."

In the Preamble of the latest (fourth) quinquennial White Paper (published December 2016) on **China's Space Activities in 2016**, the China National Space Administration (CNSA) has reiterated the importance of its space industry in the nation's overall development strategy, and reaffirmed its adherence to the principle of exploration and utilization of outer space for peaceful purposes.

"Over the past 60 years of remarkable development since its space industry was established in 1956, China has made great achievements in this sphere, **including the development of atomic and hydrogen bombs, missiles, man-made satellites, manned spaceflight and lunar probe**.

"It has opened up a path of self-reliance and independent innovation, and has created the spirit of China's space industry.

"To carry forward this spirit and stimulate enthusiasm for innovation, the Chinese government set April 24 as China's Space Day in 2016..." (2)

Following high-level US threats to nuke China during the Korean War (1950-53) and the First Taiwan Strait Crisis (1954-55), Chairman Mao Zedong decided at the Central Committee meeting on 15 January 1955 to go nuclear with Project 02.

He saw the need for nuclear weapons: "... In the world nowadays, to avoid being bullied, we can't afford not having them," Mao said to his senior colleagues. (3)

China tested its first atomic bomb (20 KT) on top of a 120-meter tower in the Xinjiang desert at 1500 hours on 16 October 1964, and then went on in record time to explode in the air its first hydrogen bomb (3 MT) at 0820 Saturday 17 June 1967 (10th day of the 5th lunar month in the year of the Fire Goat).

In 1965 China started work on developing its first long-range intercontinental ballistic missile (ICBM), known as the DF-5, capable of delivering a multi-megaton nuclear warhead to the continental United States and the Western Soviet Union. (4)

Following its successful full-range flight test in May 1980, the DF-5 was deployed in 1981 **to establish China's nuclear deterrent capability**. (5)

In 2017 China deploys 4 versions of the ICBM: DF-4 (first deployed in 1971), DF-5 (1981), road-mobile DF-31 (2008), and **DF-41** (2016), China's new strategic standard-bearer. (6)

When Deng Xiaoping returned from political oblivion to become vice-chairman of the Central Military Commission and chief of the General Staff in early 1975, he ordered speeding up R&D on strategic weapons and urged the Seventh Ministry of Machine Building to prioritize the JL-1 submarine-launched missile (SLBM), DF-5 ICBM, and satellite programs, following Mao's endorsement of the May 1975 report by the Defense Science and Technology Commission on the development of the nation's strategic missiles.(7)

John Wilson Lewis and Xue Litai have written: "... Mao embraced the weapons projects as a way to rebuild the Middle Kingdom's power and status. Nothing could shake his dream of retrieving China's proper place in the world..." (8)

China's Man-made Satellites

China has produced and launched a wide range of satellites for various missions. According to the 2016 White Paper, they include:

(1) Earth observation satellites, with improvements to Fengyun (Wind and Cloud), Haiyang (Ocean), Ziyuan (Resources), Gaofen (High Resolution), Yaogan (Remote Sensing), and Tianhui (Space Mapping) satellite series.

The China High-resolution Earth Observation System has been fully implemented: Gaofen-2 (launched 19 August 2014) capable of sub-meter (0.8m in full color) optical remote-sensing observation and capable of collecting multispectral images of objects larger than 3.2 m, Gaofen-3 (launched 9 August 2016) -- China's first satellite with a Synthetic Aperture Radar (SAR) imaging instrument that can see through clouds (9) and is accurate to one meter, and Gaofeng-4 (launched 28 December 2015) as China's first geosynchronous orbit (GEO) high-resolution earth observation satellite.

The high-resolution remote-sensing satellite has entered commercial service.

Launched May 2018, Gaofen-5 has the highest spectral resolution of China's remote sensing satellites.

Launched on 2 June 2018 in the 276th mission of the Long March series, Gaofen-6 functions like Gaofen-1, but with better cameras for its high-resolution images over a large area of the Earth, deployed largely for agricultural research such as estimating crop yields, and surveying forest and wetland resources.

"China now leads the world in remote sensing technologies for scientific purposes," said Wang Qi'an, director of the Ministry of Science and Technology's National Remote Sensing Center in Beijing, on 27 November 2017, following publication of its annual Global Ecological Environment Sensing Report 2017. 19.08.2018 10:40

(2) Communication and broadcasting satellites.
Fixed communication satellites such as Yatai and Zhongxing, and China's first mobile communication satellite Tiantong-1 have been launched.

The DFH-5 super communications satellite platform is being developed.

On 22 Dec 2018 the first of 5 technology experiment satellites (TESs) was launched to establish a global broadband communication network.

(3) Navigation and positioning satellites.
On 30 October 2000 16:02 the Long March 3A rocket launched the Beidou-1A satellite into geosynchronous orbit (GEO) to start the development of China's global navigation satellite system.

With the networking of 14 Beidou navigation satellites in late December 2012, the Beidou Navigation Satellite System (known as Beidou-2) has become fully operational in the Asia-Pacific region, providing customers services such as positioning, velocity measurement, timing, and short-message communication.

Beidou will go global by 2020 with the networking of its 35 satellites.

Tianlian-1 data relay satellite service has also been globally networked.

(4)   Space science and technology satellites.
According to press reports, China has successfully launched the Dark Matter Particle Explorer, Shijian-10 and Quantum Science Experiment Satellite for frontier scientific research.

According to the 2016 White Paper, new technological test satellites will be launched with the Shijian-9 satellite series for testing new technologies.

Regarding key developments and major tasks for the next five years of the 13th Five-Year Plan (2016-2020), the 2016 White Paper has cited further development of the three main satellite systems of remote-sensing (focus on the three series of multi-functional satellites for observing land, ocean and atmosphere), communications and broadcasting (building a space-ground integrated information network oriented toward industrial and commercial operations), and navigation and positioning system for the Beidou-2 to go global by 2020 with more accurate and more reliable services from integration of ground-based and satellite-based augmentation systems.

Regarding experiments on new space technologies to provide solid support for China's space industry, China will develop and launch technology experiment satellites, including Shijian-13 (launched 12 April 2017 as China's first high-throughput satellite to facilitate fast internet access), Shijian-17 and Shijian-18 (launched in mid-June 2017 China's first astronomical satellite with its first X-ray space telescope HXMT), and a global carbon dioxide monitoring satellite, and conduct experiments in key technologies for new electric propulsion, laser communications, and common platforms of new-generation communications satellites.

(5) Launched by China Aerospace Science and Industry Corporation (CASIC) in 2016, the Hongyun low-orbit broadband communication project to become operational around 2022 to provide broadband internet access globally to remote and rural areas in China and other remote and underdeveloped regions in the world. The first of five TES satellites was launched in late December 2018 to establish the new global network.

According to Union of Concerned Scientists (UCS) statistics 8/31/2017, out of 1,738 operating satellites (1,071 LEO, 531 GEO), China has 204, the US 803, Russia 142. China's remarkable satellite development includes high throughput satellites that can deliver 20GB bandwidth and remote sensing satellites with resolution of below one metre.

China has conducted 49 commercial satellite launches for other countries, and exported 14 homemade satellites, according to **People's Daily Online** 2017-09-20.

China National Space Administration (CNSA) has signed 117 cooperative agreements with 37 countries and 4 international organizations.

Lunar and deep-space exploration

Of 250 carrier rocket launches from Long-March 1 on 24 April 1970 to September 2017, China recorded 97% success. Following the successful maiden launch of the Long March-5, China's most powerful rocket capable of delivering a payload of 25 tons, reportedly comparable with the US Delta IV Heavy and Europe's Ariane V, China is now designing the super heavy-lift LM-9, a Saturn-V class rocket for lunar and deep-space exploration.

On 12 September 2017, China's first cargo spacecraft Tianzhou 1 and space lab Tiangong 2 successfully completed their first automated fast-docking operation – a capability considered to be important to the construction and operation of a manned space station.

Construction of China's space station is expected to start in 2019 for its completion by 2022.

The lunar launch of Chang'e 5 is reportedly scheduled for 30 November 2017 to soft land on the Mons Rumker, an isolated volcanic formation on northwest near side of the Moon, to take samples back to Earth.

Chang'e 4 is expected to be launched in 2018 to land on the far side of the Moon, for the first time in the history of space exploration.

"The moon (about 384,000 km/250,000 mi from Earth) is the first step for humanity's march towards deep space," the official **Science and Technology** said on 8 March 2017.

According to Yang Liwei, China's first taikonaut and deputy director of China Manned Space Engineering Office, China is in the preliminary stage of its manned lunar program to land Chinese astronauts on the Moon around 2030.

China will launch its Mars probe with a rover around 2020 (about three decades after the 1987 flyby of Voyager 2), and plans to retrieve soil and rock samples by 2025-2030 from the Red Planet, as far away as 400 million km at its most distant from Earth.

The 2020 Mars 3-in1 mission to enter its orbit, land, and deploy a rover, aims to explore the Red Planet's topography, environment, and atmosphere.

According to Zhang Ronggio, chief designer of the Mars mission, China aims to be first to conduct orbital and surface explorations of Mars in a single mission.

"These feats (landing on the far side of the Moon and the Mars probe) will place China firmly among the world leaders in space exploration," Dr Tamelor Macrel, Space Communications Manager, National Space Centre, Leicester, UK, commented 10/03/2017.

Wu Yanhua, deputy chief of the National Space Administration (NSA), said at a press conference in Beijing on 3 January 2017:

"Our overall goal is that, by around 2030, China will be among the major space powers of the world..."

Notes CHINA A(7) CHINA'S SPACE ASSETS

1. **globalsecurity.org Xinhua**/Beijing May 26, 2015
2. **cnsa.gov** China National Space Administration (CNSA) 2016-12-27

   April 24 commemorates the historic launching of the first Long March rocket with the first Chinese satellite Dong Fang Hong 1 on 24 April 1970 at 13:35 (UTC) which inaugurated China's space era.

   From that memorable opening shot to July 2017, a total of 250 Long March rockets have been launched, 236 of them successfully to record a success rate of 94.4%.

3. John Wilson Lewis and Xue Litai, **China Builds the Bomb**, Stanford University Press, Stanford, California, 1988, p. 36.

   In 1946 Mao had dismissed A-bombs as "paper tigers".

   In January 1955 he expressed great concern "with U.S. nuclear blackmail".

On 21 January 1958 Mao told his senior colleagues that "others don't think what we say carries weight" without the heft of atomic and hydrogen bombs.

4. John Wilson Lewis and Xue Litai, **China's Strategic SEAPOWER**, Stanford University Press, 1994, p. 167.
5. Ibid., p. 305 Note 68.
6. At the height of the Cold War in the mid-1980s, the US had 7 types of ICBM: Atlas, Titan I & II, Minuteman I, II & III, and M-X Peacekeeper (only Minuteman III and the MX MIRVed with multiple warheads).

The Soviet Union had 9 versions of the ICBM, including 3 ICBMs MIRVed: SS-7 (4 warheads), SS-18 (10 warheads), and SS-19 (6 warheads).

The US currently deploys only the single-warhead land-based LGM-30 Minuteman III ICBM. The US Air Force Global Strike Command has 405 ICBMs at 3 USAF bases.

Roughly half of the US nuclear weapons are deployed on submarine-launched ballistic missiles (SLBMs) in the formidable American fleet of 14 Ohio-class nuclear-powered submarines (SSBNs).

With 24 SLBMs each armed with up to 8 (100 KT) warheads, every Trident boomer packs sufficient nuclear firepower to unleash nuclear Armageddon. Each Trident boat is more powerfully nuclear-armed than the nuclear arsenal of either India or Pakistan.

Russia currently has seven types of ICBMs on strategic duty, with the new awesome RS-28 Sarmat (MIRVed with up to 15 X 770KT nuclear warheads) to enter service in 2018-2019.

According to Rick Fisher, a China military affairs analyst and senior fellow of the International Assessment and Strategy Center, the Chinese **DF-41** is capable of lofting up to 10 warheads.

According to Fisher, China will also MIRV its DF-31 ICBM. He also expects the new SLBM, the JL-3, to be developed as a long-range submarine-launched missile with multiple warheads.

The DF-31A is the land-based version of China's second-generation submarine-launched ballistic missile, the **JL-2 SLBM** which became operational in 2013 to render the PLA Navy's **undersea strategic nuclear deterrence capability** against the US.

"China is re-engineering its long-range ballistic missiles to carry multiple nuclear warheads," U.S. Strategic Command chief Adm. Cecil Haney said on 22 January 2016.

Both China's DF-31B and DF-5B ICBMs are reported to be MIRV-equipped to deliver multiple warheads. In January 2017, China tested its new DF-5C ICBM reportedly MIRved with 10 warheads.

According to the 2016 congressional report by the U.S.-China Economic and Security Review Commission, China is also developing maneuvering re-entry vehicles (MARVs) which "are more difficult to intercept and better able to penetrate adversary missile defences."

In a well-informed article in **THE WASHINGTON FREE BEACON** April 19, 2016, Bill Gertz wrote: "China is currently engaged in a large-scale buildup of nuclear forces and missile delivery systems that include new missiles and a hypersonic glide vehicle (the **DF-ZF/WU-14**) – a weapon that can maneuver to avoid missile defences in delivering nuclear or conventional warheads..."

7. **China's Strategic SEAPOWER** p. 181

8. Ibid., p. 237

"Chinese imagers have stated resolutions of one to thirty meters and can image in the visible, infrared, and multispectral ranges. The Yaogan and Huanjing satellites also use synthetic aperture radar (SAR) to be able to image through cloud cover or at night. Certain Yaogan satellitesare also said to have electronic intelligence services," Kevin Pollpeter has written with Eric Anderson, Jordan Wilson and Fan Yang in their report **China Dream, Space Dream**, prepared in March 2015 for the U.S.-China Economic and Security Review Commission.

"Accessing information from these satellites is facilitated by a network of three Tianlian satellites that relay communications and data between satellites and ground stations anywhere on Earth.

"Thus they play a critical role in facilitating real-time intelligence collection for China's military..." **uscc.gov** 03/02/2015

With the "Beidou" (Compass) navigation satellite project, China plans to field 138 satellites in orbit in order to acquire "the world's highest spatial resolution and time resolution space information" globally (quoting Rui C. Barboscu **NASA Spaceflight**, 7 October 2015), Andrew Erickson said in testimony on China's Advanced Weapons, 23 February 2017, for the U.S.-China Economic and Security Review Commission. **uscc.gov**

Within a couple of years of launching of the Tiantong-1 01 mobile communications satellite on 6 August 2016, **People's Daily** reported on 16 May 2018 China's official start of its own mobile satellite phone service. China's first satphone system will help eliminate its dependence on foreign satellites. China also unveiled its first all-mode satellite mobile phone.   08.09.2018 21:45

By 2020 China plans to field 60 remote sensing Jilin satellites for maritime monitoring and targeting of ASBMs such as the DF-21D and DF-26.

On November 2016 the XPNAV-1 satellite was launched to test pulsar technologies in deep space that can operate independently to improve accuracy of satellite navigation signals.

10pages 2,849 words 14.08.2017 11:57 15.08.2017 12:29 22.08.2017 13:55 24.09.2017 21.11 14.01.2017 06:21
19.08.2018 10:56 08.09.2018 21:45 15.10.2018 03:21 29.03.2019 17:47

NEW CHINA A(8)
CHINA'S QUANTUM LEAP

China's Quantum Leap in the field of communications

A. China's Breakthroughs in the new Quantum Revolution

On 16 August 2016 China's first quantum space satellite as well the world's first was launched by a Long March 2-D rocket into sun synchronous orbit (SSO) 488 km to 584 km above Earth.

Named Micius/Mozi after a 5th century BC philosopher and scientist credited to have been the first person to conduct optical experiments, the 631 kg satellite (manufactured and operated by the Chinese Academy of Sciences/CAS) is also known as the QUESS satellite, designed for Quantum Experiments at Space Scale (QUESS). (1)

Following China's robust performance in human and robotic space exploration, the Chinese government is stepping up its participation in space science. QUESS is one of the National Space Science Center's "Strategic Priority Programs", which include investigations into black holes, dark matter, and cosmic background radiation.

QUESS is a proof-of-concept mission designed to facilitate quantum optics experiments over long distances for developing quantum encryption and quantum teleportation technologies for hack-proof transfer of quantum information and secure quantum communications.

On board QUESS satellite are R&D facilities, including a quantum key communicator, quantum entanglement emitter, entanglement source, processing unit, and a laser communicator. (2)

The main instrument on board the Micius satellite is called the "Sagnac effect" (common path for light beams) interferometer, used to generate pairs of entangled photons for transmission to ground stations, through a process known as quantum key distribution (QKD) for transmission of a secure cryptographic key that can be used to encrypt and decrypt messages.

Compared with terrestrial QKD/photon transmission, sending the QKD keys from an orbiting satellite results in less scattering (destruction of entangled photons), and over much greater distances.

The estimated cost of the QUESS project is US$100 million.

Of the three salient experiments in quantum communications, the first was to test and demonstrate the feasibility of quantum key distribution (QKD) between the Xinjiang Astronomical Observatory near the provincial capital city of Urumqi and the Xinlong Observatory near the national capital Beijing, a distance of about 2,500 km (1,600 mi).

The second experiment involved testing satellite-based quantum entanglement distribution (known as Bell's inequality) for quantum cryptography to two ground stations in Delingha on the Tibetan Plateau and Lijiang in northwest Yunnan, over a record distance of 1,200 km (750 mi).

Also successful in their Bell test, Chinese physicists established the entangled pairs of photons which had retained quantum entanglement at separate ground stations.

According to Wang Jianyu, executive deputy head of the Micius project, a potentially unhackable breakthrough could lead to important applications.

"It (the successful Bell test) is a small but important step of humans into the quantum age," Wang said. (3)

According to knowledgeable observers, it could be the first essential step towards the development of an envisioned quantum internet as well as commercially usable quantum cryptography.

The third key experiment involved quantum teleportation/communication between Mencius satellite and three ground stations over 1100 km -1200 km: (1) Nanshan in Shenzhen, southeastern China, (2) Delingha on the Tibetan Plateau, and (3) Lijiang in Yunnan, southwestern China.

Chinese scientists successfully completed all the three important QUESS experiments, a year ahead of schedule.

Their unprecedented success was reported and published in **Science** June 25, 2017; they wrote that their success in distribution of entangled photons to three different terrestrial base stations over a distance of 1,200 km has opened up "a new avenue to both practical quantum communications and fundamental quantum optics experiments at distances previously unaccessible on the ground..." (4)

According to Bai Chunli, president of the Chinese Academy of Sciences (CAS), the achievements show that China has reached a leading position in the field of quantum communication research.

"Micius has ushered in the construction of global quantum communication, the study of space quantum physics and experimental verification of quantum gravity theories," Bai said.

"It helps China's race to control the command point of quantum science and technology, and enables China to become a leader in the field..." (5)

On June 2017 the Pentagon described Micius as a "notable advance in cryptography research..." (6)

QUESS lead scientist Pan Jianwei told **Reuters** (2016-08-16) that "hack-proof" communications satellite has "enormous prospects" in defence.

According to the US Department of Defense, China is pursuing and increasing its space capabilities to prevent adversaries from using their space-based assets in a crisis.

But, China has repeatedly stressed its adherence "to the principle of exploration and utilization of outer space for peaceful purposes". Beijing also strongly supports international space cooperation. "China will promote the lofty cause of peace and development together with other countries," says China National Space Administration (CNSA). (7)

China needs international cooperation to construct a global quantum communications network which, according to Pan Jianwei, could be set up around 2030. (8)

B. Beijing-Shanghai Quantum Communication Network

On 23 April 2014 Jane Qin reported in **Nature** international weekly science journal on the start of work installing the world's largest quantum communication network. At the core of the US$100 million project is the 2,000-km link using quantum key distribution (QKD) technology, between China's two leading major mega cities -- Beijing, the national capital, and Shanghai, the biggest city in the country and a global financial hub. (9)

According to project director Dr Pan Jianwei, a quantum physicist and professor at the University of Science and Technology of China in Hefei, capital of landlocked Anhui Province in eastern China, the new network "will not only provide the highest level of protection for government and financial data, but provide a test-bed for quantum theories and new technologies..."

For the Beijing-Shanghai line, 32 nodes will reportedly be used to relay the hack-proof quantum signals. (10)

According to Pan, quantum communication affords ultra-high security through generated pairs of entangled photons. As a quantum photon can neither be separated nor duplicated, it is therefore practically impossible to wiretap, intercept or crack information transmitted through quantum communication. (11)

The capital of eastern China's Shandong province, Jinan serves as the hub of the quantum communication network by virtue of its strategic location between the two principal metropolises of Beijing and Shanghai.

Zhou Fei, assistant director of the Jinan Institute of Quantum Technology, told UK **Financial Times** early August 2017, "We plan to use the network for national defence, finance and other fields, and hope to spread it out as a pilot that if successful can be used across China and the whole world..." (12)

Notes NEW CHINA A(8) CHINA'S QUANTUM LEAP

1. **Wikipedia**
2. **POPULAR SCIENCE popsci.com** March 4, 2016 report by Jeffrey Lin, P.W. Singer, and John Costello
3. **South China Morning Post** Stephen Chen 17 June 2017

The Institute for Quantum Optics and Quantum Information (IQOQI) Vienna commented that the Micius satellite was "able to send entangled photon pairs to two different ground stations simultaneously and violating a Bell's inequality (test in quantum entanglement), thereby confirming the quantum nature of their correlation.

"These promising results show that the future of quantum communication is very likely to take place in space..."

The group of Rupert Ursin (IQOQI-Vienna) is looking into possibilities of performing quantum experiments with much more economical mini-satellites, so-called "CubeSats" (5 kg or 20 kg).

"Observing entanglement and quantum correlations between space and ground would be possible with these less complex mini-satellites at a fraction of the cost (of QUESS project)," the team of Rupert Ursin and 10 colleagues reported.

"Such a mission could be the key for European researchers to keep up with the developments in the Chinese quantum community..."

iqoqi-vienna undated

The Austrian Academy of Sciences is a partner in the QUESS program.

4. **THE VERGE theverse.com** Russel Brandom June 15, 2017
5. **BBC News** David Edmonds 21.08.2017
6. **Reuters** Christian Shepard June 16, 2017
7. China National Space Administration (CNSA) 2016-12-27

White Paper on **China's Space Activities in 2016** December 2016

8. **Xinhua** August 16, 2016

4 pages 1,037 words 24.08 17:08

9. **nature.com Nature** Vol 508 Issue 7497
10. According to April 2014 report, the technology-development company Battelle has started installing a 650-km /2017 between its HQ in Columbus, Ohio to its offices in Washington, DC. Working with ID Quantique, a Swiss quantum-cryptography company in Geneva, Battelle was reported to be planning a network to link major US cities, stretching over 10,000 km.
11. **People's Daily Online** June 07, 2016
12. **m.phys.org/news** August 4, 2017

12 (a) Quantum technologies and disruptive military capabilities?

"… Even a slim possibility that <u>quantum radars or sensing</u> could one day defeat <u>stealth</u> is a powerful incentive for the Chinese military to invest, perhaps quite heavily, in its development. For the U.S., stealth has been a key enabler of military advantage, and it could be critical in any future conflict scenario in the Indo-Pacific," Elsa B. Kania has written in **Defense One,**

Defense Technology, August 2018, EBook "Sorting Hype from Reality in China's Quantum-Tech Quest" (p. 15).

"If these claims about the state of China's quantum radar prove credible, then the PLA could succeed in offsetting this vital pillar of U.S. military power in the foreseeable future.

"Beyond these notionally 'stealth-defeating' technologies, the Chinese defense industry is also progressing in the development of quantum navigation technologies, which could enable independence from satellites that might be taken out in a conflict.

"Future Chinese submarines could be equipped with quantum navigation, improving their ability to navigate precisely and covertly, and these technologies might also be applied to improve missile guidance and enhance precision strike capabilities…"

Elsa B, Kania is an Adjunct Fellow with Technology and National Security Program at the Center for a New American Security, focusing on Chinese defense innovation and emerging technologies, and author of **Battlefield Singularity: Artificial Intelligence, Military Revolution, and China's Future Military Power**   20.11.2018 01:15

12 (b)

Europe is also reported to be determined to advance to the forefront of the "quantum revolution" with its EUR 550 million investment in quantum technologies and its support for the 2016 Quantum Manifesto.

The Quantum Manifesto calls for a EUR 1 billion flagship-scale initiative for Europe to remain a leader in the "second quantum revolution" in progress, and to unlock the full potential of quantum technologies. Europe cannot afford to lag behind the US and other countries in the new global race for talent and technology.

Report by Michael Allen, UK-based science writer March 17, 2017

physicsworld.com

7 pages 1809 words 30.08.2017 14:18 14.01.2018 06:24 14.01.2018 06:27 15.10.2018 17:45 20.11.2018 01:23 15.12.2018 01:33 29.03.2019 17:55

NEW CHINA A(9)
FUXING HIGH-SPEED TRAIN

Fuxing (Rejuvenation), China's Brand-New Bulletin Train, the world's fastest in service

With the commercial debut on 21 August 2017of the **Fuxing (Rejuvenation)** bulletin train operating at up to 350 km per hour (217 mph) on the Beijing-Tianjin line (115 km), China has regained the distinction of providing the fastest train service in the world.

On 1 August 2008 China first became the champion of high-speed rail (HSR) transport when China Railway Corporation introduced its 350 kmph service on the Beijin-Tianjin route in connection with the 2008 Summer Olympic Games in Beijing on 7-24 August.

In 2012 China Railway Rolling Stock Corporation (CRRC) Qingdao Sifang started R&D on the high-speed electric multiple unit (EMU) train. The Fuxing EMU train has, as reported in **People's Daily** June 09, 2018, more than 500,000 different machine components. Following exhaustive tests in extreme weather conditions and cumulative trial runs in 2015 of over 610,000 km, equivalent to 15 round trips around the Equator, the Fuxing EMU models were declared ready for the track.

In 2015 CRRC completed its development of the CRH series of high-speed trains capable of running up to 350 km per hour.   15.10.2018 18:03

On Fuxing's maiden trip (probably a dry run before the start of its commercial service) from Beijing to Shanghai (1,433km) on 26 June 2017, Huang Jingjing reported in **Global Times** 2017/7/19 that the next-generation high-speed train is completely designed, developed and manufactured in China, and that Fuxing is capable of running at a top speed of 400 km per hour.

According to a report in **People's Daily Online** 2017-08-2017, China's brand-new Fuxing Electric Multiple Unit (EMU) completed 600,000 km of tests before given the green light to go into commercial service at 350 km/ph.

The Beijing-based China Railway Corporation (CRC), operator of China Railway High-speed (CRH), proudly touts the Fuxings as the "Chinese Standard bullet trains", opening a new era in China's high-speed rail (HSR) transport to accelerate the nation's socio-economic development.

China's HSR service was inaugurated on 12 October 2003 with the Qinshen HSR on an electrified 404 km dual-track between Qinhuangdao, Hebei and Shenyang, Liaoning, and with the first-generation **Hexie (Harmony)** trains operating at up to 250 km/ph (166 mph) on upgraded rail lines, and subsequently up to 350 km/ph (217 mph) on new passenger-dedicated lines (PDLs).

China's early high-speed trains were imported or built with transferred technologies from foreign train manufacturers, including Canada's Bombardier (the CRHA delivered in 2006), Japan's Kawasaki (CRH2A), France's Alstom (CRH5), and Germany's Siemens (CRH3C). So, China has been running bullet trains of four types with foreign pedigree.

On record, China's HSR development has been plainly phenomenal. Within the first four years of rapid expansion (2007-2011), China built and operated 8,358 km (5,193 mi) of HSR lines by January 2011, more than those of the three other major runners (Japan, France and Germany) in the aggregate.

On June 2011, the heavily-trafficked Beijing-Shanghai HSR commenced its commercial operation to the max of 380 km/ph.

After the 23 July 2011 train collision on a viaduct near Wenzhou, Zhejiang province, HSR construction was temporarily suspended, and operating speeds were limited to 300 km/ph (186 mph) on passenger-dedicated tracks.

In July 2015 when President Xi Jinping visited Changchun Railway Vehicles Co. Ltd. (co-builder with CNR Tangshan, of the CRH380BL with a top speed of 487.3 km/h/302.8 mph), China's core leader lauded the Chinese HSR system as a "name card" in the global market.

China's HSR network passed 22,000 km (14,000 mi) by the end of 2016, about 60% of the global HSR, with 2,595 high-speed trains in service. 2016 registered 1.44 billion HSR trips, over half of China's total railway passenger traffic, and the world's busiest. An estimated 2.4 trillion yuan has been invested in development of the HSR network.

On its debut on 1 January 2017, the Beijing West-Kunming South became the world's longest HSR service on its 2760 km track for a routine travel of about 12-13 hours, to overtake the 2697 km West Beijing-Behai HSR service which was inaugurated on 1 July 2016.

Although the US still maintains the world's longest rail transport network, only over 1,600 km of its lines of over 257,000 km are electrified. Though in second position, China has 87,000 km of tracks electrified (3 times more than India's 25,000 km+). China's national rail network spans 127,000 km (2017).

According to the report of the National Bureau of Statistics released on 12 September 2018, China's high-speed rail system has been extended to 25,200 km. The "four vertical and four horizontal high-speed railway network" (spanning 12,000 km) is close to its completion, which will make it the world's first of its kind in operation.

Next, the 8+8 HSR grid will be developed and completed by 2030:

(A) Eight Vertical passageways: (1) coastal passageway, (2) Beijing-Shanghai passageway, (3) Beijing- Hong Kong (Taipei) passageway, (4) Harbin-Hong Kong (Macau) passageway, (5) Hohhot-Nanning passageway, (6) Beijing-Kunming passageway, (7) Baotou (Yinchuan)-Hainan passageway, and (8) Lanzhou (Xining)-Guangzhou passageway.

(B) Eight Horizontal passageways: (1) Suifenhe-Manzhouli, (2) Beijing-Lanzhou, (3) Qingdao-Yinchuan, (4) Eurasia Continental Bridge passageway, (5) Yangtze River passageway, (6) Shanghai-Kunming, (7) Xiamen-Chongqing, and (8) Guangzhou-Kunming.

15.10.2018 18:55

China plans to have 30,000 km HSR by 2020, 38,000 km by 2025, and 45,000 km by 2030 with the expected completion of the 8+8 passenger grid with electrified, double-tracked, passenger-dedicated lines.

According to **Xinhua** 2017-06-30, CRH trains were exported to 102 countries and regions. 2016 sealed agreements worth US$18 billion.

Starting on 21 September 2017, Fuxing trains run seven round-trips daily on the 1,250km Beijing-Shanghai route, cutting travel time from 6 to 4 and half hours. With max of 400km/h, China's Fuxing (Rejuvenation) provides the world's fastest commercial bullet train service.   05.09.2017 12:39 23.09.2017 14:02

Revving up China's Rail Revolution

As posted on **Wikipedia**, on 26 February 2008 the Ministry of Science (MOS) and the Ministry of Railways (MOR) signed an agreement for joint basic research into improving China's scientific and industrial resources to develop a national high-speed system. Of the four major components of their agreement to improve train services and railway infrastructure, the most important relate to (i) developing key technologies for creating a nation-wide network capable of operating high-speed trains at speeds of 350 km/ph and higher, and (ii) establishing intellectual property rights (a prerequisite for national branding) and standards for export-oriented international competitiveness.

According to a report in **Science and Technology Daily** September 8, 2010, the Ministry of Science (MOS) expressed its aspiration of developing HSR trains capable of 500 km per hour. The Ministry was also reported to have invested nearly 10 billion yuan in this S&T project, by far its largest investment.

On 19 October 2010 MOR announced start of R&D on a "super-speed" HSR technology to max over 500 km/ph (333mph).

China was also reported to be working on ultrafast bullet trains capable of maxing up to 600 km per hour (400 mph).

China Daily reported June 06, 2016 that China was developing and testing a next-generation train that can run at 400 km/ph for operation on China's HSR network and the new 770-km Moscow-Kazan high-speed route.

According to Professor Jia Limin of Beijing Jiaotong University and head of China's high-speed rail innovation program, the new bullet train in development under the 13th Five-Year Plan (2016-2020) will have adjustable wheels to fit various gauges of railway tracks.

According to Jia, China has also developed and begun to test an ultrafast bullet train that is potentially able to speed at 600 km per hour. The ultra train is being used to test cutting-edge technologies, advanced materials, and operational limits. Its development means that China can now design and manufacture trains that can travel at least 500 km per hour.

5pages 1365 words 05.09.2017 19:18 23.09.2017 14:02 14.01.2018 06:28 15.10.2018 18:57
28.11.2018 18:59 29.03.2019 18:05

NEW CHINA A (10) CONCENTRATED URBANISATION (UPDATED COPY)

Integrated and Concentrated Urbanisation in China: Urban agglomeration and city clustering

According to a mid-2015 **Hitachi** report, 56% of the world's population will live in the cities by 2020. (1)

By 2025, China will have over 200 cities each with a population of more than one million. China will be 65.4% urbanised, with an estimated urban population of 921 million – about 2.6 times the total population of the US.

Mega cities are expected to contribute nearly US$6.24 trillion to China's GDP in 2025. (According to the 5 September 2014 press statement by the US-based **IHS Inc**, a global industrial data and analysis company, China is expected to become the world's largest economy with a nominal GDP of US$28.25 trillion in 2024.)

According to the Hitachi report, China In 2030 will have 13 megacities, 4 mega regions and 7 mega corridors.

According to the **Economist Intelligence Unit (EIU)**, a London-based think-tank, China's urbanisation will reach 61% by 2020, and

67% in 2030 with an urban population close to 940 million and around 450 million in rural China.

According to the 2014 EIU report, China's march towards becoming an urbanised society will continue in the next 20 years "when China will remain the main force driving global urbanisation".

According to World Bank report April 2014, China will be 70% urbanised by 2030, when one of every six urbanites in the world will live in China.

By 2030, one-fifth of China's cities will be on a par in terms of overall development with the cities in developed economies. (2)

15.09.2017 15:25

According to the **McKinsey Global Institute (MGI)**, world's leading think tank in business and economics research, China's urban population will increase by 350 million (more than the US population) in 20 years (2010-2030), including some 240 million migrants from rural China, to reach **one billion** by 2030.

By 2030 the world will be 61% urbanised (66-70% by 2050), Asia 55%, and China about 70%.

It took the world 10,000 years to achieve the first one billion urban dwellers in the early 1950s, but only 25 years to add another billion. In 2008 for the first time in history, more people lived in the cities and towns than in the rural areas of the world.

According to **MGI**, more concentrated urbanisation in China could produce 15 supercities (or megacities) averaging 25 million people each, or could spur further development of 11 clusters of cities, each of them with a strong economic network and an aggregate population of over 60 million.

"The research suggests that concentrated urban growth scenario could produce 20 percent higher per capita GDP than that yielded by China's current urbanisation path, would have higher energy consumption but also higher energy efficiency, and would contain the loss of arable land (to urban development)," Jonathan Woetzel et al reported. (3)

"Concentrated urbanisation would also have the advantage of clustering the most skilled workers in urban centers that would be engines of economic growth, enabling China to move more rapidly to higher-value-added activities..."

Released on 16 March 2014, China's **National New-type Urbanisation Plan (2014-2020)** stresses that people-based urbanisation is the road for China's modernisation drive, serving as a strong engine for sustainable growth, improving social equity, balancing urban-rural development with its emphasis on building up the less-developed central, west and north-east regions, spurring domestic demand, and pursuing green and low-carbon development.

In brief, China's sustainable, integrated and inclusive urbanisation.

On 25 March 2014 the World Bank and the Development Research Center of China's State Council released their joint report **Urban China: Toward Efficient, Inclusive and Sustainable Urbanization**.

Among other key measures, the new approach in urbanisation recommends curbing rapid urban sprawl by reforming land acquisition (to be based on market value), giving migrants urban residency and equal access to basic public services, promoting more local financing, and reforming urban planning and design to price land on market value, to optimise use of existing urban land through flexible zoning for denser and more efficient urban development, to link transport infrastructure with urban centers, and to promote coordination among cities to better manage congestion and pollution.

"Urbanization is a powerful engine for China's sustained and healthy economic growth," said Lou Jiwei, Minister of Finance.

"It is necessary to put people at the core of urbanization, supported by institutional and systemic innovation, and unleash the development potential of urbanization through reform..."

In the last 30 years, China's phenomenal economic growth lifted well over half a billion people out of the pits of poverty, with rapid urbanisation providing employment for abundant labour resource, availability of cheap land and good infrastructure to keep pace with development.

"More than any other country in the world, China has made huge progress in ending extreme poverty. It now has an opportunity to make further gains by improving the lives of the hundreds of millions residents moving into cities," said Sri Mulyani Indrawati, Managing Director and Chief Operating Officer of the World Bank Group. (4)

"If China stays committed and implements the necessary reforms, it could become a global model on urbanization, while winning the war on pollution, sustaining high growth rates for its economy, making cities more livable and allowing more people to benefit from development."
15.09.2017 17:10

According to the UN Habitat World Cities Report 2010, cities are pushing beyond their limits and are merging into new massive conurbations, known as mega-regions, which are linked physically as well as economically. Their expansion drives economic growth, but also leads to ungainly and unwholesome urban sprawls, rising inequalities, and urban unrest.

The world's 40 mega-regions have less than one-fifth of the global population residing on only a tiny portion of the planet's habitable surface. But, they account for two-thirds (66%) of all economic activity and about 85% of scientific and technological innovation, according to Eduardo Lopez Moreno, co-author of the 2010 UN Habitat report. (5)

According to Moreno, China's five largest cities account for half (50%) of its national wealth.

On February 2016, Beijing issued a new urbanisation blueprint for more concentrated and higher density development in view of the anticipated move of 100 million more people to China's metropolises by 2020. (6)

In China the three leading mega-regions are the **Pearl River Delta (PRD)** in southern China, the **Yangtze River Economic Belt (YREB)** covering one-fifth of the country in central China, and the **Beijing-Tianjin-Hebei (BTH)** northern metropolitan region, known in short as **Jingjinji (JJJ)** mega-region.

Deng Xiaoping's bold and timely initiatives in launching China's economic reforms and opening up the country in 1979 drew the curtains for the miraculous performance and historic transformation of the Chinese economy, starting with the creation of the three Special

Economic Zones of Shenzhen (1May 1980), Shantou and Zhuhai in Guangdong province, and the Xiamen SEZ in neighbouring Fujian province.

The further urbanisation planned in the expansive YREB and BTH/JJJ regions came into the limelight in the mid-2010s with President Xi Jinping's strong and determined leadership, far-sighted vision and personal acumen. Each of the three regions presently contributes over 10% of China's GDP.

1,220 words 15.09.2017 18:00

1. **Pearl River Delta (PRD), the Golden Delta of Guangdong**

Mainly agricultural land before 1979, the Pearl River Delta in the coastal Guangdong province of southern China was incredibly transformed within a short period of rapid development following the crucial decision of the Third Plenum of the 11th Congress of the Communist Party of China (CPC) in December 1978 to re-orient the national economy toward the external market, to shift from a "socialist planned commodity economy" to a "socialist market economy", and the launching of economic reforms and opening up the country to the outside world in 1979.

Within three decades, within the span of one human generation, the Pearl River Delta (PRD) emerged from the backwater to become the world's largest (40,000 sq km/15,200 sq mi) and most populous (42 million) urban area by 2010, according to the World Bank. (7)

The Pearl River Delta has since become "the crown jewel of the Chinese economy". The PRD Economic Zone has been described as "the fastest growing portion of the fastest growing province in the fastest growing large economy in the world". (8)

Soon after his visits to Bangkok, Kuala Lumpur and Singapore in November 1978, Deng Xiaoping fully returned to power in Beijing late December 1978 when he had the foresight and gumption to change China's economy with its GDP of slightly over one-fifth trillion dollars

(US) and a per capita of US$227 for a population close to one billion (956 million). He could have made up his mind for a sea change after his meeting with Lee Kuan Yew.

"Deng wanted (like Mao Zedong before him) to create a wealthy and powerful China," Daniel Yergin and Joseph Stanislaw wrote in their 1998 book **THE COMMANDING HEIGHTS**. (9)

"I have two choices," said Deng. "I can distribute poverty or I can distribute wealth…"

And, it's generally glorious (for any nation) to be both rich and strong.

17.09.2017 16:50

In his last inspection journey to southern China on January 1992 before his political retirement at the age of 88, Deng re-visited **Shenzhen** where he was astounded when he saw for himself the phenomenal progress on the ground.

To quote Yergin and Stanislaw: "… What he saw was enormously changed from what he had viewed in 1984, when Shenzhen was still very much a rough, unfinished city in the making. Now it was a modern high-rise urban area…

"It had been a "flying leap" – the real great leap forward. Shenzhen was no longer an experiment; now it was the model for the future…" (10)

From a market town of 30,000 people in 1979, Shenzhen now has a population close to 12 million (11,906,400 in 2016). Its GDP came to CNY 1.95 trillion, US $284 billion in 2016. China's GDP was US$261.59 billion in 1979. (11)

According to Michael Parker, head of Asia Pacific Strategy at Sanford C. Bernstein & Co, Shenzhen's GDP could jump to US$350 billion in 2018, ahead of ncighbouring Hong Kong's projected US$345 billion. (12)

Originally a fishing village, Shenzhen has become the world's third busiest container seaport, aftcr Shanghai and Singapore.

According to HSBC, Shenzhen is now China's de facto 'Silicon Valley', hosting major ICT companies like nationwide ISP and Tencent, and global players like ZTE and Huawei. (13)

With 101 skyscrapers over 150 metres high in an area of 2,050 sq km (790 sq mi), Shenzhen is 8th in the global list, with one more skyscraper than the provincial capital Guangzhou with its history of over 2,200 years.

Ranked as an Alpha-Global city (14), **Guangzhou** is the manufacturing hub of the Pearl River Delta where heavy industry came in the 1990s with hi-tech electronic equipment and machinery, chemical production and the automotive industry. Guangzhou is one of China's three major automotive manufacturing bases. (14)

As a sub-provincial city of 7,434sq km (2,070 sq mi), Guangzhou has a population of 14 million (2016). Metropolitan Guangzhou has 11.5 million people (2016) on a land area of 3,843 sq km (1,483 sq mi). Its GDP came to CNY 1.96 trillion/US$284 billion in 2016, more than Shenzhen's by a whisker. (15)

In 2008 China announced its plans to integrate the nine key PRD cities of Guangzhou, Shenzhen, Dongguan, Zhaoqing, Foshan, Huizhou, Jiangmen, Zongshen, and Zhuhai into a single megacity.

And, according to HSBC, this move set in motion a series of massive infrastructure projects, merging transport, energy, water and telecoms networks, and further boosting economic development.

The PRD now has a complete network for air, land, and sea transportation. The entire region is covered by a rail network and by 2018, an express rail will connect Guangzhou, Shenzhen and Hong Kong. PRD also has some of China's key sea and inland port facilities, including Shenzhen container port (the world's third largest).

On November 2015, PRD National Independent Innovative Demonstration Zone (PRD NIIDZ) was approved by the State Council as the first and only region-wide NIIDZ, to promote innovation and high-tech industry development. (16)

The PRD generates over 10% of China's GDP annually and a quarter of its exports.

2. Yangtze River Economic Belt (YREB)

In 2014 the development of the massive Yangtze River Economic Belt (YREB) became one of the cardinal features of the new national strategy for sustainable growth and further modernisation.

It's China's largest development network along the designated 1,800-km stretch of the "golden waterway" of the 6,300-km Yangtze River.

The Yangtze River runs through 9 provinces and the two municipalities of Shanghai on eastern China's central coast and Chongqing in the south-west.

The huge YREB development embraces the two municipalities of **Shanghai**, China's largest city on its central coast, and the country's largest municipality of **Chongqing** (twice the size of the Netherlands) in south-western China, as well as the nine provinces of Jiangsu, Zhejiang, Anhui, Jiangxi, Hubei, Hunan, Sichuan, Yunnan, and Guizhou.

Designed and planned for coordinated inter-regional development, the total YREB area of over 2 million sq km covers one-fifth of China's mainland, with a population of 600 million (40% of total Chinese population). YREB produces over 40% of China's GDP.

The YREB is twice the area of Egypt with about one-tenth of the YREB's population, and is twice bigger than France and Germany together, and slightly larger than Indonesia with a population of over260 million.

According to Premier Li Keqiang (as reported in **People's Daily** April 29, 2014), it's logical to use China's strategically routed and largest river to connect relatively developed east China with less developed central and western regions.

Speaking on 28 April 2014 at a symposium held in Chongqing on the construction of the golden waterway of the YREB, Premier Li said its development would provide a new and important driving force for the sustainable development of the Chinese economy, involving development of the delta, city clusters along the middle stretches of the mighty Yangtze River, and Chengdu-Chongqing city cluster and economic zone.

According to the 2015 ADB Report on its proposed YREB development, three major urban agglomeration areas are involved: (1) the Yangtze River Delta Global Mega Agglomeration focused on Shanghai, (2) the Middle Yangtze City Cluster focused on Wuhan, commercial centre and capital of Central China's Hubei province, and a major transportation hub (China's "Chicago"), and (3) the Yangtze Upper Reaches, focused on Chongqing. (17)

According to Premier Li, the Yangtze River's transport system is the most trafficked among the world's inland rivers, but with its remarkable potential for further transport capacity expansion.

On April 2014 the State Council issued guidelines to enhance the traffic capacity of the Yangtze River and its tributaries. Its integrated transport system will connect roads, railways, waterways, and air routes by 2020.

The government plans to further develop railways, highways, waterways, airways, and underground pipelines along the Yangtze River to build a multimodal transport corridor.

On 11 June 2014 the State Council made public its decision to construct a multi-tier transport system along the "golden waterway" of the Yangtze River to promote inter-regional economic integration and to inject fresh energy (chi) into China's economic growth. (18)

As reported in **China Daily** 12 June 2014, the Yangtze River will be dredged to increase the navigation capacity of the Three Gorges Dam, which construction was completed in 2006 to produce electricity with its world's largest hydropower station (22,500 MW) as well as to enhance the Yangtze River's shipping capacity.

China will build railways, roads and airports that connect with ports along the Yangtze River to form a multi-tier transport network. Oil and gas transportation facilities will be improved.

Water resources will be protected through rigorous control over river pollution. Speaking in Chongqing on 5 January 2017, President Xi Jinping said belt development must prioritize ecology and green development, including green manufacturing to reduce pollution and boost economic growth. (19)

On June 2017 the Ministry of Environmental Protection (MEP), National Development and Reform Commission (NRDC), and Ministry of Water Resources (MWR) jointly issued a mandatory environmental protection plan for the Yangtze River Economic Belt (YREB).

On 9 March 2016 the NRDC, Ministry of Industry and Information Technology (MIIT), and Ministry of Science and Technology (MST) jointly issued a blueprint for the YREB development through innovation and industrial restructuring to modernise the industrial system by 2020. By 2030, the YREB will lead the world in innovation and become a major engine to drive further China's economic transformation.   (20)
18.09.2017 16:21

3. **Beijing-Tianjin-Hebei (BTH) Regional Development**

On the back burner for about three decades, the development of Northern China has moved to the fore since 25 February 2014 when President Xi Jinping firmly called for the integrated and coordinated development of Beijing (the national capital), Tianjin (port city and industrial centre) and Hebei (industrial and transportation hub) in the Bohai Bay area in coastal north-eastern China. (21)

Covering an amalgamated area of 216,000 sq km (2.2% of mainland China), with a population of well over 100 million (over 7% of China's) and an aggregate GDP of over US$1 trillion (10.5% of the national), the envisioned development of Beijing (Jing), Tianjing (Jin) and Hebei (Ji) will lead to the emergence of the so-called Jing-Jin-Ji (JJJ) megalopolis.

Bigger than Syria, Tunisia, and Uruguay, the BTH/JJJ region is twice the area of South Korea, slightly bigger than Belarus, Guyana, and New Zealand. Though slightly smaller than the UK, its population is nearly twice as big; though half the size of France, its population is also nearly twice the French.

Though geographically contiguous (both Beijing and Tianjin were once part of Hebei province), the region lacks hitherto the socio-economic cohesion of the Pearl River and Yangtze River Deltas.

With 14 districts and two counties, Beijing occupies an area of 16,410.5 sq km with a population of 20.7 million in 2014 (and estimated 22.8 million in 2015, close to Taiwan's 23.5 million, and with GDP of RMB 2.3 trillion/US$339 billion. After the 2008 Summer Olympic Games, Beijing will host the 2022 Winter Olympics.)

About 120 km (75 mi) to the east of land-locked Beijing is Tianjin on the west coast of the Bohai Gulf. With 13 districts and 3 counties in an area of 11,946.9 sq km, Tianjin is the largest coastal city in northern China with a population 14.1 million in 2014. Though its economic output of RMB 1.65 trillion (US$243 billion) in 2015 was about a quarter less than Beijing's, Tianjin ranked first in China in terms of its per capita GDP.

With 11 prefectural cities, 172 counties and 2,207 townships in an area of 187,700 sq km, and a population of over 72.9 million in 2014 and nearly 75 million in 2015 with GDP of RMB 2.94 trillion (US$434 billion), Hebei has rich natural resources and is China's largest steel producer (about 300 million tonnes per annum, about one quarter of the national output in 2015), but besmirched by smog.

As the northern region has for long been dogged by environmental issues, its coordinated development will prioritize urban traffic management and environmental protection as well as energy security, industrial upgrades and improved public services. (22) Also, the "strictest" management of water resources.

According to an urbanisation document issued on 2 April 2014, Hebei will enlarge its Baoding city, about 150 km/93 mi southwest of Beijing, to accommodate administrative organs, colleges and universities, research institutions, medical and nursing services on transfer from Beijing. With a population of over 11 million, Baoding is a metropolitan area of 1,840 sq km/710 sq mi, slightly twice the size of Singapore.

Midway between Beijing (to the north) and Tianjin (to the east), Hebei's "corridor" city of Langfang (population of over 4 million) will boost its service sector to serve as an ecological and recreational zone for the national capital.

On 8 August 2014 **China Daily** reported on the setup of a leading team and office headed by Vice-Premier Zhang Gaoli, to promote the synergetic development of the BTH/JJJ region.

On 12 December 2014 **Beijing News** reported on the planned investment of 10 billion yuan (US$1.61 billion) to build a Beijing-Tianjin-Hebei (BTH) railway transportation company in order to break the gridlock and spur regional development after nearly three decades of sluggish growth.

On October 2015 Beijing-Tianjin-Hebei Inter-City Railway Investment Company signed an agreement with Tianjin Economic-Technological Development Area (TEDA) to invest RMB 30 billion/ US$4.3 billion) to roll out Binhai-Beijing inter-city line in 2020 and cut travel time to less than an hour.

Within the Tianjin Municipality, Binhai has a population of well over one million in an area of 2,270 sq km/ 880 sq mi. and is fast developing as a new growth area.

Officially referred to as the Tianjin Binhai New Area (TBNA), Binhai plays a key part in the Tianjin Free Trade Zone (FTZ) established in April 2015. It's designed as a national hub for financial and high-end services as well as advanced and high-tech industries. Binhai hosts 6 industrial clusters from microelectronics and steel to chemical engineering and new energy, and 14 industrial chains from mobile communication products and microelectronics to green food processing and new building materials.

Tianjin's new Dongjiang port area is planned to complement the TBNA and to serve as a focal point for trade and logistics.

"Every administration since Deng Xiaoping's has taken on an ambitious economic project that defines its legacy," Cary Huang commented in **South China Morning Post** 25 June 2014.

"For President Xi Jinping, that project is to link 130 million people (a trickle more than Japan's) across Bejing, Tianjin and Hebei province into a single megalopolis, the so-called Jing-Jin-Ji (JJJ) region.

"Xi has held out the model as a template for China's urbanisation in the future..."

On 24 August 2015 the State Council in Beijing posted on its website a guideline on JJJ coordinated development "Confirmed Positioning for Jing-Jin-Ji Co-ordinated Development Functions", entailing (1-2-3-4):

One Core: Beijing to alleviate its congestion through removal (offloading) of economic activities not crucial to its operation as the nation's capital;

Two Cities: Beijing and Tianjin to function and operate as the "twin engines" of regional development;

Three Axes: three main corridors for industrial development and urbanisation forming Jing-Jin-Ji's geographical backbone: (1) Beijing-Tianjin (BT) axis from east to west, (2) Beijing-Baoding-Shijiazhuang (BBS) axis through Hebei's south-west, and (3) Beijing-Tangshan-Qinhuangdao (BTQ) axis;

Four Zones: (1) a central co-ordinating zone around Beijing, (2) an eastern zone around Tianjin's Binhai port area for development support, (3) a southern zone for Greenfield development, and (4) a north-west zone for ecological conservation. (23)

According to the document issued on 24 August 2015 by the office of the leading group for Beijing-Tianjin-Hebei integrated development in the next 15 years, an improved economic structure and better public services will be provided with a cleaner environment in the region by 2030. BTH will also emerge with "strong competitiveness and influence globally". (24)

Beijing will become the national center for politics, culture, international exchanges, and scientific and technological innovation.

Tianjin will be a national research and development base for advanced manufacturing, a hub for international shipping in North China, a zone for financial innovation and services, and a pilot zone for economic reform.

Hebei province will be an important national base for trade and logistics, a pilot zone for industrial transformation and upgrading, a demonstration area for modern urbanisation and urban-rural integration, and an ecological buffer zone.

Development of three city clusters will be closely coordinated: (1) Beijing (population of over 22 million) and Tianjin (over 14 million),

(2) Beijing, Baoding (over 11 million), and Shijiazhuang (Hebei's capital and largest city with population of 10.7 million in 2015), and (3) Beijing, Tangshan (industrial and Qinhuangdao (port city with about 3 million residents and about 300 km/200 mi east of Beijing).

On 1 April 2017 China announced the creation of the **Xiongan New Area (XNA)** in Hebei, about 100 km southwest of downtown Beijing, to advance the coordinated development of the BTH/JJJ region. President Xi has ordered the building of a modern urban district, guided by new development concepts, "world vision, international standards, Chinese characteristics and high goals" to build Xiongan into a new model of innovative and optimised urban development in densely-populated areas. (25)

4. **The millennial call of Xiongan New Area (XNA)**

The development of the Xiongan New Area (XNA) will initially focus on its three rural counties of Xiong, Rongcheng and Anxi with a combined area of 100 sq km, which will eventually expand 20-fold to 2,000 sg km, as big as Shenzhen. (26)

Xiongan is the 19th "national new area" created since 1992.

According to Chen Gang, CCP district chief in Hebei Province, Xiong's development will follow "a thousand-years strategy" in President Xi's millennial development project for China.

Xiongan will take over Beijing's non-capital functions and accommodate the capital's colleges, universities and research institutions, hospitals, business headquarters and state enterprises, and financial as well as public institutions in keeping with its envisioned status and development.

By 2035, Xiongan will basically develop into a modern city that is green, digital/intelligent/smart, and livable as well as competitive with innovative high-end and high-tech industries, a fast and highly-efficient transportation network, shared quality public services, and a modernized city security system to boot. It's also expected to house about 4.5 million people from Beijing.

According to an estimate by Morgan Stanley, American multinational investment bank and financial services company, up to 2.4 trillion yuan (US$362 billion) (over 13 times Three Gorges' 180 billion yuan) is expected to be invested in Xiong's development over the next couple of decades.

"The establishment of Xiongan New Area in Hebei Province is a significant decision and arrangement by the CPC Central Committee with Comrade Xi Jinping at the core to push forward the coordinated development of Beijing, Tianjin, and Hebei," states the 2018-2035 master plan document (published on 21 April 2018).

Described as "a significant national event", the development of Xiongan will be according to "a strategy that will have lasting importance for the millennium to come..."

It will include developing a scientific and reasonable layout, shaping the city landscape for a new era, building a beautiful natural ecology and environment, developing high-end service and high-tech industries, providing quality shared public services and amenities, constructing a fast and highly-efficient transportation network, building a green and smart new city, fostering a modernized city security system, and ensuring the orderly and effective implementation of the development plan. (27)

According to plan, Xiongan is expected to become "a model city in the history of human development."

Associate Professor Liu Chunsheng of the Central University of Finance and Economics commented on **CGTN** 21 April 2018:

"... The master plan aims to build a world-leading smart city, set up intelligent transportation networks, create a high-quality ecological system and green area. Develop high-tech industries and high-end service industries, establish platforms for innovation, foster a modernized city security system, gather top talents and provide efficient and effective public services..."

Major industries include information, biotechnology, new materials, modern services, and green agriculture,

By high-speed railway, it will take only 20 minutes to travel from Xiongan to Beijing's planned new airport in Daxing District, 30 minutes to Beijing and Tianjin, and one hour to Shijiazhuang, the capital of Hebei Province.

Xiongan will serve Beijing's role as an international exchange center. A pilot Free Trade Zone (FTZ) is also expected to be set up in Xiongan.

Intergovernmental cooperation programs will be developed as well as a comprehensive bonded zone.

High-quality development

Over 100 high-end and high-tech enterprises have set up branches in Xiongan, accumulating resources for innovation. (28)

The plan has 38 key targets to build Xiongan into a smart city, including over 90% smart infrastructure and a smart management system for big data assets, to provide a model of high-quality urban development.

A digital version of the city will be built in tandem with the physical metropolis to form a digital-physical city system that allows the testing of crucial decisions in a simulated Xiongan before their implementation on the ground.

By using the latest technologies in the smart Internet of Things (IoT) platform and cloud computing, etc., the new city will be able to monitor, analyze, and optimize the deployment and management of public resources.

A green and livable city

About 70% of XNA will be covered by trees and water. Parks will stand in the suburbs, downtown areas, and residential communities for the dwellers to enjoy a close-to-nature life. All roads and streets will be tree-lined.

Forest coverage will be extended from 11% to 40%, prioritizing ecological protection and green development. The Baiyandian National Park will be established after restoration of the Baiyandian Lake to 360 sq km.

New-type villages will be developed in a demarcated area of 50 sq km, to feature a pleasant living environment with thriving businesses, sound infrastructure facilities and public services.

No large-scale real estate development. Population density not to exceed 10,000 people per sq km.

The XNA plan emphasizes green, smart, and innovative development by promoting a green and low-carbon way of living as well as clean urban construction and operation. Environment-friendly and energy-saving materials and techniques will be widely used.

Its construction will be people-centered; all its public amenities, facilities and services will be shared by all to make this new modern city a very attractive, livable and highly sustainable urban environment for the fortunate Xiongan ("Bold Peace") residents and enterprises.   09-10.01.2019 00:34

5. **Greater Bay Area (GBA) Development**

On 13 January 2019 Beijing gave its blessings to the development blueprint for the "Greater Bay Area" in southern China to agglomerate the quartet of major cities of Hong Kong, Macau, Guangzhou and Shenzhen, and seven other neighbouring mainland cities in the Pearl River Delta, to create a mega regional zone of 56,500 sq km (bigger in area than Costa Rica, Croatia, and many other countries in the world).

In creating its own "Silicon Valley", China will build a high-tech hub by facilitating the free flow of talents, goods and services as well as other resources among the Special Administrative Region (SAR) of Hongkong, the SAR of Macau, and the 9 mainland cities of Guangzhou, Shenzhen, Zhuhai, Dongguan, Huizhou, Zhangshan, Foshan, Zhaoqing, and Jiangmen in southern China's Guangdong Province.

Though occupying only 0.6% of China's total land area, the GBA commands some 13% of its GDP, about 10 trillion yuan (US$1.48 trillion) in 2017. According to Morgan Stanley, the GBA's economy will more than double by 2030.

The GBA has a population of about 71 million, bigger than that of Britain or France, or South Korea, and many other nations.

On 18 February 2019, the Central Committee of the CPC and State Council unveiled the development plan for the GBA to transform it into one of the world's top bay areas like New York, Tokyo and San Francisco, with a world-class smart city cluster as well as a world-class technology industry innovation centre, and to provide a role model for China's further opening up as well as a new driver for regional and national economic growth.

Lin Chunsheng, associate professor of Central University of Finance and Economics in China, has written that having developed a fairly complete high-tech industrial chain, the GBA is expected to develop into one of the most influential technological innovation centers in the world (as reported by **CGTN** Feb 20, 2019).   29.03.2019 19:32

Notes NEW CHINA A (10) CONCENTATED URBANISATION

1. **hitachi.en**
2. **People's Daily Online** March 19, 2014
3. **mckinsey.com**
4. Press release 2014/395/EAP by World Bank, Beijing, March 25, 2014
5. John Vidal 22 March 2010 2010 **theguardian.com**
6. **Bloomberg**/Beijing report in **New Straits Times** April 25, 2016
7. World Bank Report March 2015: **East Asia's Changing Urban Landscape: Measuring a Decade of Spatial Growth**. **worldbank.org**

    According to the World Bank press release issued in Singapore on January 26, 2015, there was a movement of about 200million people to urban areas from 2000 to 2010.

    "...The Pearl River Delta in China – which includes the cities of Guangzhou, Shenzhen, Foshan and Dongguang – has overtaken

Tokyo as the world's largest urban area in both size (land area) and population, with more inhabitants than countries such as Argentina, Australia or Canada..."

8. **wikipedia.org**
9. Touchstone/Simon & Schuster, New York, 1999, p. 198
10. **THE COMMANDING HEIGHTS** p. 206

Yergin and Stanlislaw have written (p. 214):

"... Reform launched China on high growth. Between 1978 and 1995, China's foreign trade increased from $36 billion to $300 billion. Per capita income doubled between 1978 and 1987 and doubled again between 1987 and 1996 – a rate unheard of in modern history. It took Britain sixty years to double its per capita income; the United States fifty years. In instituting reforms with such effect, Deng did something that no one else in history has ever accomplished – he lifted upward of 200 million people out of poverty in just two decades..."

11. **wikipedia.org**
12. **Bloomberg**/Shenzhen report in **New Straits Times** September 7, 2017
13. **business.hsbc.uk**
14. **wikipedia.org**
    According to a report released on 5 May 2018 by the Guangdong Academy of Social Sciences, the GDP of Guangdong province will reach 26.2 trillion yuan (about US$4.14 trillion) by 2035 to account for 12.4% of China's total GDP, and to catch up economically with France, the UK, etc. to become the world's 6th largest economy.

    CHINA DIGEST/ASIA TIMES (atimes.com) May 7, 2018   19.08.2018 20:30

15. **wikipedia.org**
16. **HSBC business.hsbc.uk**
17. **adb.org**
18. **BBC News** 12.06.2014
19. **Global Times** 2017/7/22
20. **chinadaily.com Xinhua**/Beijing 2016-03-9
21. **cityofbeijing.gov.cn** 2014-02-08
22. **CHINESE SOCIAL SCIENCES TODAY csstoday.com** 2015-05-21
23. **The Economist Corporate Network corporatenetwork.com/ ecn-jingji-2016-pdf China's Jing-Jin-Ji regional economic strategy: 2016 progress update** (14 pages) sponsored by JLL real estate agency **joneslanglasalle.com.cn** 15 pages 4,032 words 27-28-09.2017 04:15
24. **Xinhua/China Daily** August 24, 2015 **china.org.cn**
25. **XINHUANET xinhuanet.com** 2017-04-01 08:56

Expected to start operating by end of 2020, HSR service will cut commuting time between Xiongan and Beijing to about 30 minutes.

President Xi Jinping has called the coordinated and integrated development of the BTH/JJJ region a "major national strategy" for China's sustainable growth.

The envisaged development is of an economic powerhouse in Northern China to rival the Pearl River Delta (PRD) and the Yangtze River Economic Belt in the triad of national turbochargers, of China's concentrated urbanisation, coordinated regional development, modernisation and rejuvenation.

26. Xie Yu 20 Jul, 2018 **SCMP South China Morning Post**

In Jan 2019 the Chinese authorities approved the 2018-2035 Master Plan for developing the Xiongan New Area (XNA) into a high-level socialist modern "city of the future" by 2035, a new engine of growth for China's modern economic system, and as a national model for high-quality development in the new era. **CCTV** March 31, 2019

The industrial layout of the XNA's development plan will prioritize artificial intelligence (AI), big data, cloud computing, mobile internet, biopharmaceutical development, genetic engineering, high-end medical equipment, and satellite communication, to form a world-class high-tech industrial cluster.

As of March 2019, 2,582 enterprises have registered to operate in the XNA, more than half of them from information and technology industries.Technology giants like Tencent, Alibaba, and Baidu are among the pioneers, having relocated to the XNA in Sept 2017. **CGTN** Apr 01, 2019

27. According to a blog by Artem Risukhin November 5, 2018 **KITCAST.TV**,

A city is "smart" when investments in human/social capital and information technology infrastructure (data centers & hubs, ISPs, digital signage & communication technologies) support sustainable growth and enhances the quality of life through participatory governance.

Simply put, a SmartCity is a municipality that uses IoT (Internet of Things) and communication tech to increase its efficiency, share information and goods with its citizens and improve services and welfare…

When we say Smart, we mean efficient. When we say Smart City, we mean technologically advanced and inclusive. However controversial and challenging the new urbanistic paradigm might be, it creates a whole new technological environment for citizens, investors and technologically augmented companies.... 09.01.2019 08:06

From 2017, 12 top planning and design teams from China and abroad took part in the formulation of the 2018-2035 master plan for the development of Xiongan, including over 300 world experts. **CGTN** Apr 21, 2018

28. Zhang Xudong, Qi Leijie, Wang Min, An Bei & Yu Qiongyuan: <u>Xiongan: A City of the Future</u> **China Today** 2018-08-10 13:19:00

20 pages 6,292 words 18.09.2017 16:27 27-28.09.2017 06:06 14.01.2018 06:35
19.08.2018 20:32
10.01.2019 00:37 29.03.2019 19:36 01.04.2019 17:11

NEW CHINA A(11)
CHINA'S INFRASTRUCTURE (UPDATED COPY)

China's Infrastructure and Built Assets

According to a report released on 25 July 2017 by Global Infrastructure Hub (GIH) and Oxford Economics, China accounted for almost 30% of global infrastructure investment in 2007-15. China will have to invest about $28 trillion in infrastructure projects from 2016 to 2040 -- 30% of the global total $97 trillion.   21.08.2018 21:00

(A) Railways

Rail is the primary and major mode of long-haul transport in China, and it has developed considerably from a network of 21,800 km (13,546 mi) in 1949 to 120,970 km /75,167 mi (including 19,000 km/11,806 mi High Speed Rail, the world's largest HSR system) in 2015 – the world's second largest rail network after the US railway of over 250,000 km.

China has built and operated 127,000 km of railway infrastructure, up by 150% from 1978 when the country started its reform and opening up to the outside world.   16.10.2018 16:29

Nearly half (47%) of the Chinese railroad track was electrified by 2010. (1) Close to 70% of China's 127,000 km rail transport network was electrified by the end of 2017 (87,000 km/over 68% electrified).

China will invest 3.5 trillion yuan (US$503.3 billion) in railway construction during the 13th Five-Year Plan (13FYP) period (2016-2020).

According to the White Paper on **Development of China's Transport** issued by the State Council Information Office in Beijing on 29 December 2016, the HSR network will be extended to 30,000 km by 2020 to link over 80% of the big cities in the country.(2)

According to the White Paper, high-speed rail (HSR) has become a symbol of Made-in-China and going-global products, and "China's technologies for high-speed, alpine, plateau and heavy-haul railways have reached the world's advanced level..."

On 28 December 2016, the day before the release of the White Paper, China launched one of the world's longest HSR railways – the 2,252-km Shanghai-Kunming line, crossing 5 provinces and cutting travel time from 35 to 11 hours.

On 28 December 2016, China also launched another HSR line from Kunming, capital of southwest China's Yunnan province, to Nanning, capital of Guangxi region in southern China near the border with Vietnam.

The White Paper states: "High-performance railway equipment technologies with proprietary intellectual property (IP) rights, represented by high-speed railways and high-power locomotives, have reached the advanced world level, with some of them leading the world..."

Moreover, China's key construction technologies for offshore deep-water ports, improved technologies for large estuary waterways, and construction technologies for large-scale airports are leading the world.

And, according to the White Paper, China will build a faster, greener public transport system throughout the country by 2020.

(B) Public Roads

China's roads and highways expanded from 1 million km in 1990 to 4.3 million km (including over 90,000 km expressways) in 2013.

China has built 4.77 million km by the end of 2017, up 440% from 1978, including over 136,000 km of expressways.   16.10.2018 16:34

All major cities will be linked by a 108,000 km/67,108 mi interprovincial expressway system by 2020. (3)

(C) Expressways

China's first expressway, Shanghai-Jiading Expressway (17.57 km/10.79 mi) opened on 31 October 1988. China's expressway network exceeded 10,000 km (6,200 mi) in late 1999. (4)

1989 147 km (91 mi)
1994 1,145 km (711 mi)
1996 2,141 km (13,330 mi)
1997 3,422 km (2,126 km)
1998 4,771 km (2,965 mi)
1999 8,733 km (5,426 mi)
2000 11,605 km (7,211 mi)
2002 19,453 km (12,088 mi)
2004 29,800 km (18,500 mi)
2008 53,913 km (33,500 mi)
2011 74,113 km (46,052 mi)
2012 84,946 km (52,783 mi)
2014 104, 500 km (64,900 mi)
2017 (early) 131,000 km (81,000 mi), 136,400 km by end of 2017, ranking first in the world, covering 97% of cities with a population of 200,000 or more.

From zero in 1988, China's expressway network overtook the American Interstate Highway by late 2011. (5)

The world's largest, China's National Trunk Highway System (NTHS) comprises 7radial expressways from Beijing, 11 north-south expressways, and 18 east-west expressways.

China's expressways are slated to surpass 139,000 km (93,000mi) in 2020.

(D) Metro/Rapid Transit Systems

From 2009 to 2015, China built 87 mass transit rail lines totalling 3,100 km in 26 cities at an estimated cost of 988.6 billion yuan (about US$150 billion).

China can boast the world's longest and second longest metro systems as well as four of the 10 busiest.

As of early 2017, China has 30 metros operating 3,586 km across the country, including some of the world's largest and busiest subway networks. While 17 new projects are under construction, 39 cities have been signalled the green light to proceed with their planned metros. (6)

China is reportedly in the midst of a massive expansion and upgrading of its transportation infrastructure. With the need to sustain the momentum of economic growth, rapid urbanisation and mounting traffic demand, the government has reportedly relaxed and lowered the minimum criteria for a city to build its subway system from over 3 million people and annual revenue of 10 billion yuan (US$1.53 billion) to an urban population of over 1.5 million. (7)

Opened on 1 October 1969, the Beijing Subway presently operates 19 lines (including 1 airport express line), 345 stations, and a track system of 574 km (357 mi). It's the world's second largest after the Shanghai Metro.

Beijing Subway is the world's busiest with 3.66 billion trips (2016), averaging 9.998 million per day with a daily record of 12.69 million on 1 May 2016.

Beijing Subway is building 6 fully automated lines totalling 300 km (over 190 mi); China's first driverless metro is expected to be inaugurated in 2017.

In early 2017, China has 5,636.5 km of rail transit lines under construction. Under the 13FYP, about 3,000 km of new tracks will be added to the urban rail transit system by 2020.

Beijing Subway will expand its track to 999 km (621 mi) to deliver 18.5 million trips per day by 2020.

Opened on 28 May 1993, the Shanghai Metro operates 14 lines, 364 stations, and a track network of 588 km (365.4 mi). Its annual ridership of 3.4 billion (2016) averaged 9.29 million per day in 2016, with a record 11.867 million on 28 April 2017.

Shanghai Metro became the world's largest in early 2010.

The 13FYP envisions a more sustainable transport system, prioritizing high-capacity public transit particularly urban rail transit and bus rapid transit.

All cities with over 3 million residents will start or continue to develop urban rail networks.

In 2017, 43 third-tier cities have received approvals to develop subway lines, mainly in Shandong, Henan, Guangdong, Anhui and Hebei provinces.

Regional railway networks will connect and integrate urban agglomerations such as the Jingjinji/JJJ in northern China, the Yangtze River Delta, and the Pearl River Delta in southern China where their intercity railway networks will be completed by 2020.

China reportedly plans to spend 4.7 trillion yuan (US$706 billion) on transport infrastructure in 2016-2018.

(E) 13FYP Outlays on Transportation and Infrastructure

According to the Minister of Transport Li Xiaopeng at a press conference on 28 February 2017, the 13th Plan (2016-2020) will invest RMB 15 trillion (US$2.17 trillion) on transportation and infrastructure:

- Railways RMB 3.5 trillion (US$510 billion)
- Roads RMB 7.8 trillion (US$1.13 trillion)

- Civil aviation RMB 650 billion (US$94 billion)
- Water transportation RMB 500 billion (US$72 billion).

2020 targets: 150,000 km of railway lines (120,970 km in 2015)

: 5 million km of roads (3.98 million km in 2011)
: 260 airports (170 in 2010)
: 2,527 berths for vessels over 10,000 tonnes
: HSR 30,000 km to connect over 80% of cities with population of over one million each. (8)

(F) Construction Sector

Despite projected slowdown (especially in housing construction), China remains the world's largest construction market.

According to the report by Global Construction Perspectives and Oxford Economics released on 10 November 2015, China will contribute US$2.1 trillion to construction output by 2030 and account for almost a quarter of global construction activity (slightly higher than present levels, having peaked in 2013). (9)

(G) China's Built Assets Top the World's

According to the most recent (October 2015) Global Built Asset Wealth Index published by Arcadis, design and consultancy firm for natural and built assets, China has overtaken the US as the world's wealthiest country as measured by the value of its built environment – the value of all the buildings and infrastructure contributing to economic productivity.

With its built asset wealth of $47.6 trillion, China leads and tops the world; the US with its built asset wealth of $36.8 trillion loses its global leadership for the first time.

China has invested $33 trillion in its built assets since 2000.

China's investment in its infrastructure is 9% of its GDP, compared with 2% of the US.

According to Tom Morgan, vice president, head of business advisory, North America at Arcadis, "a strategically planned, highly developed and well maintained built environment is critical to the economic and social success of a nation..." (10)

According to a recent report by McKinsey & Company, a global management consulting firm, the world will require around $49 trillion in new economic infrastructure investment by 2030. (11)

Of the global investment of $31.4 trillion in 2000-2015, China spent 26%, North America 22%, and Europe 16%.

Over the next 15 years up to 2030, China will invest around $14 trillion. While North America will continue to invest around 22% of the total (about $10 trillion), Western Europe will invest 12%.

According to Arcadis, the global investment of over $217 trillion in built assets generated a return of about $36 trillion in 2016 (about 40% of global GDP), including China's $10.4 trillion and US share of $5.4 trillion. China will benefit by almost $18 trillion by 2026, more than double the US return of about $7 trillion. (12)

Notes NEW CHINA A (11) China's Infrastructure

1. **wikipedia.org**
    In 1992 China launched a large-scale rail project known as the "New World's Silk Road" aka "Eurasian Continental Bridge", involving development of a 4,131 km/2,567 mi railroad route from Lianyugang, Jiangsu through central and northwestern China to Urumqi, Xinjiang, to the Alatau Pass in Kazakhstan, the historical Dzungarian Gate mountain pass between China and Central Asia over a distance of 4,800 km/3,000 mi, and thence over 6,800 km/4,225 mi to Rotterdam, a major port city in the Dutch province of South Holland in the Netherlands in northwestern Europe.

2. **Xinhua/Shanghai Daily** December 30, 2016
3. **wikipedia.org**
4. **wikipedia.org**

Also known as the Hujia Expressway, near Shanghai's Hongqiao Airport but across town from the Pudong International Airport. Jiading is located in the northwestern part of Shanghai.

5. **wikipedia.org**

With a total length of 77,017 km/47,856 mi, the US Interstate Highway System (IHS), officially named the Dwight D. Eisenhower National System of Interstate and Defense Highways, took some 35 years to construct and complete at an estimated cost of around $425 billion (equivalent to $526 billion in 2016).

An estimated 2 trillion yuan (about US$300 billion in 2016) was invested in development of China's NTHS expressway network.

6. **wikipedia.org**   680 words 07.10.2017 21:03
7. **Economic Daily** May 16, 2016

According to Wu Chungeng, spokesperson for Transport Ministry (as reported in **People's Daily Online** 2017-09-21), urban buses provided over 70 billion passenger trips in 2016 while rail transit delivered 16.15 billion passenger trips.

China had 608,600 electric buses in service by end of 2016, on operating routes of 981,200 km.

Also in service were 165,000 clean-energy buses.

8. **CHINA MONEY NETWORK** PAN YUE March 1, 2017 By 2011, China overtook the US and EU to become the world's

largest investor in infrastructure, having invested 8.5% of GDP in 1992-2011 vis-a-vis 2.6% of GDP in the US and EU. **mckinsey.com**

9. **South China Morning Post** Jessie Lau 10 Nov 2015 **scmp.com**

According to **TRADING ECONOMICS tradingeconomics. com** Oct 2017, China GDP from Construction 1992-2017 averaged 9416.04 CNY HML from 1992 until 2017, reaching an all time high of 49522 CNY HML in the fourth quarter of 2016 and a record low of 181.90 CNY HML in the first quarter of 1992.

10. **THE MARITIME EXECUTIVE** Mar Ex 2015-1**0-19** **maritime-executive.com**
11. **consultancy.uk** 02 Jan 2017
12. **consultancy.uk** 04 Jan 2017

Note on the Cement Industry in China.

China consumed over 6 billion tons of cement in three years from 2011 to 2013, and used more cement than the US did throughout the 20th century.

With nearly 60% of global cement production capacity, China's is 30 times that of the US.

In 2011 the cement industry produced over 2000 MT (2 billion tons) for the first time in China. Production was 2,403 million (2.4 billion) tons in 2016, from 166 million tons in 1986. **CISION prnews. wire.com**

Anhui Conch, China's largest cement producer with 34 plants, made 219.13 MT in 2015.   8 pages 1,976 words 27.12.2017 20:10 14.01.2018 06:41

9 pages 2 211 words 08-09.10.2017 02:41 03:11 21.08.2018 21:16 16.10.2018 16:40 18.10.2018 19:54

NEW CHINA A(12)
CHINA'S SHIPBUILDING SURGE

China's Shipbuilding's Surge
To Global Leadership

By mid-2010, China sailed past South Korea which had in 2001 displaced Japan as the leader in the shipbuilding world. Japan had for long been the world's top shipbuilder, having produced about half of global new ship tonnage since the early 1960s.

In the first half of 2010, China accounted for about 41% of global shipbuilding capacity, 46% of new orders (about 16.4 million deadweight tons/dwt), and 38% of the volume of backlog orders of the world market, despite difficulties in the wake of the 2008 global financial crisis.

In the first half of 2010, China's shipbuilding enterprises completed and exported 24.3 million deadweight tons (dwt).

China's takeoff in the modern shipbuilding industry took place shortly after the establishment on July 1999 of the country's two largest state-owned shipbuilders – the China State Shipbuilding Corporation (CSSC) and the China Shipbuilding Industry Corporation (CSIC).

"China has witnessed remarkable achievements in the shipbuilding industry in recent years. The shipbuilding industry has become one of the industries with world-class competitiveness in China, and an important window for countries worldwide to understand the level of China's industrial development," said Zhang Changtao, chief researcher of the Economic Research Center of China Shipbuilding. (1)

Central government has introduced effective policies guiding the industry's development. China has fully mastered the technologies required for constructing oil tankers, bulk carriers and container ships, and presently owns a series of standardized ship brands.

As also reported in **People's Daily** August 13, 2010, China has independently developed a series of ships such as the eco-friendly bulk carriers with a displacement of 175,000 tons and new-generation ships that meet international standards. China has started mass production of domestically-designed large container ships for the world market. (2)

"Announced by China, the programme "5-3-1" put down a marker to reach global leadership by 2015," Rima Mickeviciene of Lithuania's Klaipeda University has written. (3)

"However, fortune was kinder to China than it might have expected. Its emerging economy (its high growth rate averaging 10.7% per annum over the decade 2002-2012), huge human potential, and State support have resulted In its target accomplishment in half the time (by mid-2010)..."

As Mickeviciene has put it, China's leadership in global shipbuilding was propelled by acceleration of economic growth, fuelled by lowest labour cost in the market (nearly 50% of Japan's and 30% of South Korea's in 2006), by State development programmes and government subsidies as well as by growing shipyard capacity.

With strong government support and huge investments, Chinese shipbuilding was further boosted by its price competitiveness and cooperation with foreign equipment manufacturers.

As reported by Global Security.org, China is the leading shipbuilding country in the world. As of the end of October 2010, China's production completion of shipbuilding was 50.90 million deadweight tons (dwt) which was 58.4% more than in the corresponding period in 2009, and new orders of the industry came to 54.62 dwt – 2.9 times that of the same period in 2009. (4)

China overtook South Korea as the world's top shipbuilder in the first half of 2010, and kept ahead in terms of three major industry indicators, including new orders, order backlogs and delivery.

According to data released on December 2016 by Clarksons Research, a highly respected and authoritative provider of intelligence for global shipping, Japan had a backlog of 20.64 million compensated gross tons (CGT) to surpass South Korea's (19.91 CGT) for the first time in 17 years. (5)

China remains the world's largest shipbuilding nation with roughly 30 million CGT.

According to a July 2017 report in **Seatrade Maritime News**, the recession following the 2003-2008 boom has exacted quite a heavy toll on Chinese shipyards. The number of "active" Chinese shipyards ("active" with at least one 1,000+ gross tonnes unit on order) has dropped considerably from their record 934 at the start of 2009 to 358 on July 2017. (6)

Those in the "White List" (first released in September 2014 as a guide to the yards deserving of government support) number 70, including 37 state-owned and 24 privately-owned.

According to an official statement published 17 January 2017 on the website of the Ministry of Industry and Information Technology (MIIT), China aims to capture up to 40% of the global high-end marine equipment market over the years through 2020 while reforming and supporting its money-losing shipbuilding industry. (7)

With the global shipping industry in a severe downturn, demand for new vessels has plunged. Many shipyards, which build mainly mid-to-low-end vessels such as cheap dry bulk carriers and tug boats, have shut down.

"Our shipbuilding industry is facing its most difficult challenge since financial crisis, making the task to restructure and upgrade the industry urgent and arduous," the government stated.

Government will encourage industry to increase spending on research and to focus on building more high-end products such as offshore equipment, with the aim of 35-40% of the market by 2020.

France's CMA CGM, a leading worldwide container transportation and shipping company, has recently signed a letter of intent (LOI) with Hudong-Zhonghua Shipyard and Shanghai Waigaoqiao Shipbuilding to construct 9 22,000 TEU container ships. The two Chinese companies clinched the world's largest container ship deals, and **The Medi Telegraph** reported from Seoul on 21 August 2017 that the South Korean shipbuilding industry was in shock.

The US$1.44 billion deal is to build 9 ultra-large container ships with dual-fuel propulsion systems operating on either LNG or fuel oil.

According to foreign container shippers, Chinese shipyards' technology and price competitiveness have caught up with Korea's.

"China's shipbuilders have surpassed their counterparts in Western Europe, Japan, and South Korea in terms of the number and types of ships they can produce," the U.S.-China Economic and Security Review Commission reported to Congress on November 2014. (8)

"China's shipbuilders could reach the technical proficiency of Russian shipbuilders by 2020 and approach the technical proficiency of U.S. shipbuilders by 2030..."

The Department of Defense reported to Congress in November 2016:

"... China's two largest state-owned shipbuilders – the China State Shipbuilding Corporation (CSSC) and the China Shipbuilding Industry Corporation (CSIC) – collaborate in shared ship designs and construction information to increase shipbuilding efficiency.

"China continues to invest in foreign suppliers for some propulsion units, but is becoming increasingly self-sufficient.

"China is the top ship-producing nation in the world..." (9)

In its May 2017 Report to Congress, the DOD has reiterated: "... China is the top ship-producing nation in the world and has increased its shipbuilding capacity and capability for all types of military projects, including submarines, surface combatants, naval aviation, sealift, and amphibious assets..." (10)

In its August 2018 Report to Congress, the DoD has stated (p. 86): "... China now produces its naval gas turbines and diesel engines domestically -- as well as almost all shipboard weapons and electronic systems -- and is almost entirely self-sufficient with little dependence on traditional foreign suppliers for shipbuilding."   30.03.2019 33:55

Notes NEW CHINA A(12) China's Shipbuilding Surge

1. **People's Daily Online** 16:15 August 13, 2010
2. According to **People's Daily Online** 2017-09-22, Fujian Mawei Shipbuilding (MS), is building the world's first deep sea mining vessel to be operational in 2018.

    Measuring 227 meters long and 75 meters high, the new vessel will be capable of working to depths of 2,500 meters and carrying 40,000 tons of ore; it will integrate advanced technologies, including deep sea mining robots, a deep sea lift system, water-storage and cargo-loading systems. It will accommodate 200 people.

3. Chapter 11 of **The Economic Geography of Globalization**, edited by Prof. Piotr Pachuva, page 202 **intechopen.com InTech-Global** 27 July 2011
4. **Globalsecurity.org** page last modified on 27-02-2017.

    GlobalSecurity.org is a leading source of news and security information, directed by John Pike.

5. **gcaptain.com** Jan 4, 2017
6. **seatrade-maritime.com** posted 21 July 2017 by Lee Hong Liang.
7. **Reuters**/Shanghai report Jan 12, 2017 in **Business Times**
8. **uscc.gov/pdf** page 290
9. 2016 Annual Report to Congress on China's Military Power

    globalsecurity.org page last modified 27-02-2017 19:48:01 ZULU

10. **Annual Report to Congress** May 15, 2017 **defense.gov**

China's first home-grown aircraft carrier Type 001A was launched on 26 April 2017. 313 m long and 75 m wide, the new carrier has a displacement of 50,000 tonnes and a cruising speed of 31 knots.

The PLA Navy's new destroyer Type 055, a 10,000-ton domestically designed and manufactured vessel, was launched on 28 June 2017.

The new Chinese destroyer is reported to be Asia's most advanced and largest warship, and the world's second most powerful destroyer after the US Navy's Zumwalt class DDG-911. **chinamil.com.cn** 2017-10-16

China is constructing a very large new-generation amphibious assault vessel, the 075 Landing Helicopter Dock, a variant of aircraft carrier.

China is also building new nuclear-powered ballistic missile submarines (SSBNS) to further boost its undersea nuclear deterrent power.

According to CSIC statement on 23 October 2017, China's first permanent magnet propulsion motor was successfully tested on 18 October 2017.

According to Rear Admiral Ma Weiming, the PLA Navy is outfitting its latest nuclear attack submarines (SSNs) with a "shaftless" rim-driven pump jet, considered to be a revolutionary low-noise propulsion system.

Chinese shipyards are outperforming their South Korean rivals in the construction of high-end mega-container ships, cruise liners and other special-purpose vessels, having already sharpened their manufacturing cutting-edge and grabbed a larger share of the global market, according to Jin Peng, secretary-general of China Association of National Shipbuilding in Beijing.

In the first eight months of 2017 January to August, China's shipbuilders received new orders amounting to 13.34 dwt – 32.9% of new orders worldwide vis-a-vis South Korea's 27%.

COSCO Shipping Heavy Industries is building 4 of the world's biggest offshore subsea support vessels for Maersk Supply Services, the Danish company providing marine services to the offshore energy sector worldwide. The first of four, Maersk Installer, was delivered in Oct 2017.

On 13 Oct 2017, Hudong-Zhonghua Shipbuilding in Shanghai delivered the first of four 174,000-cubic-meter trifuel diesel electric liquefied natural gas (LNG) carriers to an Australian client. **China Daily** 2017-10-24

About as big as an aircraft carrier, China's largest LNG carrier "Pan Asia" (290 m long and 46.95 m wide) entered service on 14 Oct 1017. "This tanker showcases the peak of China's shipbuilding industry," Huang Guoliang, Pan Asia project manager, told **CCTV**.

7 pages 1832 words 16.10.2017 06:59 26.10.2017 05:47 10.11.2017 10:55 27.12.2017 20:23 14.01.2018 06:45 16.10.2018 16:54 15.12.2018 23:05

30.03.2019 23:05

NEW CHINA A(13)
CHINA'S AVIATION

The Making of A Global Aviation Power

(A) China's Military Aviation

One year after Mao's decision on January 1955 to initiate China's nuclear weapons programme, he directed to start R&D on aircraft and missile delivery systems for the future nuclear bombs and warheads.

On February 1956, shortly after missile engineer Qian Xuesen's return to China from his stint at the Jet Propulsion Laboratory in California, the rocket scientist submitted a report on defence aviation to the Central Military Commission (CMC) in Beijing, following which the CMC established the Aviation Industrial Commission under Vice Premier Marshal Nie Rongzhen, to manage the development of guided missiles and military aircraft. (1)

However, China's twin top priorities were nuclear weapons and missiles; warplanes were backburnered for quite a while.

The 1991 Gulf War, which revolutionised military operations, transformed China's military perspective, and the country's unprecedented and phenomenal economic growth in the 2000s, the first decade of the 21st century, provided much-needed funds for its military modernisation.

From the paper on "New Changes in Air Defence Operations" penned by Colonel Ming Zengfu of the Air Force Command Institute in Beijing, and published in **Military Science** (Spring 1995), there are at least three salient points which strongly merit iteration:

(1)   What the Chinese authorities term the "informatisation" or "informationisation" of weapons and operational systems.

"Nowadays, modern aircraft (referring to information-equipped third-generation and fourth-generation aircraft) has become an information-dominated weapon," Col Ming has written.

"Compared with that of WWII, the efficiency of the battle aircraft of the 21st century will increase more than 100 times..."

(2)   The ascendant role of the air force in military operations, as displayed in the decisive application of air power in large-scale offensives in the Gulf War.

To quote Col Ming:

"Joint operations of various services means air power joins in an equal partnership with the army and the navy. This symbolises a qualitative change from previous history. In the past, the air force assisted the army or the navy to carry out missions..."

The air force has ascended to the level of parity with the army and the navy. Ming has added in writing: "Air power is mainly used in strategic depth and campaign depth..."

(3)   Globalization of the air wing: Global Reach and Global Strike.

"Any target in any part of the world is within striking range of air power," Col Ming emphasized.

"After the Gulf War, the main military powers in the world decided to enhance their air power's ability to carry out global strike and all-depth operations..." (2)

Under the wings of the Aviation Industry Corporation of China (AVIC), the state-owned aerospace and defence company founded on 6 November 2008, but with a history rooted in that of the Aviation Industry Administration (AIAC) formed on 1 April 1951 during the Korean War, China has recently produced advanced bombers and fighters comparable to the best warplanes in the US and Europe.

For example, the Xian H-6K strategic bomber has been listed by **Military Today** among the world's top 7 bombers.

China is developing its long-range stealth strategic strike bomber H-20 to rival the US B-2 Spirit and possibly the future B-21 stealth bomber.

On 6 July 2016, two Y-20 long-range transport planes, China's largest homemade transport aircraft, officially joined the PLA Air Force (PLAAF), registering its entry into the world's "large aircraft club" of aviation powers.

On 28 September 2017, China's fifth-generation stealth fighter jet was officially commissioned into service. Chengdu J-20 is the third stealth fighter to enter service after the US super stealthy air superiority fighter F-22A Raptor (2005) and the trouble-ridden F-35 Joint Strike Fighter (IOC with the US Marine Corps in 2015).

China's second 5-G stealth fighter, the FC-31 Gyrfalcon will reportedly attain IOC (Initial Operational Capability) by 2022   669 words

(B) China's Civil Aviation Industry

While China's military aviation has reached the world's advanced level, its fast-growing civil aviation has yet to catch up with its leading commercial counterparts in the West.

Nevertheless, notable progress has been made. On 23 July 2016, China completed production of the massive amphibious Ag600 with a reported range of 4,500 km, the world's largest of its kind and about the size of a Boeing 737, to be deployed in fighting forest fires and marine rescue operations.

On 19 October 2017 China's first domestic regional jetliner ARJ 21-700 was delivered to Chengdu. Commercial Aircraft Corp of China (COMAC), its maker, has of mid-October 2017 received 433 orders of the 90-seat plane.

With a flight range of 2,25-3,700 km, the ARJ 21 made its commercial debut om 13 December, flying from Chengdu, capital of southwestern Sichuan province, to Shangrao City in east China's Jiangxi province.

COMAC has also built the large passenger aircraft C919, a narrow-body 108-seat jumbo with a range of up to 5,556 km designed to compete with Airbus A320 and new #Boeing#B737.Following its third successful test on 3 November 2017, Reuters reported that China has taken a step closer to its goal of becoming a global civil aerospace player. However, the C919 is not expected to enter commercial service before 2020, according to a report by Chinese-owned leasing company Avolon on 30 October 2017.

With the C919, China has become the fourth jumbo jet producer after the US, Europe, and Russia.

According to **Reuters**/Beijing report 19.09.2017, orders for the C919 single-ailse aircraft total 730 planes from 27 customers.

According to **AFP**/Shanghai report 3 Nov 2016, COMAC and Russia's United Aircraft Corp (UAC) have agreed to invest US$20 billion to develop a 280-seat wide-body jet with a range of 12,000 km, which will make its maiden flight in seven years' time. It will sell less than the 280-seat Airbus A350 listed at US$272.4 million, and the 290-seat Boeing 787 costing US$264.6 million.

According to **People's Daily Online** September 02, 2017, quoting reports in **South China Morning Post**, China and Russia will jointly develop and make the aero engine for the C929 passenger jet. The new giant long-distance passenger plane is set to be completed by 2025.

According to **CRI Online** June 11, 2018, the CR929 is expected to make its maiden flight in 2023.   16.10.2018 17:04

As reported by Katherine Koleski, Research Director and Policy Analyst, Economics and Trade, U.S.-China Economic and Security Review Commission, the Chinese government has made COMAC a national champion in commercial aviation. Under the 13th Five-Year Plan (2016-2020), the government has initially provided over US$7 billion to develop its own commercial industry, as a foundation for technological innovation and national defence. (3)

According to Koleski, Aviation Industry Corporation of China (AVIC) formed a joint venture in 2011 with General Electric(GE) to "develop and market integrated, open architecture avionics systems to the global commercial aerospace industry for new aircraft platforms," particularly the C919. This joint venture aims to eventually become a global commercial avionics supplier, and to provide avionics directly to Airbus, Boeing, and Embraer (a Brazilian aerospace conglomerate).

According to the August 2018 report by US Department of Defense, China's aviation industry continues to advance with the initial delivery of its domestic Y-20 large transport aircraft and with the first flight of the world's largest seaplane, the AG-600. The new transports will supplement and eventually replace China's small fleet of strategic airlift assets of a limited number of Russian-made IL-76 aircraft.   16.10.2018 17:12

Under the 10-year blueprint (2015-2025) for innovation-driven and quality-controlled manufacturing to make China a leading world manufacturer by 2049, **Made in China 2025** calls for speeding up development of large scale commercial single-ailse aircraft, starting R&D on wide-body aircraft, encouraging foreign participation in R&D of large helicopters, and promoting regional aircraft, helicopters, unmanned aerial vehicles (UAVs), and industrialization of general aviation. (4)

According to Boeing's China Current Market Outlook2016, China will require 6,810 new airplanes (17% of world total) through 2035, costing US$1.025 trillion (17% of world total), including 5,110 new single-ailse airplanes with 90-230 seats. (5)

The list also includes: 140 regional jets with 90 seats and below for $10 B, 870 small body/wide with 200-300 seats for $240 B, 630 medium body/wide with 300-400 seats for $220 B, and 60 large body/wide with 400 seats and over for $20 B.

According to the 13th Five-Year Plan (2016-2020), China will launch at least 100 key projects over the next 15 years (2016-2030), including manufacturing aviation engines, gas turbines, and large aircraft, to step up the country's technological capability and improve people's livelihood.

On 28 August 2016 Aero Engine Corporation of China (AECC) was established in Beijing as a state-owned enterprise with a registered capital of 50 billion yuan (US$7.5 billion). Its objective is to become a world-class aircraft engine company on the wings of innovation. Its task and mission, to develop China's own aircraft engine, and to complete the industry chain from R&D, design, experiment to manufacture of large aircraft.

As reported by **Xinhua** and **Reuters** August 29, 2016, President Xi Jinping called on the new company to accelerate independent research, development and manufacture of aircraft engines and gas turbines to help China become an aviation power.

On 28 August 2017, AECC teamed up with Nanchang Hangkong University to establish China's first aero engine institute, in Nanchang, capital of Jiangxi Province in southeastern China, to train high-end talents and conduct scientific research on engine-making. According to **Xinhua**, China plans to catch up or surpass the major players in the West in 20 years. (6)

"The aviation industry is the crown industry in the manufacturing industry," said Geng Ruguang, deputy manager of Aviation Industry Corporation of China (AVIC). "The large aircraft is the exclusive capacity of a great power, with its will and strength..." (7)

(A) Flying in the Hypersonic Future

On December 2015 China's scramjet test was successfully conducted up to 30 km (about 20 miles) high up and at up to Mach 7 speed. It took off from a land-based launcher while American scramjet tests were airdropped before firing rocket boosters. (8)

According to Beijing Power Machinery Research Institute (BPMRI), China's turbo-aided rocket-augmented ram/scramjet engine (TRRE), which uses rocket augmentation to push to supersonic and hypersonic (from Mach 6/4,000 mph to Mach 10 or more), could be the world's first combined cycle engine to fly by 2025 and to pave the way for hypersonic near-space (20-100 km/12-60 miles) planes and single-stage space launchers.

Such a hypersonic spacecraft could circumnavigate the world in a couple of hours and out of reach of conventional air defences.

China has the world's largest wind tunnel for hypersonic testing. According to China Academy of Aerospace Aerodynamics (CAAA), the FD-21 556-foot-long wind tunnel (completed in 2016) can reach speeds of Mach 10-15, and large enough to test full-sized components of hypersonic propulsion, like gliders and scramjets.

Lockheed Martin, an American global aerospace company, hopes to fly its Mach 6 SR-72 hypersonic twin-engine reconnaissance unmanned aircraft on a turbine rocket combined cycle (TRCC) engine by 2030. (9)

Boeing is developing its dual-stage-to-orbit (DSTO) "Phantom Express" XS-1 spaceplane, which fires an expendable rocket at stage two in near space (18-62miles) to ascend into orbit with its 1.5 ton payload. The carrier rocket plane will return on its own to land on a runway, where it will be prepped for another launch within 24 hours.

In China, China Aerospace Science and Industry Corporation(CASIC) is developing the DSTO Teng Yung spacecraft with a Mach 6 hypersonic 'carrier' aircraft with TRCC engine to fly 18-25 miles up and deploy a reusable rocket in the second stage to go into orbit. According to CASIC Vice President Liu Shiquan, the two-stage space plane will fly by 2030, as part of a US$16 billion research programme.

Manned as well as unmanned, Teng Yung's second stage can be a launch rocket, or it can reportedly take five taikonauts to a future Chinese space station.

Its payload of 10-15 tons could include sensors and weapons as well as additional fuel (with its modifications).

The DSTO Teng Yung spacecraft will be deployed in near space on fast global reconnaissance and strike missions.

Under CASIC 1st Academy, the 10th Research Institute (aka Near Space Flight Vehicle Research Institute) is reported to be developing China's hypersonic glide vehicle (HGV), the DF-ZF/WU-14, which has been tested seven times (the first on 9 January 2014 and the seventh on 22 April 2016).

If China's veritable HGV can attain IOC by 2020, it will be the first to do so in the world. (10)

China Aerospace Science and Technology Corporation (CASC) is also building a hypersonic spacecraft.

Announced on August 2016, CASC's hypersonic spaceplane is also expected to fly by 2030. CASC plans to use a scramjet engine powerful enough for an SSTO (single-stage-to-orbit) hypersonic plane to fly directly to orbit.

CASC is also reported to have a DSTO programme to include (1) a reusable vertical takeoff suborbital carrier rocket plane with an expendable upper stage rocket, (2) a reusable rocket-powered aircraft with second/upper stage which can return to land on a runway, and (3) a TRCC hypersonic carrier aircraft like the DSTO Teng Yung for extended near space recce and strike operations.

The future belongs to hypersonic 'high-flyers' in near space.

Notes NEW CHINA A(13) CHINA'S AVIATION

1. John Wilson Lewis and Xue Litai, **China's Strategic SEAPOWER**, Stanford University Press, Stanford, California, 1994, p. 130.
2. **CHINESE VIEWS OF FUTURE WARFARE**, edited by Michael Pillsbury, Institute for National Strategic Studies **au.af. mil** 11/2/2004
3. Staff Research Report February 14, 2017 **uscc.gov**
4. PLANNING FOR INNOVATION. A report prepared by Tai Ming Cheuny et al for the U.S.-China Economic and Security Review Commission, July 2016 **uscc.gov**

5. China Country Commercial Guide, prepared by US Embassies abroad.
    export.gov 7/25/2017

According to Boeing Co (BA.N), China will buy 7,690 new planes worth 1.2 trillion over the next two decades up to 2037, to account for 18% of the world's commercial airplane fleet (from current 15%):

Three quarters of the total being single-ailse aircraft, and 1,620 new widebody (3 times the present fleet).

"The growth in China can be attributed to the country's growing middle class, which has more than tripled in the last 10 years and is expected to double again in the next 10," said Randy Tinseth, Boeing Commercial Airplanes' vice-president of marketing, in a statement.

To keep pace with the booming consumer and business demand for air travel. **Reuters**/Beijing Sept 11, 2018   16.10.2018 17:34

6. **People's Daily Online** 2017-08-29

According to **Made in China 2025**: To indigenously manufacture advanced engines and make breakthroughs in high thrust to weight ratio, and advanced turboprop engines and high bypass ratio turbofan engines.

7. **Xinhua/People's Daily** October 01, 2016   1,555 words

The US Department of Defense has stated in its August 2018 Report to Congress (p. 86):

China's aviation industry has advanced to produce a large transport aircraft; modern fourth- to fifth-generation fighters incorporating low-observable technologies; modern reconnaissance and attack UAVs (Unmanned Aerial Vehicles); and attack helicopters.

China's commercial aircraft industry has invested in high-precision and technologically advanced machine tooling and production processes, avionics, and other components applicable to the production of military aircraft.

However, China's aircraft industry remain reliant on foreign-sourced components for dependable, proven, high-performance aircraft engines.

China's infrastructure and experience for the production of commercial and military aircraft are improving as a result of China's ongoing C919 commercial airliner and Y-20 large transport programs.   16.10.2018 17:51

8. **POPULAR SCIENCE** Report by Jeffrey Lin and P.W. Singer April 19, 2017 **popsci.com**
9. **POPULAR SCIENCE** Report by Jeffrey Lin and P. W. Singer June 16, 2017
10. According to report in the **Diplomat**, the PLA Rocket Force successfully tested the new **DF-17 HGV** on the 1st and 15th November 2017.

According to Song Zhongping, a former member of the PLA's Second Artillery Corps, the **DF-17** is the weaponised model of the hypersonic **DF-ZF/WU-14** prototype, which has been tested seven times (Jan 2014 to April 2016) in the open field as well as probably many times in the JF-12 shockwave hypersonic wind tunnel in Beijing.

According to US intelligence, the **DF-17** could be operational by around 2020. **South China Morning Post** 01 Jan 2018 report by Minnie Chan.

Harry Pettit reported in **Daily Mail** 16 Nov 2017 that China is developing a nuclear-capable hypersonic aircraft with max speed of up to Mach 35 (43,200 kmh/27,000 mph), capable of reaching the US mainland in 40 minutes. It will tested in the world's fastest wind tunnel which will be completed by 2020.   30.03.2019 23:27

"... U.S. competitors are making enormous investments in hypersonic delivery vehicles, artificial intelligence (AI), and other advanced technologies.

"With respect to hypersonics in particular, the United States finds itself trailing China and perhaps Russia as well," the National Defense Strategy Commission has submitted in its report to the US Congress PROVIDING FOR THE COMMON DEFENSE (p. 10), released on 14 November 2018.

"All this (the proliferation of advanced technology eroding US advantages and creating new vulnerabilities) raises the possibility that America may find itself at a technological disadvantage in future conflicts," the group of 12 senior national security officials and military experts have warned.

"Because the American way of war has long relied on technological supremacy, this could have profoundly negative implications for U.S. military effectiveness..."   20.11.2018 02:28 03.01.2018 06:36

10 pages 3,000 words 25-26.10.2017 05:15 10.11.2017 11:15 03.01.2018 06:41 14.01.2018 06:50
24.08.2018 02:14 16.10.2018 17:51 20.11.2018 02:39 30.03.2019 23:27

NEW CHINA A(14) ECOLOGICAL CIVILIZATION

From Environmental Crisis to Ecological Civilization

At the 16th National Congress of the Communist Party of China (CPC) led by outgoing President Jiang Zemin, 8-15 November 2002, the ruling Party called for pursuing "comprehensive, balanced and sustainable development for the people..."

The imperative of "sustainability" is deeply and strongly rooted in the concept and development strategy of "ecological civilization", as proposed by President Hu Jintao at the CPC's 17th National Congress on 15-21 Oct 2007.

Describing it as "a future oriented guiding principle based on the perception of the extremely high price we have paid for our economic miracle", an enlightening opinion piece in **China Daily** 2007-10-24 commented that the new concept must entail a list of elements for sustainable development, including the right (harmonious) relationship between man and nature (not its wanton exploitation), balanced economic growth, ecological balance as well as social justice for disadvantaged people to fairly enjoy the benefits of development.

It's stated in the article: "From the Outlook in Scientific Development (Hu's concept of people-oriented, comprehensive and sustainable development) to harmonious development and ecological civilization, we can see where the Party is trying to (re-) orientate the country's economic and social progress."

When President Hu proposed creating an eco-civilization on October 2007, it was about a couple of years after China had overtaken the US as the world's largest emitter of greenhouse gases.

According to Zhu Guangyao, vice president of the Chinese Ecological Civilization Research and Promotion, it's got to be human co-existence (with nature).

Yea, and overdue respect for nature as well. And, symbiosis of humankind and nature.

At the 18th National Congress held on 8-14 November 2012, which led to the election of Xi Jinping as successor to Hu Jintao as general secretary of the CPC Central Committee, "ecological civilization construction" was incorporated and enshrined in the Party's Constitution.

"We must give high priority to making an ecological civilization, work hard to build a beautiful country, and achieve lasting and sustainable development of the Chinese nation," President Hu Jintao said when presenting his report on 11 November 2012. (1)

Hu gave prominence to ecological progress in listing it with economic, political, cultural, and social progress in the country's overall development.

In his 2012 report, Hu also called for efforts to keep more farmland for farmers (2), and to leave for future generations a beautiful homeland with green fields, clear water, and blue skies.

Hu's report stressed improving energy, resources, ecological and environmental conservation, and enhancing China's capacity for sustainable development.

"Adhering to the basic state policy of conserving resources and the environment is vital to the immediate interests of the people and the survival and development of the Chinese nation," Hu reported.

"We must give prominence to building a resource-conserving, environment-friendly society in our strategy for industrialization and modernization and get every organization and family to act.

"We will improve laws and policies to promote energy, resources, ecological and environmental conservation, and speed up the formation of systems and mechanisms for sustainable development...

"We will develop environmental conservation industries. We will increase spending on energy and environmental conservation with the focus on intensifying prevention and control of water, air and soil pollution and improving the living environment for both urban and rural residents.

"We will improve water conservancy, forestry and grasslands, intensify efforts to bring desertification under control and prevent the spread of stony deserts, and promote restoration of the ecosystems.

"We will enhance our capacity to respond to climate change and make new contributions to protecting the global climate..." (3)

The **key tenets of ecological civilization** include the need to respect, protect, and adapt to nature, to promote resource conservation, environmental protection and restoration, reuse/recycling, low-carbon use, and sustainable development.

Having Clean Water and Conserving Water

When Hu Jintao proposed the concept of eco-civilization in mid-October 2007, **China Daily** 2007-10-24 commented:

"... This concept is proposed at a time when 62 percent of the country's major rivers have been seriously polluted, 90 percent of waterways flowing through urban areas are contaminated, more than 300 million residents (the population of the US) are yet to have clean water to drink, and quite a number of localities fail to fulfil the required quotas for pollution emission reduction and energy saving..."

NATIONAL GEOGRAPHIC Atlas of China (2008) reported (p. 45):

"China's incredible economic expansion, industrialization, and urbanization -- coupled with inadequate water treatment infrastructure – has resulted in widespread water pollution. Most urban sewage is dumped directly into lakes and rivers..."

According to **Choke Point**, an environmental NGO initiative, water depletion and pollution are among China's biggest environmental challenges. Overconsumption and widespread contamination have produced severe shortages, affecting nearly 70% of agriculture and 20% of coal industry, and polluting over 60% of China's rivers and 90% of urban underground water. About two-thirds of 660 cities are short of water.

Xinhua reported (30 August 2013) that 298 million people in rural areas did not have access to safe drinking water at the end of 2012.

According to Li Guoying, vice-minister of water resources, all the rural population would have safe water supply by 2015.

The four indicators of safe water are: quality, quantity, convenience of access, and assurance/reliability of supply. Government allocated nearly 179.1 billion yuan (US$29 billion) for safe drinking water projects 2005-2015.

The 12th Five-Year Plan (2011-2015) allocated nearly RMB 700 billion (US$112 billion) to upgrade water treatment and piping systems as well as to safeguard water quality. (4)

On 16 April 2015, the State Council issued the Water Pollution Prevention and Control Action Plan, also known as the "Water Ten Plan", and described as probably the most comprehensive water policy, including its major objectives to control pollution discharge, to promote economic and industrial transformation (entailing tough controls on polluting industries, technological upgrading, boosting clean production), and to conserve/recycle resources as well as to fully improve the quality of the ecological environment for the ecosystems to "realize a virtuous cycle" by mid-21st century. (5)

Among 238 specific actions, <u>(1) to greatly reduce the **percentage of badly polluted water bodies** -- over 70% of the seven key rivers (Yangtze, Yellow, Pearl, Songhua, Huai, Hai, and Liao) shall reach Grade III or above (for supply of safe drinking water)</u>

<u>(2) To improve the quality of drinking water</u>—over 93% of urban drinking water sources shall reach Grade III or above by 2020, and 95% Grade I-III by 2030.

<u>(3) To reduce groundwater over-extraction and to control groundwater pollution by 2030.</u>

According to the Ministry of Water Resources (MWR), China's total annual water consumption will stay within the 2020 cap of 630 billion cubic metres/138.6 trillion gallons, or 379.76 billion gallons per day.

Blue skies and Fresh Air

In **Atlas of China** (2008), **NATIONAL GEOGRAPHIC** reported (p. 44) that China's CO2 emissions began to increase dramatically in the early 21st century, in tandem with the country's tremendous economic growth.

"By 2005, China was the world's second highest overall greenhouse emitter (after the United States), with coal combustion for industrial uses being by far the largest source," **NG** reported. The world's largest coal producer and consumer, China overtook the US in 2007.

In January 2013 the city air in Beijing had readings of concentration of PM2.5 (tiny airborne particles) close to 1,000 microgrammes per cubic metre – 40 times above the World Health Organization's recommended maximum of 25 microgrammes.

At the end of November 2015, Beijing issued an orange-level pollution alert (the second highest below the top red in its four-tier warning system) when over 560 microgrammes per cubic metre (22 times above healthy limits) were registered.

A month earlier, a record high smog of 1,400 microgrammes per cubic metre had covered the city of Shenyang, the capital and largest city of northeastern Liaoning province (some 658 km/409 mi away by "trunk road" from Beijing)

A recent study by Greenpeace (international environmental NGO) found nearly 80% of cities in China with very high pollution levels over the first nine months of 2015. (6)

According to Professor Eloi Laurentin in a Project Syndicate article published in **South China Morning Post** 28 Dec 2018, China now contributes 28% of global carbon dioxide emissions, twice as much as the US, from 1.5 billion tons in 1978 to 10 billion tons in 2016, and from 1.8 tons to 7.2 tons per capita, compared to world average of 4.2 tons.   30.03.2019 21:47

China's Air Pollution Prevention and Control Action Plan was released on September 2013, backed by 1.7 trillion yuan in investment. (7)

According to Hu Angang's report in **People's Daily** March 12, 2014, China also faces an enormous problem of "ecological poverty" with an estimated 200 million people living in ecologically deprived conditions, although over 400 million Chinese had been liberated from income poverty within a couple of decades, from 499 million in 1990 (GDP US$394.57 billion) to 86.4 million in 2010 (GDP $6.1 trillion to overtake Japan as world's second largest economy).

In what's reportedly the world's largest pollution treatment programme, China plans to get rid of 50,000 coal-fired furnaces and old polluting coal-fuelled power stations, and to push through a renovation project covering slightly over one-third of the total coal-generating capacity (960 GW at the end of 2016): to desulphurize 15 million KW of coal-fired generation, denitrate 130 million KW, and "dedust" 180 million KW. (8)

World's largest electricity consumer, over 60% of China's electric power is coal-generated.

The World Nuclear Association (WNA) has described China as well advanced in developing and deploying supercritical and ultra-supercritical coal plants. Almost 70% of the power plants in China were built in the last decade. (9)

In March 2014 Premier Li Keqiang declared "war on pollution" to prevent and control air pollution in large cities and regions frequented by smog, and to counter microscopic particulate matter PM2.5 (micrometers) and PM10 (micrometers) – designated the deadliest form of air pollution as these airborne particles can penetrate deep into human lungs and bloodstreams to cause nonfatal heart attacks, and premature death in people with heart or lung diseases (according to US Environmental Protection Agency).

In May 2014 government amended the 1988 Environmental Protection Law to provide guidelines and legal grounding for stronger responses to air pollution.

In an article in **New Straits Times** March 25, 2017, Lina Gong has written that environmental pollution "now poses a major non-traditional security (NTS) challenge to the Chinese society, and smog is its most visible element..." (10)

Minister of Environment Protection Li Ganjie said on 23 Oct 2017 that China's aim is to reduce PM2.5 concentration from 47 microgrammes per cubic metre in 2016 to 35 microgrammes per cubic metre by 2035. (11)

7 pages 2,008 words 12.11.2017 08:55 14.11.2017 08:02

Conserving Farmlands and the Good Earth

According to **NATIONAL GEOGRAPHIC Atlas of China** (2008, p. 45), more than 40% of China is affected by land degradation.

According to a late December 2006 report by Xu Qi, a journalist with **China Environmental Times**, a scientific sampling of China's cultivated land found 150 million mu (100,000 sq km, area of South Korea) polluted, with contaminated water being used to irrigate a further 32.5 million mu (21,670 sq km, size of Israel). Solid wastes were found to cover or destroy another 2 million mu (1,300 sg km, twice the area of Singapore). (12)

In total, polluted soil reportedly accounts for one-tenth of China's arable land.

Branded as China's "invisible pollution", soil contamination has spread, largely unnoticed, across the vast Chinese landscape.

With one-fifth of the world's population, China has less than one-tenth of the global farmland.

Conserving farmlands entails land protection as well as ecological remediation.

"The earth lay rich and dark," Pearl S. Buck (1892-1973) wrote in her classic novel of China in the 1920s **The Good Earth**, which won the Pulitzer Prize in 1935.

In late 2012, President Hu called for efforts "to keep more farmlands for farmers, and leave for future generations a beautiful homeland with green fields, clear water and blue skies..."

Controlling Desertification, Rolling Back Stony Deserts & Afforestation

As depicted in **NATIONAL GEOGRAPHIC Atlas of China** (2008, p.45), China suffers from some of the world's worst soil erosion, and its rate of desertification has doubled since the 1950s.

Barren land and desert occupy 14.7% of China.

Overgrazing and deforestation contribute to harsh and severe erosion, with China losing over 1,000 sq miles (over2,700 sq km, larger in area than Luxembourg) to desertification each year.

At the 18th Congress November 2012, President Hu reported that China would "intensify efforts to bring desertification under control and prevent the spread of stony deserts..."

Wikipedia has reported on the "Great Green Wall of China" project to roll back the encroaching Gobi desert, and to reforest and restore most desert land by 2050.

Launched in 1978 as long-term ecological protection along with reform and opening up of China, the plan is to plant some 88 million acres of protective forests on a belt nearly 3,000 miles long and as wide as 900 miles in some places. The government has also subsequently implemented other major afforestation projects which altogether come to the largest tree-planting program in human history.

Over the past 40 years, China has cultivated some 30 million hectares of forest reserves, raising its green area coverage from 5.05% in 1978 to 13.57%. China has planted some 70 billion trees.

In 2000-2017, China contributed a quarter of the global greening through afforestation.

According to Zhang Jianlong, head of National Forestry and Grassland Administration (as reported by **Xinhua/China Daily** 13 March 2019), rural China is 20% green and urban China has achieved 37.9% green coverage.

As part of the plan to build a "Beautiful China", the country will increase its forest coverage from about 22% in 2017 to slightly over 23% by 2020, and then to 26% by 2035.

According to Zhang, the target entails annual afforestation of about 6.7 million hectares while protecting forestry resources.

In 2018, 7.1 million hectares of trees were planted, and 6.7 million hectares of degraded grassland were treated.

China has nearly 410 million hectares of natural grassland, covering 41.7% of the country. Protection and restoration of grassland resources will be strengthened, according to Zhang.

China's Afforestation:

2014 6 million ha
2015 6.3 million ha
2016 6.8 million ha
2017 7.3 million ha
2018 7.1 million ha   30-31.2019 01:05

The Ecological Way Ahead

"We built an agricultural, then an industrial, and now must build an ecological civilization," James Thornton, environmental lawyer, said to Jane Gleeson-White, **theguardian.com** 10 September 2017.

Founder of ClientEarth, a London-based public interest environmental law firm set up in 2007, Thornton was first invited to Beijing in 2014 to help implement China's new law allowing NGOs to sue polluting companies.

"My job is to try and clean up the environment for future generations. The Chinese really want to do that," he said to Gleeson-White.

Thornton then added, "They said, we have a long-term vision, we want to be here in another 2,000 years and that will only happen if we clean up the environment. So we have determined that we're going to do so in a very thoroughgoing way."

For China, it's the way of eco-civilization.

After pledging in February 2013 to promote China's developmental philosophy of ecological progress, the United Nations Environment Programme (UNEP) published on 26 May 2016 its maiden report **Green is gold: The strategy and actions of China's ecological civilization**.

The Chinese eco-civilization blueprint has listed a series of 2020 targets, including forestation of nearly one quarter of China (from 15.8% of land cover in 2007), cutting water consumption by 23%, energy use by 15%, and carbon emissions per unit of GDP by 18%. (13)

Also, increasing prairie vegetation coverage by 56%, reclaiming over half of reclaimable desert, and preserving at least 35% of natural shorelines. China has a coastline of 14,500 km.

"Building an ecological civilization is vital to sustain the Chinese nation's development," President Xi Jinping said in his report to the 19th CPC National Congress on 18 October 2017. (14)

"We will adopt a holistic approach to conserving our mountains, rivers, forests, farmlands, lakes, and grasslands, implement the strictest possible systems for environmental protection, and develop eco-friendly growth models and ways of life.

"We must pursue a model of sustainable development featuring increased production, higher living standards, and healthy ecosystems.

"We must continue the Beautiful China initiative (its goal to be basically attained by 2035) to create good working and living environments for our people and play our part in ensuring global ecological security..."

President Xi also said: "Taking a driving seat in international cooperation to respond to climate change, China has become an important participant, contributor, and torchbearer in the global endeavour for ecological civilization..."   14.11.2017 09:29

I

The new path of national high-quality development prioritizes ecology, highlights green development, and entails accomplishing the two major tasks of pollution control and environmental protection.

President Xi's call is to transform China into "the ecological civilization of the 21st century". The target to do dso by mid-century.   31.03.2019 01:19

Notes NEW CHINA A(14) Ecological Civilization

1. **china.org.cn**
2. Meijun Fan and Zhihe Wang of The Institute for the Postmodern Development of China have aptly described farmers as "people who live close to the Earth and to one another". They have also righltly observed that while agriculture is bearing "the roots of ecological existence", growing vast amounts of food has incurred "the high cost of serious pollution in the countryside and almost irreversible destruction of rural lands". Both experts are promoting ecological agricultural development, including organic farming.
3. **Xinhua/China Daily**   700 words 10.11.2017 12.56
4. Hongqiao Liu, **CHINA'S LONG MARCH TO SAFE DRINKING WATER** A China Water Risk/chinadialogue Report March 2015, translation by Hannah Short **chinawaterrisk.org/pdf**

According to Liu Wenju, director of Safe Water Drinking Insititute of Tsinghua University, only about 5% of waterworks have facilities for advanced treatment (e.g. ozone-activated membrane/carbon filtration technology). According to him, all waterworks need to have advanced treatment to guarantee good water quality. Probably referring to polluted water.

"Water is a basic human need; it's not an optional requirement," Liu (rightly) said.

According to Song Lau, chief engineer at the Urban Water Quality Monitoring Centre of the Ministry of Housing and Urban-Rural Development (MOHURD), at least 20-30% of waterworks in China need to adopt advanced treatment processes as soon as possible.

Hongqiao Liu concludes: "...China's march to safe drinking water is still long but there is hope if the various challenges are tackled.

Declaring "war on pollution" in 2014, Premier Li Keqiang observed that the remaining tasks are all "hard bones"…

5. **chinawaterrisk.org**
6. **AFP** report in **theSun** December 1, 2015

According to Greenpeace Asia, at least 80% of 367 cities with real-time air quality monitoring, failed to meet national small-particle pollution standards during the first three quarters of 2015. **The Economist** Aug 10 2013

7. **Xinhua/People's Daily** March 09, 2014
8. Hu Angang, **People's Daily** March 12, 2014

Coal accounted for 65% of China's total electricity generating capacity in 2016.

9. **nuclear.org** August 2016
10. Lina Gong is a research fellow with the Centre for Non-Traditional Security Studies (NTS), S. Rajaratnam School

of International Studies (RSIS), Nanyang Technological University, Singapore.

11. **Xinhua** October 23, 2017

12. **chinadialogue.net** 29.01.2007

13. Report by Joshua Marks **inhabitat.com** 05/30/2016

According to 2017 data, China's forested area totals 2,083,210 sg km (21.8% of China's total land area of 9,596,961 sq km/3,705,408 sq mi).

According to **NATIONAL GEOGRAPHIC Atlas of China** (2008, pp. 42-43), China has 1,977 national protected areas totalling 145.38 million hectares (15% of total land).   25.11.2017 03:59

According to China's forestry plan, the country's forest cover will be increased from 21.6% in 2018 to 23.04% by 2020, and 26% by 2035.

The greening of rural China will expand from 30% in 2020 to 38% by 2035, and 43% by 2050. **CGTN** Jan 07, 2018

According to the 2015 guidelines on ecological civilization construction, China aims to tame 50% of its deserted land by 2020. Scientists are working on targeted desertification control, reported **People's Daily Online** June 22, 2018.

14. **China Military/PLA Daily chinamil.com.cn**

13 pages 3,535 words 14.11.2017 09:32 25.11.2017 04:01 14.01.2018 07:03 24.08.2018 02:43 16.10.2018 18:12 17.12.2018 23:23 23:27 31.03.2019 01:55

NEW CHINA A(15)
BELT AND ROAD INITIATIVE

The Belt and Road Initiative (BRI): Going Global, Forging A Shared Future

Addressing students and faculty at Nazarbayev University in Astana, capital of Kazakhstan, on Saturday 7 September 2013, President Xi Jinping called for enhanced regional cooperation and a closer economic partnership to embrace Eurasia's "golden opportunity of development". (1)

"Both China and Central Asian countries are at a crucial stage of development with unprecedented opportunities and challenges," Xi said. (2)

"Our strategic goals are the same, which are to ensure sustained and stable economic development, build prosperous and strong nations and achieve national rejuvenation..."

Across-the-board cooperation, he added, would be needed to turn good regional relations into drivers of sustained growth for mutual benefit as well as the common good.

"To forge closer economic ties, deepen cooperation and expand development space in the Eurasian region, we should take an innovative approach and jointly build an economic belt along the Silk Road," Xi then proposed.

Coming out of the blue, it was a challenging and tempting proposal to rejuvenate and transform the ancient network of trade routes (going back a couple of millenniums to the Han Dynasty (206 BC-220AD) of China) linking China to central and western Asia, India, and the Mediterranean region in northern Africa and southern Europe.

"This will be a great undertaking, benefitting the people of all countries along the route," Xi said.

Xi then listed five key steps in regional cooperation in constructing the new economic belt along the historic Silk Road: improving policy communication and road connectivity, promoting unimpeded trade, enhancing monetary circulation, and increasing understanding among the peoples in the region.

The bottom line: "win-win progress in the region".

"The proposed economic belt along the Silk Road is inhabited by close to three billion people, and represents the biggest market in the world with unparalleled potential," Xi emphasised. (3)

About a month later, on Thursday 3 October 2013, President Xi Jinping addressed the Indonesian parliament, Dewan Perwakilan Rakyat, in Jakarta, capital of Indonesia, where he proposed joining hands with the countries in Southeast Asia to build a new "Maritime Silk Road" and link it with the overland trade routes. (4)

Stressing the "shared destiny" of China and Asean countries, Xi expressed his country's readiness to open itself wider to enable them to benefit more from China's development.

The proposed 21st Century Maritime Silk Road connects southern China to Southeast Asia via the South China Sea and thence to India through the Indian Ocean and on to Africa and the Mediterranean.

The coupling of the proposed Silk Road Economic Belt and the 21st Century Maritime Silk Road completes President Xi's innovative and far-reaching formulation of what's universally known as the "Belt and Road Initiative" (BRI), for unprecedented international connectivity, cooperation and development across three contiguous continents, including the world's two largest and most populous in Asia and Africa, and the wealthiest in Europe.

The BRI community is presently described as comprising 65 countries and regions, 4.4 billion people (63% of the world's population), and aggregate GDP of US$23 trillion (29% of global).

The humongous BRI economic network is geographically structured along six main corridors: (1) China-Indochina Peninsula Economic Corridor, from southern China to Singapore; (2) Bangladesh-China-India-Myanmar Economic Corridor, from southern China to Bangladesh; (3) China-Pakistan Economic Corridor, from southern China to Pakistan; (4) China-Central Asia-West Asia Economic Corridor, from western China to Turkey, which is described as a transcontinental country in Eurasia/Western Asia/Southeast Europe, bounded by seas on three sides with the Aegean Sea to the west, the Black Sea to the east, and the Mediterranean Sea to the south; (5) New Eurasian Land Bridge, from western China to western Russia via Kazakhstan, a former Soviet republic in Central Asia, extending from the Caspian Sea in the west to the Altai Mountains at its eastern border with China and Russia; and (6) China-Mongolia-Russia Economic Corridor, from northern China through Mongolia (located in East Asia between China to the south and Russia on the north) to Eastern Russia. Although the world's two largest landlocked countries Kazakhstan and Mongolia do not have a common border, they are only 36.76 km (22.84 mi) apart.

For Xi, the BRI is the brand new vehicle to drive China's globalisation further along the chosen path of "open and win-win cooperation" across the globe.

"China is committed to a fundamental policy of opening-up and pursues a win-win opening-up strategy," Xi said at the plenary of the World Economic Forum annual meeting at Davos, Switzerland, on 17 January 2017. (5)

"China's development is both domestic and external oriented; while developing itself, China also shares more of its development outcomes with other countries and peoples...

"China will keep its door wide open and not close it. An open door allows both countries to access the Chinese market and China itself to integrate with the world..."

Xi told the distinguished gathering at the Alpine town of Davos that since the launching of reforms and its opening up from late 1978, China has attracted over $1.7 trillion of foreign investment and made over $1.2 trillion of foreign investment. Following the 2008 financial crisis, China has also contributed over 30% of the annual global economic growth.(6)

According to Xi, China is expected in the coming five years (2017-2021) to import $8 trillion worth of goods, attract $600 billion of foreign investment, and invest $750 billion abroad. Also, 700 million overseas visits (an outbound tourist traffic twice the size of the US population).

"Through the BRI, China is proposing to share its immense financial and industrial resources and capabilities, as well as its experience of four decades of reform and opening-up, while securing its own long-term development," Michael Buehler and four learned colleagues have written in their analytical piece on the "New Silk Road". (7)

The five co-authors have written that the BRI "has the potential to prompt a profound shift in the global order towards a new multilateralism..."

According to them, the BRI will need about $6 trillion to finance infrastructure projects over the next 15 years, and the Chinese plan to invest $4 trillion (having committed about $1 trillion) – about 20 times the American investment in the post-World War II Marshall Plan of $17 billion (about $190 billion today). (8)

"Comprehensive development of infrastructure, including transport, telecommunications and energy, will serve as the basis for integration," President Vladimir Putin has written on expanding regional economic cooperation and Eurasian partnership. (9)

"It is our hope that through the 'Belt and Road' development, we will unleash new forces for global economic growth," Xi said in a brief press conference at the close of the high-level BRI forum in Beijing on 15 May 2017. (10)

"China has not just the resources, which is key, but also the vision and desire and strategy to push its engagement outside its borders,"

Afghan ambassador to Beijing Janan Mosazai said on the eve of the BRI forum. (11)

"Belt and Road may be a Chinese initiative, but it is a global effort involving developed and developing countries, and international organisations," says Stuart Gulliver, Group Chief Executive for HSBC Holdings plc. (12)

"China has put forward the Belt and Road Initiative and is pursuing it in a spirit of extensive consultation, joint contribution and shared benefits," President Xi said in his keynote address at the 25th Asia-Pacific Economic Cooperation (APEC) Economic Leaders' Meeting on 11 November 2017 in Danang, Vietnam.

"Going forward, China will deepen policy, infrastructure, trade, financial and people-to-people connectivity with our Asia-Pacific partners, seek interconnected development and move toward a community of shared future..." (13)

In his report to the 19th CPC National Congress on 18 October 2017, President Xi described the Belt and Road Initiative (BRI) as building "a new platform for international cooperation to create new drivers of shared development".

Xi declared: We, the Chinese, are ready to work with the people of all other countries to build a community with a shared future for mankind and create a brighter tomorrow for all of us..."

Xi stressed China's three heroic tasks: (1) advancing its modernization, (2) national reunification, and (3) world peace and common development. (14)

Notes NEW CHINA A(15) Road and Belt Initiative (BRI)

1. 2.7 million sq km (1 million sq mi) in area, Kazakhstan is the largest country in strategically located Central Asia, the world's largest landlocked country, and the ninth largest in the world, with an estimated population (2016) of very close to 18 million.

2. Michelle Witter, BUSINESS **astanatimes.com/2013** 11 September 2013

3. As envisioned, the Silk Road Economic Belt extends from China through Central Asia to Europe, linking Xian, capital of Shaanxi Province in Central China, to Dushanbe, capital of Tajikistan in Central Asia, Moscow in western Russia, Rotterdam, a major port city in the Dutch province of South Holland in northwestern Europe, and Venice, the port city of canals in northeastern Italy in southern Europe, and in the heart of the Mediterannean.

   President Xi was named Honorary Professor of Nazarbayev University.

4. **Xinhua/People's Daiy Online** November 15, 2017.

   At the 20th ASEAN-China, Japan, and South Korea (10+3) Leaders' Meeting in Manila on 14 November 2017, Premier Li Keqiang offered a 6-point proposal to forge an economic community in East Asia, concerning regional cooperation, sustainable development, social progress, joint responses to non-conventional security threats, innovation of security concepts, and improving the regional security framework.

5. **weforum.org**

6. According to Xi, Christine Lagarde, Managing Director of International Monetary Fund (IMF), recently told him that emerging markets and developing countries have contributed 80% of the growth of the global economy.

   "Rapid growth in China has been a sustained, powerful engine for global economic stability and expansion," Xi stated at Davos in mid-January 2017.

   "The inter-connected development of China and a large number of other countries has made the world economy more balanced..."

Xi extended his invitation to all countries to come aboard "the express train (Fuxing HSR) of China's development..."

According to Zhang Xiao, Chinese Ambassador to Kazakhstan, in his article published in **People's Daily** September 10, 2018, China's trade with the BRI-participating countries exceeded $5 trillion, and China invested over $60 billion in these countries in the past five years, including $43 billion in Kazakhstan (where President Xi first proposed his OBOR/BRI vision in a speech at the Nazarbayev University in Astana on 3 September 2013).

Five years after the BRI roll-out, China's trade with the BRI countries has exceeded $5.5 trillion. **Xinhua/People's Daily** 08.10.2018   16.10.2018 18:28

7. Posted on **European Business Review** website October 30, 2017.
8. Officially labelled as the European Recovery Program (ERP), the Marshall Plan was an American $13 billion initiative (about $135.4 billion in exchange value as of September 2017) to help rebuild Western European economies at the end of World War II. A four-year operation, it started on 8 April 1948. **wikipedia. org** last edited 22.11.2017
9. Article published in **New Straits Times** November 9, 2017.
10. **AP** report in **New Straits Times** May 16, 2017.
11. **AP** report in **New Straits Times** May 13, 2017.
12. **hsbc.com** 11 May 2017 27 September 2017
    HSBC has been named Best Overall International Bank for Belt and Road Initiative (BRI) in the inaugural Asiamoney New Silk Road Finance Awards, reflecting the Bank's commitment to being the leading financial partner to clients engaged in Belt and Road projects.

According to HSBC, Belt and Road will reshape the 21st century economy.

$4 trillion invest.

900 projects planned or under way benefitting more than 80 countries.

Projects in Asia alone will require $1.7 trillion a year to 2030.

The top BRI priority is in infrastructure development, focusing on transportation, particularly railways, as well as telecommunications and energy sectors.

13. **Xinhua/People's Daily** 2017-11-12
14. **chinamil.com.cn**

2046 words 7 pages 25.11.2017 09:30 24.08.2018 02:50
16.10.2018 18:36

NEW CHINA A(16)
GLOBAL CHIP CHAMP?

Can China Become A Global Chip Champ By 2030?

A. The Vital Role of Semiconductors

"Think of (the) little computer (microprocessor). Its value isn't in the sand (silicon) from which it is made, but in the microscopic architecture designed into it by ingenious human minds," President Ronald Reagan said in May 1988 when he addressed students at the Moscow State University. He spoke on the essence of the new knowledge economy.

"In the new economy, human invention increasingly makes physical resources obsolete. We are breaking through the material conditions of existence to a world where man creates his own destiny..." (1)

The first-generation semiconductor, also known as the microchip or simply chip, had only one to ten transistors (electronic switches or electrical power amplifiers) in the early 1960s. It was the early period of Small-Scale Integration (SSI).

The year 1971 marked the entry of Large-Scale Integration (LSI) when the chips were made from 500 to 20,000 transistors. 1980 introduced Very Large-Scale Integration (VLSI) with up to one million transistors, followed in 1984 by Ultra-Large-Scale Integration (ULSI) with one million plus.

"The new industrial revolution is a revolution of mind over matter," US economist George Gilder wrote in a magazine article in1989. "Chip producers build volume not chiefly by processing more silicon but by placing more circuits on a given area which is almost entirely a function of accumulated knowledge and experience..." (2)

In his book **Microcosm: The Quantum Revolution in Economics and Technology** (1989), Gilder wrote:

"Combining millions of components on a single chip, operating in billionths of seconds, these devices (microchips) transcend most of the previous constraints of matter...

"Today, transcendent nations and corporations are masters, not of land and material resources, but of ideas and technologies..." (3)

The billion-transistor chip or integrated circuit (IC) came in 2005, and 2007 ushered in chips with tens of billions of transistors! (4)

Semiconductors are the "brains" of all modern electronics, in data processing, communications, consumer and industrial electronics, automotive and aerospace, and national defence. They are driving the world's digital economy.

From $6 billion in 1964, the global semiconductor market grew to $354 billion in 2016. US semiconductors sold for $164 billion in 2016.

According to the US Semiconductor Industry Association (SIA), semiconductors are not only America's #3 Manufactured Export after automobiles and airplanes, but also vital as a key driver of the nation's economic strength, national security, and global competitiveness.

According to the SIA, semiconductors are strategic in building America's Innovation Economy, Economic Strength, National Security, and Technology Leadership. (5)

"A strong national semiconductor industry underpins a country's competitiveness across the entire IT (Information Technology) sector," Tom Forester, a leading Australian IT expert and author, has written. (6)

"A state-of-the-art semiconductor capability is also vitally important for national security, because modern military systems are now wholly dependent on semiconductor technology…"

806 words 25.04.2017 10:59

B. China's Semiconductor Industry

In 2015, American firms supplied 56% of China's imported semiconductors worth $98.6 billion. The towering leader in the global semiconductor market with about half of its share, the US sells over 80% of its semiconductors abroad, more than half of which to China.

While the US is the world's leading producer, China is its largest consumer of semiconductors.

They are the two Goliaths in the semiconductor world: the US with its technological supremacy and manufacturing predominance, and China with its huge presence and pre-eminent position in the global market. While one delivers superbly, the other can often call the shots.

As the world's largest manufacturer of consumer electronics, China is also the world's largest consumer of semiconductors – over half of the global consumption – nearly 60% in 2015, for which China paid over $200 billion, much more than its annual expenditure on crude oil imports. (Back in 1978, China's GDP slightly exceeded $216 billion.) (7)

More than 90% of China's demand for semiconductors is supplied by other countries including the US, Japan, South Korea, Taiwan, etc.

China's IC consumption increased from $46 billion in 2006 to $176 billion in 2015 (almost 64% of worldwide).

Based on data from US technology firms Gartner and IDC, China accounts for 20% of global personal computer (PC) consumption, 29% smartphone, 17% tablet, 27% automobile, and 23% of global telecommunications equipment capital expenditures.

As reported by PricewaterhouseCoopers (PwC), China's semiconductor industry grew at a 18.7% compounded annual growth rate (CAGR) from 2005 to 2015 to net $89.3 billion or 16.2% of worldwide semiconductor revenues. The US sold about twice as much worth of semiconductors.

China's IC design, the fastest growing segment of China's semiconductor industry, developed from a revenue of $0.13 billion in 2000 (when the Chinese semiconductor industry was reportedly privatized) to $1.52 billion in 2005, $5.38 billion in 2010, and $21.09 billion in 2015.

From 2005 to 2015, China's IC design industry grew at a 30.1% CAGR from $1.52 billion to just over $21 billion, and from 6.4% to almost 7.5% of the worldwide IC market.

Of China's semiconductor consumption in 2015, IC accounted for over 80%. China contributed slightly over 16% of the worldwide semiconductor production market, according to a report by PricewaterhouseCoopers in January 2017.

According to the China Center of Information Industry Development (CCIID), the number of IC design enterprises in China increased from 15 in 1990 to 98 in 2000, 200 in 2001, 463 in 2003, 518 in 2012, and 715 by the end of 2015 with a total of about 155,000 employees.

July 2016 marked the first merger of two major players in the semiconductor industry when Tsinghua Unigroup, China's largest chip designer, acquired a majority stake in XMC, one of China's leading chip makers, and established a holding company for XMC, called Yangtze River Storage Technology (YRST).

According to Hui He, a senior analyst with IHS Technology, XMC is developing the leading-edge 3D NAND chips for testing by the end of 2016 and initial mass production in the first half of 2018. (8)

On 28 February 2017, Xiaomi unveiled its own processor known as the Surge SI, designed by its subsidiary Pinecone (formed in 2014). "The ability to create its own chipsets is the pinnacle achievement for any smart phone company," said Xiaomi, in joining an elite group of smartphone manufacturers with their self-designed processors.

On March 2017 Tsinghua Unigroup obtained new funding of 150 billion yuan ($21.8 billion) from China Development Bank and China

Integrated Circuit Industry Investment Fund, a major state-owned investment vehicle established to help China become self-sufficient in semiconductors.

Dubbed as one of the "national champions", Tsinghua is leading China's self-sufficiency as well as global competitiveness drive in the highly competitive semiconductor industry.

According to Tsinghua Group Chairman Zhao Weiguo, Tsinghua aims to be among the top 5 memory chip makers by 2025. Tsinghua is focusing on advanced 3D NAND flash memory chips which are used in smartphones, mobiles and other connected devices, long-term data storage, SSD storage in PCs and data servers, and which are now all made by non-Chinese companies.

Tsinghua's subsidiary Yangtze River Storage Technology (YRST), also known as Changjiang Storage, will reportedly build two memory chip facilities in Wuhan and Nanjing. Wuhan will begin production by 2018.

Also owned by Tsinghua, Spreadtrum Communications, a home-grown mobile chip supplier, is a rival of Mediatek, Taiwan's top chip designer, and US-based Qualcomm, world's largest smartphone chip maker. Spreadrum is developing the 5G chips for the market by 2020 to catch up with Qualcomm and MediaTek, the world's two leading mobile chip providers. (9)

China's production capacity of wafers (slices of semiconductor material used in IC fabrication) grew from 1.5% of worldwide in 2001 to 10.5% in 2010, and 12.7% in 2015 with 169 wafer plants out of the global 1,031. Of the 118 fabs worldwide making 300 mm (12 in) wafers, China has only 10.

At the high end, China's share of advanced technology node (28 nanometers (nm) or less) capacity comes to only about 5%.

In 2015 China had 123 SPA&T (semiconductor packaging, assembly, and test) facilities in operation, the most in the world (22% of worldwide), occupying 34% of global SPA&T manufacturing floor space.

In 2015, 70% of China's SPA&T manufacturing floor space was dedicated to semiconductor assembly and test services (SATS).

Of the world's 10 largest SATS companies with their total of 125 SATS facilities, nine of them had a total of 27 facilities in China, with 42% of their manufacturing floor space worldwide.

Of the world's top 20 SATS companies in 2015, China had three: Jingsu Changjiang Electronics Technology (JCET) in fourth place, Tianshui Huatian Microelectronics (TSHT) ninth, and Nantong Fujitsu Microelectronics (NFME) #14.

According to International Trade Administration (ITA) 2016 Top Market Report, China accounts for over 50% of the world's electronics production and nearly one-third of the global market for semiconductors. (10)

Raman Chikara, Global Technology Industry Leader at PricewaterhouseCoopers (PwC), said: "For China's semiconductor industry, all signs point to continued moderate but sustainable growth over the next few years. Government incentives and market conditions should continue to benefit the now-mature industry, leading to long-range moderate growth and a further narrowing of the consumption/production gap." (11)

1,682 words02.05.2017 23:41

C. China's quest for technological mastery, global competitiveness, and self-sufficiency in the strategic semiconductor industry

At a 12.8%CAGR from 2016 to 2020, China's semiconductor industry is expected to further grow from $83.67 billion in 2015 to $157.68 billion by 2020. (12)

According to International Data Corporation, the global semiconductor market will be worth $389.4 billion in 2019 at a 3.1% CAGR from 2014 to 2019, slowing down substantially after four decades of rapid growth. (13)

"For approximately the past two decades, U.S. headquartered firms have accounted for half of global semiconductor sales. Other leading firms are based in South Korea, Japan, Taiwan and Europe. No Chinese-headquartered company is in the top 20," the President's Council of Advisors on Science and Technology reported to the US President on 6 January 2017, in a32-page report "Ensuring Long-Term U.S. Leadership in Semiconductors". (14)

"China's starting position in its quest for semiconductor prowess is well behind that of the United States," the presidential advisors stated in no uncertain terms.

To "foster innovation and keep the U.S. industry at the technological frontier", the presidential experts recommended pursuing a sustained long-time and multi-dimensional innovation strategy, but to focus on areas of major challenge such as game-changing biodefense systems. The good advisors also called for "moonshots" (like the Apollo project) in order "to drive computing and semiconductor innovation forward together..."

To upgrade China's semiconductor industry, to catch up with the global leaders, and to forge further ahead, the State Council in Beijing has recently issued: (1) the "National Semiconductor Industry Guidelines" June 2014 for China to reach an "advanced world- level in all major segments of the industry by 2030", and (2) the "Made in China 2025" blueprint May 2015 with targets for self-sufficiency, and strengthening advanced manufacturing and innovation capabilities in IC design, fabrication and production.

The self-sufficiency targets are 40% by 2020, 70% by 2025, and up to 80% by 2030 with US$305 billion worth of made-in-China (MIC) chips ($65 billion in 2016).

The MIC 2025 prioritizes the world best practice in IC design cores and design tools, next-generation multi-component semiconductors (MICOS), and 3D IC micro-packaging technology to speed up processing, improve yield, reduce fabrication cost and power consumption, enhance circuit security, expand bandwidth, etc. (15)

"China's leadership views China's (overwhelming) reliance on foreign semiconductors as a major national security concern. Because semiconductors are foundational to information and communication technologies (ICTs), China's leadership views the industry as a cornerstone of China's goal of securing its ICT ecosystem and technologies of the future through indigenization (domestication and "indigenous innovation") of the ICT supply chain while concurrently transforming and upgrading China's economy (on a more stable and sustainable basis)," International Trade Administration (ITA) submitted in its 2016 Top Market Report. (16)

"The Chinese government has begun implementing ambitious policies aimed at supporting domestic semiconductor design and manufacturing in order to develop a globally competitive semiconductor industry by 2030..."

To quote Anton Peisl of Germany's Siemens: "The nation or continent that aspires to be ultimately independent and competitive in the information technology (IT) sector must command the entire electronic 'food chain' (aka national value chain) from semiconductors to end products..." (17)

A nation creates its destiny from the freedom to create – "the most precious natural resource" (to quote President Ronald Reagan).

2,487 words 02-03.05.2017 01:27 05.05.2017 00:25 16.04.2019 02:13

APPENDIX: A TALE OF TWO ASIAN MAJORS

APPENDIX (A): Japan's Rise And Decline

Japan's rise has been concisely narrated by Tom Forester in his book **SILICON SAMURAI** (18):

"The Japanese government targeted electronics and what was to become known as "microelectronics" back in 1957, when it passed the Electronics Industry Promotion Law. Under the law, the Ministry of International Trade and Industry (MITI) was given extraordinary powers to direct electronics research and development, to provide subsidies and to ensure bank loans for producers, to select promising new products, to set production quantity and cost targets, even to create cartels and to do whatever else was necessary to enable the Japanese electronics industry to "catch up" with the United States.

"At the time, few in the US seemed bothered: innovative US electronics companies reigned supreme with vast assets and a huge domestic market. Because of their success, the culture and management style of US companies was never questioned. Besides, everyone knew that the Japanese were just a bunch of third-rate "copy-cats."

"That sort of complacent misjudgement has clearly cost America dear. The Japanese did more than merely "catch up" with the Us. Exactly 30 years later, in 1987, a definitive report from the Defense Science Board, commissioned by the United States government, confirmed the West's worst fears: Japan had **overtaken** the US in key areas of semiconductor technology and had become the world's No. 1 producer of semiconductors..."

In 1986, Japan (43% of the world semiconductor market) edged ahead of the US (41%).

How did Japan do it? In 1975 the Japanese government launched the 10-year (1975-85) VLSI (Very Large-Scale Integration) cooperative research project, involving all major Japanese semiconductor manufacturers, for Japan to catch up in semiconductor technology, design and manufacturing.

"The project developed state-of-the-art semiconductor technology, and Japanese semiconductor companies gained world leadership soon after," Michael Porter reported. (19)

Tom Forester reported: "Japan's conquest of the microchip industry followed the familiar pattern of Japanese companies importing and creatively refining key semiconductor technologies from the West; building up production and experience in a protected domestic market in which consumers were made to pay high prices for their chips; attacking overseas markets by cutting the prices of key components and commodity chips and by absorbing losses until the competition surrendered; and finally raising prices for overseas consumers on key components and more sophisticated products in order to reap healthy profits which could be used to help keep the lead in the industry..." (20)

Forester concluded: "...It is hard to see how anyone can now take the "rice" industry (the grain of electronics) from the Japanese." (21)

In 1993, the year Forester's book was published, the US reclaimed its original leadership in the global semiconductor industry to end Japan's seven-year reign, and America has maintained its predominance and the lion's share of the worldwide market over the past couple of decades.

In 1988 six Japanese companies ranked among the world's top 10, with three of them on the podium: NEC, Toshiba, and Hitachi. In 1992 when Forester was writing his classic, Intel climbed to the very top on the back of its new microprocessor.

In 2000 when Japan had only three among the top 10, Michael Porter, the world's leading thinker on competitive strategies, and his colleagues Hirotaka Takeuchi and Mariko Sakakibara reported after a decade of research: "...Today, Japan must move beyond just quality competition to competing on **strategy and innovation**...Genuine innovation not only in products but also in approaches to competing (towards the next great transformation)..." (22)

3,105 words 05.05.2017 01:59

APPENDIX (B): South Korea's Great Leap

The Koreans started to make headway in the early 1980s when three Korean manufacturers – Samsung, Goldstar and Hundai – entered the large-scale integration (LSI) semiconductor chip business "with iron determination", according to T.W. Kang, an alumnus of MIT and Harvard Business School, and the then general manager of the systems business of Intel Japan (Intel rose to become #1 in 1992).

"The business had already become very competitive, with some of the toughest competitors being large Japanese companies. It was a bit like jumping onto a fast-moving train. The Koreans have been attracting a lot of attention because they are moving up the technology curve rather fast," Kang wrote in his in-depth study of the Korean economy and industries, published in 1989 **IS KOREA THE NEXT JAPAN?** (23)

Kang described Korea's technology acquisition moves as ***"superaggressive"*** and partnerships with more advanced foreign companies as also aggressive "in order to accelerate the technology learning curve."

For example, Samsung obtained its consumer component technology from Sharp, bought up the 64K DRAM (Dynamic Random Access Memory) design and process technology from Micron Technology, and partnered with Intel Corporation in a number of semiconductor-related product lines.

According to Kang, the Japanese acquired foreign technology at a very reasonable cost when they negotiated 42,000 technology contracts from 1951 to 1984 for $17 billion. The Koreans negotiated 3,500 technology contracts from 1962 to 1985 for $1.3 billion. (24)

Kang said that Korea had "a lot of room for catch-up". He also pointed out that the supply of generations of technology had "to be licensed without divulging the state of the art." (25)

Though the Koreans were in the very late 1980s still far behind the Japanese in manufacturing technology, Kang noted that Korean achievements in the high-technology arena had been "miraculous". And he wrote: "Much of this success has been due to the Korean ability to import technology, products, and know-how through means that are perhaps much more flexible than the Japanese would tolerate..." (26)

Korea's great leap was then astoundingly accomplished well within half a decade.

In 1993 Samsung became the world's largest memory chip maker. The 1994 list of the top 10 had three Korean companies, headed by Samsung; mastery of technology in manufacturing products has come from a very steady and continuous improvement in basic R&D.

On June 1997 WTEC (US-based World Technology Evaluation Center) reported: "...The growth of the Korean semiconductor industry has been stunning. Within a 10-year period, Korean "chaebols" (family-based conglomerates) went from being virtual non-players to capturing one-quarter of the world semiconductor market in 1994. Samsung is now the world's largest DRAM manufacturer. Korean players in their semiconductor markets are regarded by U.S. and Japanese counterparts as formidable competitors..." (27)

On 27 March 2007, Samsung Electronics, the world's top memory chipmaker, said it had developed the industry's first fusion semiconductor by combining two different types of flash memory, labelled the Flex-OneNAND to help make handsets for mobile phones and multimedia gadgets much more compact at cheaper prices. (28)

In 2010 Samsung mass-produced 30 nm (nanometer)-class DRAMS and 20A nm class NAND flashes, both for the first time in the world.

In 2013 South Korea (16.2%) overtook Japan (13.4%) to become the world's second largest semiconductor producer, after the US (52.4%).

In 2017 two Korean companies stood on the podium, with Samsung Electronics at the top with over $62 billion in revenue and SX Hynix in third place ($26.6 billion) below Intel ($61.4 billion).   3,762 words
07.05.2017 09:43

SEMICONDUCTOR UPDATE 2018

According to PwC, China led worldwide semiconductor growth for the sixth consecutive year in 2016 to account for 60.6% of the global semiconductor market of US$354 billion in 2016.

According to research firms Gartner and IHS Markit, global semiconductor revenue topped $400 billion in 2017. The quartet of Samsung Electronics, Intel, SK Hynix, and Qualcomm dominated the market.

In 2017 China imported US$260 billion worth of semiconductors ($227 billion in 2016), substantially more than its crude oil imports of $162 billion.

According to World Semiconductor Trade Statistics (WSTS), China accounted for 32% of global semiconductor sales in 2017; the global market will grow by 15.7% to $477.1 billion in 2018.

While about 400,000 professionals worked in China's IC sector at the end of 2017, the country will need 720,000 by 2020.

According to Jimmy Goodrich, vice president of global policy at the Washington, DC-based trade group Semiconductor Industry Association (SIA), the R&D necessary to further develop and advance chip design can take decades. By the time it takes 5,000 engineers in another country to reverse-engineer a chip, the American maker is "already two generations ahead of you," says Goodrich. (29)

And that says quite a bit on the ballyhoo about IP infringements and technology thefts.

According to industry experts, semiconductors are among the most complicated products to design and produce.

With such complex machines for etchings and moldings and other operations at extremely low millimeter and nanometer levels, an alpha fabricating facility (fab) can cost a bomb of US$10-15 billion, the money's worth of the new Ford-class aircraft carrier in the US Navy.

According to the statement issued 29 August 2018 by State-owned defense company China Electronics Technology Group Corporation (CETC), the company has independently developed high-tech machines used to make integrated circuit (IC) chips, including 28-nanometer (nm) ion implanters and 200-millimeter (mm) chemical mechanical polishing equipment.

According to Zhang Cong, CETC technical director, foreign companies are only willing to sell first generation (1G) military chips although they have developed third generation (3G) technologies.

China spends more than $200 billion a year (more than its GDP of about $150 billion in 1978) on IC imports, including high-end chips due to foreign restrictions on manufacturing equipment, base materials and fabricating technologies.

According to Zhang, foreign companies greatly reduced their prices for first generation machines and agreed to sell second generation equipment to China following the country's recent mastery of second generation technology. But still behind the cutting edge in IC chip production, China must further upgrade its own technology.

"China's competitive edge (in the IC industry) lies in its huge domestic market and its rich supply of talent. That said, the huge market is also a challenge for Chinese semiconductor companies as they tend to focus on the domestic market and pay less attention to expanding in overseas markets," Dr Joseph Xie, founder and president of .IC Engineering and Business School (ICEBS), responded to Credit Suisse (as published online 10.10.2018), about a month ahead of its China Investment Conference in Shenzhen. (30)

"In terms of its supply chain, China's semiconductor industry needs to catch up in the areas of manufacturing equipment and materials, while in IC design it's slightly better. Therefore despite reports that the country has around 1,700 design companies, only about ten of these companies have achieved good business scale."

Dr Xie is more upbeat on China's IC design:

"China's IC design sector will be the first aspect of the domestic supply chain to catch up to the international peers. Chinese design companies can leverage leading foundries to produce advanced chips, and there is significant IC talent in China.

"Also, some Chinese IC design companies are already ahead of Taiwanese IC design companies in terms of their technology.

"I think Chinese IC design companies may overtake US IC design companies in the future. Currently, the second phase of the China IC fund's investment will focus on the IC design sector."

While China has improved its competencies in IC design for application processors, artificial intelligence (AI), and cryptocurrency, Dr Xie is also highly positive about the Chinese AI chip firms:

"Both the US and China have leading AI chip firms, but China has some advantages over the US. The development of AI chips requires complex algorithms, computing power and big data -- all of which China has as well as many different applicant scenarios currently being tested for further development. Moreover, the China market is very open to new technologies."

Founded by engineers Zhu Jinghui and Ning Song, the four-year-old start-up in Guangzhou Gowin Semiconductor has since mid-2018 begun mass production of its low- and mid-density field-programmable gate array (FPGA) chips, for which it holds full intellectual property (IP) rights.

Currently for sale in the mainland China market, these special chips are used in various sectors including automotive, video interfaces, electronics, telecommunications, defense and aerospace. From the company's first order for only 10 chips in Jan 2017, Gowin expects to sell 10 million FPGA chips in 2018.

Moreover, GS is spunky enough to take on the world leaders in the US, Xilinx, Altera and Lattice with their 90% control of global FPGA market. (31)

China's domestic leader Semiconductor Manufacturing International Corporation (SMIC) makes 28 nm chips for other companies, though lagging technologically behind the global leader contract producer, Taiwan-based TSMC. While Intel is working on 10 nm technology, TSMC is preparing to make 5 nm chips by 2020 and planning 3 nm chips for 2022.

E-commerce giant Alibaba Group Holding has moved aggressively into AI and big data, and expects to launch its first neural network chip in April 2019.

AGH is also developing smart chips for building an internet of things (IoT) infrastructure, and for building a smart city.

The world's largest telecoms equipment manufacturer, Huawei Technologies is also working on specialized chips, having launched a 7 nm system-on-chip product in late August 2018.

On September 2018 Huawei released the Kirin 980 chip set used in mid-to-high-end smartphones.

On October 2018 Huawei unveiled two AI-enabled microchips -- the Ascend 910 and Ascend 310 in its corporate surge into cloud infrastructure and its "all scenarios" AI strategy.

On 7 January 2019 Huawei unveiled its new cutting-edge central processing unit (CPU) Kunpeng 920 (7nm processor) and TaiShan servers, powered by Kunpeng 920, as reported by Li Tao o7 Jan, 2019 in **South China Morning Post**.

Primarily for use in big data and distributed storage, they also support China's move to become a world leader in such frontline technologies as AI, chip design, automation, and next generation mobile networks.

"Huawei has invested patiently and intensively in computing innovation to continuously make breakthroughs. We will work with our customers and partners to build a fully connected, intelligent world," said Eric Xu Zhijun, Huawei rotating chairman.   09.01.2019 06:26

"China has plenty of development opportunities, the (home) market is deep," Wang Huixuan, co-president of Tsinghua Unigroup, said at a technology forum in Beijing, August 2018. "China is the manufacturing hub and a big market for smart devices…"

A $24 billion chip maker jointly established by Tsinghua Unigroup, National Integrated Circuits Industry Fund and Hubei provincial government, Yangtze Memory Technologies unveiled a 32-layer 3D NAND flash memory chip in November 2017.

Yangtze Memory is developing a 64-layer NAND chip, not far behind the global leaders Samsung, Hynix and

Micron (US) currently developing 72-layer NAND chips. (32)

According to Bernstein Research, China makes over 90% of the world's smartphones, 65% of personal computers, and 67% of smart televisions.

China's chip imports have exceeded US$200 billion annually since 2013; its spending of over $260 billion on imported chips in 2017 accounted for over 60% of **global chip sales. (33)** 24.11.2018 03:45

According to Deloitte Global (as reported by Chris Arkenberg, Dec 11, 2018), China's semiconductor industry will grow by 25% from estimated US$85 billion in 2018 to US$110 billion in 2019. DG has also predicted that a Chinese chip foundry will begin producing specialized chips to support AI and machine learning (ML) tasks.

Chinese manufacturers, however, can meet only about 30% of national demand.

Local design has become competitive, but local fabrication remains in the shadow of the technological cutting-edge of the global leaders.

Huawei has designed its new mobile chipset at 7nm, and although it still relies on Taiwan's TSMC for fabrication, "it signals that Chinese companies can produce specs at the bleeding edge of technology" (to quote Deloitte).

16.04.2019 01:27 02:45 09.01.2019 06:31

NOTES NEW CHINA(A) GLOBAL CHIP CHAMP?

1. Quoted in Richard Crawford, **IN THE ERA OF HUMAN CAPITAL**, USA, HarperCollins, 1991, p. 74.
2. George Gilder, "The world's next source of wealth," **Fortune**, August 28, 1989, pp. 78-82. As quoted in Tom Forester, **SILICON SAMURAI**, Blacksmith Publishers, Cambridge, MA, USA/Oxford, UK, 1993, p.4.
3. Published by Simon & Schuster, New York, 1989, p. 17. As quoted in Tom Forester, **SILICON SAMURAI**, p. 3.
4. **wikipedia.org** last modified 18 April 2017, at 09:59

The transistor was invented towards the end of 1947 at the Bell Telephone Laboratories in North Jersey by three American physicists John Bardeen, Walter Brattain, and William Stockley (director). They got the 1956 Nobel Prize in Physics for their "supreme effort" (to quote Prof E.G. Rudberg) in reaching the "summit of Everest" in the pristine semiconductor world.

The fundamental building block of modern electronic devices, the transistor has revolutionized the field of solid-state electronics as well as the global economy. Regarded as one of the greatest inventions of the 20th century, the transistor inaugurated the Information Age. **wikipedia.org** 19 April 2017 17:42

On 12 September 1958 Jack S. Kilby demonstrated the first working integrated circuit to the managers at Texas Instruments in Dallas, Texas.

Originally used in military applications, the integrated circuit (IC) quickly became the core of commercial and consumer electronics – from personal computers (PCs), cell phones and digital cameras to anti-locking brakes to ear and eye implants, medical diagnostic devices, etc. From $29 billion in 1961, the electronics industry has grown to $1.5 trillion in 2015. **ethw. org** 31 December 2015 03:30

Jack Kilby was awarded in 2000 the Nobel Prize for Physics for his part in the invention and development of the integrated circuit, the chip.

"Through his invention microelectronics has grown to become the basis of all modern technologies," to quote from the press release on 10 October 2000 by the Royal Swedish Academy of Sciences.

His work also contributed to laying the foundation of modern information technology, IT. **Nobelprizes.org**

5. **semiconductors.org**

Congress and the Donald Trump administration should enact policies that "keep America in pole position at the tip of the technology spear," said John Neuffer, president and chief executive of the 38-member Semiconductor Industry Association (SIA) after releasing its 16-page report "Winning the Future" on 3 April 2019.

The SIA's report reiterates its longstanding position that the chips are critical for the US's economy, defense, and technological leadership.

Report by Mark Maguier, 04 Apr, 2019 **South China Morning Post**
04.04.2019 22:19

6. **SILICON SAMURAI**, p.43
7. Data from report by PricewaterhouseCoopers, **China's impact on the semiconductor industry: 2016 update** January 2017 **pwe.com**

In 2015 China paid US$134.5 billion for importing a record 335.5 million tonnes of crude oil, or 6.71 million barrels per day. **Reuters**/Beijing report in **NEW STRAITS TIMES** January 14, 2016

8. **THE WALL STREET JOURNAL** July 26, 2016
According to research firm IHS, the NAND sector is expected to earn US$35.7 billion in 2017. **Reuters**/Seoul report in **NEW STRAITS TIMES** December 23, 2016

9. **NIKKEI ASIAN REVIEW asia.nikkei.com** April 24, 2017
Report by Cheng Ting-Fang, Nikkei staff writer

10. **trade.govt**

11. **consultancy.uk** January 26, 2017

12. **marketandmarket.com**

13. **marketrealist.com** Paige Tanner September 10, 2t015

14. **obamawhite.archives.govt**

15. Dieter Ernst, East-West Center, Honolulu, Hi, "From catching up to forging ahead: China's new role in the semiconductor industry"
electroi.com/blog/2016/05

16. **trade.govt**

17. As quoted in **Harvard Business Review**, September-October 1990, p. 180, and as also quoted in Tom Forester, **SILICON SAMURAI**, Blackwell Publishers, Cambridge, MA, USA/ Oxford, UK, 1993, p.6.

18. **SILICON SAMURAI**, pp. 43-44.

19. Michael E. Porter with Hirotaka Takeuchi and Mariko Sakakibara, **CAN JAPAN COMPETE?** Cambridge, Massachusetts, 2000, p. 40.

20. **SILICON SAMURAI**, pp. 45-46

21. Ibid., p. 83.

22. **CAN JAPAN COMPETE?** pp. 189-190.

23. Published by the Free Press, New York.

24. **IS KOREA THE NEXT JAPAN?** p. 54.

25. Ibid., p. 92.
26. Ibid., p. 109.
27. **wtec.org**
28. **AFP**/Seoul report in **NEW STRAITS TIMES** March 28, 2007
29. Joseph Horwitz July 25, 2018 **qz.com**
30. Also Professor at China's Fudan University, School of Microelectronics, Dr Xie was one of the founding members of SMIC, and founder of QST Corp, a motion sensor chip company in China.

    Founded in 1856, Credit Suisse is a leading wealth manager operating globally in about 50 countries with over 46,840 employees.

31. He Huifeng 25 Sept 2018 **South China Morning Post**
32. Elaine Chan 25 Sept 2018 **South China Morning Post**
33. Sarah Dai 24 Aug 2018 **South China Morning Post**

21 pages 5706 words 06.05.2017 08:55 07.05.2017 09:45 16.10.2018 20:37 24.11.2018 04:19
04.04.2019 22:20 16.04.2019 01:31 03:09

NEW CHINA B
INTRO (UPDATED COPY)

China's Need For A Strong Military

On 14 March 2013 Xi Jinping was elected as the 7th president of the People's Republic of China (PRC), making him the leader of the Chinese state, its ruling party and military (having earlier been elected on 15 November 2012 as the CPC General Secretary and Chairman of the Central Military Commission).

As the CMC Chairman, Xi has said that a strong military is needed for the great renewal of the Chinese nation.

"The armed forces need to be ready to assemble at the first call of the CPC (the Communist Party of China) and be capable of fighting and winning any battle," Xi said. (1)

While vowing to never allow the country's sovereignty, security and development interests to be infringed, Xi has also reiterated that China will always remain a staunch force in upholding world peace, as the nation suffered from past wars.

"A new technological and industrial revolution is brewing, a global revolution in military affairs is accelerating, and the pattern of international military competition is experiencing historic changes," President Xi told Chinese military officials in a keynote speech on December 2014. (2)

"The United States is the leader of the pack in this revolution in military affairs, and in many areas it holds the initiative, and it is also striving to gain new advantages in military technology.

"The United States is accelerating development of global rapid-strike offensive capabilities, and some advanced weaponry has technologies broken through spatiotemporal (space-time) boundaries.

"Once they are deployed for actual combat, they will fundamentally transform the traditional array of offense and defense in warfare…"

In brief, the new game-changers in global military conflict. 31.03.2019 17:27

"… Chinese leaders have characterized modernization of the People's Liberation Army (PLA) as essential to achieving great power status and what President Xi Jinping calls the "China Dream" of national rejuvenation," the Office of the US Secretary of Defense reported to Congress on April 2016.

"They portray a strong military as critical to advancing Chinese interests, preventing other countries from taking steps that would damage their interests, and ensuring that China can defend itself and its sovereignty claims.

"China's leaders understand that instability or conflict would jeopardize the peaceful external environment that has enabled China's economic development, which is central to the perpetuation of the CCP's domestic legitimacy…" (3)

To China, its peaceful development will be covered and sustained by building a strong military.

"We will adapt to the trend of a new global military revolution and to national security needs; we will upgrade our military capabilities, and see that by the year 2020, mechanization is basically achieved, IT application has come a long way, and strategic capabilities have seen a big improvement," President Xi stated in his report o the 19th CPC National Congress on 18 October 2017. (4)

"In step with our country's modernization process, we will modernize our military across the board in terms of theory, organizational structure, service personnel, and weaponry.

"We will make it our mission to see that by 2035, the modernization of our national defense and our forces is basically completed; and that by the mid-21st century our people's armed forces have been fully transformed into world-class forces..."

Until very recently regarded by the US as a near-peer, China has since been acknowledged by the top brass in the Trump Administration as a major power competitor.

"We should be prepared to be surprised" in any conflict with China, not only because it has invested heavily in modernizing its armed forces, but also how it has invested in next-generation military technology, said former Deputy Secretary of Defense (2014-2017) Robert Work at a forum sponsored by the Center for a New American Security on 21 June 2018.

According to Work, China "wants to be a first mover" in AI, incorporatig the Internet of Things (IoT), big data, robotics and machine learning (ML). "That will be how they will get ahead of the United States," he said.

Chinese progress is evident in electronic warfare, cyber and counter-space systems, hypersonics and rail-guns. 31.03.2019 17:55

"... China is reaping the fruits of a multi-decade military buildup. Beijing has invested in systems designed to counter American power-projection and thereby prevent the United States from protecting its allies, partners, and economic interests," the National Defense Strategy Commission has stated in its report to Congress PROVIDING FOR THE COMMON DEFENSE (p.7) released on 14 November 2018.

"China is also modernizing its nuclear forces, developing sophisticated power-projection capabilities, and undertaking the most thoroughgoing military reforms since the founding of the People's Republic (October 1949)," the committee of 12 senior national security officials and military experts reported.

"China already presents a severe test of U.S. interests in the Indo-Pacific and beyond and is on a path to become, by mid-century, a military challenger the likes of which America has not encountered since the Cold War-era Soviet Union (1945-89)..."

According to **GLOBAL FIREPOWER**, China will be the most powerful nation in the world by 2050.   17.11.2018 23:23

Notes.

1. **xinhuanet.com** 2013-03-17
2. Quoted in recently released 272-page book of Xi's remarks in Chinese on national security **XINHUANET.com** 2018-04-15

    Also in "What keeps Xi Jinping awake at night", report by Chris Buckley and Paul Mozup May 11, 2018 **nytimes.com**

3. **freebeacon.com ANNUAL REPORT TO CONGRESS CHINA 2016** generated April 26, 2016   279 words 23.09.2017 15:06
4. **China Military/PLA Daily chinamil.com.cn**

"The global situation is sobering," Secretary of Defense Jim Mattis wrote in his statement for the record of the Senate Armed Services Committee on April 26, 2018. **armed-services.senate.gov**

"Russia is modernizing its full range of nuclear systems while espousing a theory of nuclear escalation in military conflict.

"China, too, is modernizing and expanding its already considerable nuclear forces (280 nuclear warheads including 75-100 ICBMs as compared with the US nuclear arsenal of over 6,000, including 450 ICBMs on full alert and up to 800 nuclear warheads that can be launched in 10 minutes), pursuing entirely new capabilities.

"China is also modernizing its conventional military forces to a degree that will challenge U.S. military superiority…

"Modernizing the Nation's nuclear deterrent delivery systems, including our nuclear command and control, is the (Defense) Department's top priority…" (p. 6)

For the Budget Hearing on April 26, 2018, General Joseph F. Dunford, Jr, USMC 19th Chairman of the Joint Chiefs of Staff submitted in his statement:

"… The United States military is in fierce competition to harness the benefits of emerging technologies -- including hypersonics, artificial intelligence (AI), directed energy (DE), and biotehnology -- as these developments will fundamentally change the character of war…

"China intends to become a global military power and is building the capability to do so…

"They are developing a full range of air, maritime, space, and cyber capabilities while modernizing their nuclear enterprise…" (p.4)

"… Indeed, the PLA is pursuing next-generation capabilities, ranging from hypersonic missiles to counterforce weapons or military applications of artificial intelligence," Elsa B. Kania, adjunct fellow with Technology and National Security Program at the Center for a New American Security, has written in her article <u>China's strategic arsenals in a new era</u>, published in **Bulletin of the Atomic Scientists** 20 April 2018.

"Beyond its traditional endeavors in military modernization, China is increasingly pursuing a new agenda of military innovation, seeking to "leapfrog" ahead through rapid innovation in strategic emerging technologies.

"Significantly, Xi (Jinping) has called for the People's Liberation Army to "accelerate the development of military intelligentization". This new concept represents a progression beyond the PLA's existing strategy for informatization…

"In the course of modernization, the PLA has thus created a range of instruments for military deterrence with the precision and flexibility to defend against threats and advance core interests. Taken together, space, nuclear, and cyber capabilities -- along with newly emerging technologies -- could act as a "new triad" for this new era…"

"It takes first-class military talent, theory, and science and technology to build the PLA into a world-leading military," Xi said at a high-level military symposium in Beijing on 19 July 2017.

Xinhua/PLA Daily chinamil.com 2017-07-20   22.08.2018 22:00

"President Xi significantly accelerated China's military modernization goals in late 2017, requiring the PLA to become a fully "modern" military by 2035 and a "world-class" military by mid-century. This new guidance moves China's military modernization timeline up nearly 15 years," the U.S.-China Economic and Security Review Commission reported to Congress on 14 November 2018.

"Beijing is currently capable of contesting U.S. operations in the ground, air, maritime, and information domains within the second island chain (from Japan down south to Guam, Palau, and Indonesia), presenting challenges to the U.S. military's longstanding assumption of supremacy in these domains in the post-Cold War era. By 2035, if not before, China will likely be able to contest U.S. operations throughout the entire Indo-Pacific region.

"China continues to develop and field medium- and long-range air, sea, and ground-launched missile systems that substantially improve China's capability to strike both fixed and moving targets out to the second island chain. China's ability to threaten U.S. air bases, aircraft carriers, and other surface ships presents serious strategic and operational challenges for the United States and its allies and partners throughout the Indo-Pacific..."
21.11.2018 04:15

6 pages 1,671 words 10.11.2017 10:36 12.12.2017 13:55 21.01.2018 01:23 22.08.2018 22:02
17.10.2018 18:15 17.11.2018 23:27 18.11.2018 01:38 21.11.2018 04:19
12.12.2018 03:54
31.03.2019 18:05

NEW CHINA B(1)
INFORMATION WARFARE (UPDATED COPY)

B(1) Waging Information Warfare (Iw) Against A Technologically Stronger Foe

"In the near future, information warfare will control the form and future of war," Major General Wang Pufeng, a former Director of the Strategy Department, Academy of Military Science, Beijing, wrote in a seminal paper THE CHALLENGE OF INFORMATION WARFARE published in **China Military Science** (Spring 1995).

"We recognize this developmental trend of information warfare and see it as a driving force in the modernization of China's military and combat readiness. This trend will be highly critical to achieving victory in future wars..."

On developing the necessary hardware through information technology (IT) to prosecute information warfare successfully, Gen Wang has written: "Information technology itself is a pinnacle of high technology. The key technologies are remote-sensing technology, communications technology, and computer technology.

"Key information weapons include precision-guided weapons systems and electronic warfare weapons systems as well as C4I systems (command, control, communications, computers, and intelligence) which form the central nervous system. These hardware items are necessary and essential to adapt to and achieve victory in information warfare, and we must make efforts here..."

Gen Wang has also emphasized developing three main aspects of information technology:

(1) <u>A Reliable Reconnaissance and Remote Sensing System</u>
The goal is to obtain timely information, to understand the enemy and ourselves (the great military strategist Sun-tze's precept of knowing self and adversary), and to achieve clarity about our situation with great determination. It is especially necessary to establish a strategic reconnaissance warning and air defense system to achieve a capacity for early detection of enemy movements, in order to be forewarned and ready.

(2) <u>Information Warfare Systems</u>

The most important of these are air defense weapons systems, offensive tactical guided missile attack systems, landing and touchdown operations equipment systems, electronic warfare equipment systems, and underwater mine-laying systems. These will give China (breakthrough) over-the-horizon (OTH), high-precision, concealed, sudden defensive attack capability and a stronger survival capacity and make the enemy terrified and worried, providing an effective threat.

(3) <u>Computer Technology and Battlefield Information Networks</u>

First, we should establish battlefield information networks and battlefield databases for the battlefields in priority strategic directions. By bringing all branches of the military into an information network, information may be shared on the network. Near-real-time communication can be gained in all directions and a better solution can be achieved for the problem of vertical and horizontal coordination in warfare.

"To achieve victory in information warfare, the central issue is control of information," General Wang has strongly stressed the need for firm control of battlefield information, which has also been translated by both Chinese and American military experts as <u>information dominance or information superiority</u> over the enemy's.

During the 1991 Gulf War, according to Gen Wang, at least half a dozen types of information offensives were launched by fighter aircraft: (1) information reconnaissance to gain information on targets, (2) electronic interference to paralyse opponent's communications, (3) information suppression by using counter-radiation guided missiles to destroy air defense radar systems, (4) information attack by using precision-guided warheads to attack pre-set targets, (5) computer viruses to destroy systems of Iraq's air defense system, and (6) stealth aircraft to drop precision-guided bombs against the communications building and the command center.

Operation Desert Storm (aka the 1991 Gulf War) started on the morning of 16 January 1991, with a 43-day air offensive known as Desert Shield, involving a total of nearly 110,000 sorties.

Gen Wang has emphasised <u>cultivating and developing human talent</u>, the main factor of combat power, information control and conduct of information warfare, "<u>for China to achieve comprehensive victory even under the conditions of inferiority in information technology.</u>"

To quote Gen Wang:
<u>"The basic great plan is to cultivate talented people suited to information warfare. One aspect is to cultivate talent in information science and technology</u>. (1)

"The development and resolution of information warfare can be predicted to a great degree in the laboratory. Information science and technology talent is the forerunner of science and technology research. The achievements and practical use of their research will play a key role in the development and advancement of society and military construction and warfare.

"The second aspect is talented people in command and control. They especially need to have the ability to conduct comprehensive analysis and policy-information processing, to understand themselves and the enemy, as well as the battlefield, and also to have a capacity for scientific strategic thinking and a comprehensive point of view.

"Senior command personnel especially need to have information knowledge and the ability to control information warfare and must be adept at using information technology to organise and command warfare.

"Combat personnel must also be familiar with the technical and strategic aspects of the weapons and equipment in their hands and must be very well versed in the operation of those weapons and equipment. They must be able to understand the combat plan and resolutely and flexibly utilize weapons and equipment to wipe out the enemy.

"The combat personnel of information warfare are not only the warriors who charge enemy lines for face to face struggles of life or death, but sometimes are the operating technical personnel who sit behind computers and instruments. They stand at the first line in electronic warfare and in the resistance against C4I (command, control, communications, computers and intelligence) systems and on the front line in information technology conflicts.

"Rear support and technical support are very important in information warfare. Information technology relates to a number of high-technology groups of people and touches on new energy, new materials, artificial intelligence, space travel, marine engineering, systems engineering, and other high-tech subjects.

"The demands for the technical level of support personal are quite high. They are required to guarantee that weapons and equipment are always kept in excellent condition. While carrying out rear and front-line support, the use of information technology is a support method just like other methods. In Information warfare, the support of information technology penetrates the contents of information resistance and is also one method of warfare support…"

With portentous words has Gen Wang concluded his classic treatise on information warfare (IW) – the prime manifestation of the new military revolution on the eve of the 21st century:

"The large-scale importation of information technology deep into the field of warfare will inevitably bring about a military revolution. This revolution has actually already started (with the 1991 Gulf War). (2)

"Those who perceive it first will swiftly rise to the top and have the advantage of the first opportunities.

"Those who perceive it late will unavoidably also be caught up in the vortex of this revolution. Every military will receive this baptism.

"This revolution is first a revolution in concepts, then it is a revolution in science and technology, equipment, troop strength, strategy, and tactics as well as a revolution in training. Thus, the issue of how to adapt to and achieve victory in the information warfare which we will face from now on is an important question which we need to study carefully." (3)

1.045 words 25.10.2016 18:32

In Information Warfare and the Revolution in Military Affairs, 1995, General Wang Pufeng has encapsulated the essence of IW in one sentence: "At its heart are information technologies, fusing intelligence war, strategic war, electronic war, guided missile war, a war of "motorization" (*jidong zhan*), a war of firepower (*huoli*) – **a total war…**"

In 2007, the US Secretary of Defense reported to Congress (4):

"… There has been much writing on information warfare among China's military thinkers, who indicate a strong conceptual understanding of its methods and uses…

"The PLA is investing in electronic countermeasures, defences against electronic attack (e.g. electronic and infrared decoys, angle reflectors, and false target generators), and computer network operations (CNO).

"China's CNO concepts include computer network attack, computer network defense, and comprehensive network exploitation. The PLA sees CNO as critical to achieving "electromagnetic dominance" early in conflict...

"The PLA has established information warfare units to develop viruses to attack enemy computer systems and networks, and tactics and measures to protect friendly computer systems and networks. In 2005, the PLA began to incorporate offensive CNO into its exercises, primarily first strikes against networks..."

The **2010 White Paper on China's National Defense** has spelt out its four major goals and tasks in the new era.

On its third goal and task, it's categorically and concisely stated:

"<u>Accelerating the modernization of national defense and the armed forces.</u> Bearing in mind the primary goal of accomplishing mechanization and <u>attaining major progress in informationization by 2020</u>, the People's Liberation Army (PLA) perseveres with mechanization as the foundation and informationization as the driving force, making extensive use of its achievements in information technology (IT), and stepping up the composite and integrated development of mechanization and informationization.

"The PLA has expanded and made profound preparations for military struggle, which serve as both pull and impetus to the overall development of modernization.

"It intensifies theoretical studies on joint operations under conditions of informationization, advances the development of high-tech weaponry and equipment, develop new types of combat forces, strives to establish joint <u>operation systems in conditions of informationization, accelerates the</u> transition from military training under conditions of mechanization to military training in conditions of informationization, presses ahead with implementation of <u>the strategic project for talented people</u>, invests greater efforts in building a modern logistics capability, and enhances its capabilities in accomplishing diversified military tasks in order <u>to win local wars under the conditions of informationization</u>, so as to accomplish its historical missions at the new stage in the new century.

"The state takes economic development and national defense building into simultaneous consideration, adopts a mode of integrated civilian-military development...

"China vigorously and steadily advances reform of national defense and the armed forces, strengthens strategic planning and management, and endeavours to promote the scientific development of the national defense and armed forces..."

On Modernization of the People's Liberation Army (PLA):

"Over the 60 years and more since its founding (1 August 1927), the PLA has made great achievements in its modernization. It has grown from a single service into a strong military force featuring a range of services and arms (5), and is now beginning to make progress towards informationization.

"In recent years, the PLA has enhanced its comprehensive development in accordance with the principle of integrating revolutionization, modernization and regularization (6), and continuously accelerated revolution in military affairs (RMA) with Chinese characteristics (as the only way to modernize the Chinese military)..."

Accelerating Informationization:

"... The fighting capabilities of the armed forces in conditions of informationization have been significantly raised...

"A step-change development has been achieved in information infrastructure. The total length of the national defense optical fiber communication network has increased by a large margin, forming a new generation information transmission network with optical fiber communication as the mainstay and satellite and short-wave communications as assistance.

"Significant progress has been made in building information systems for reconnaissance and intelligence, command and control, and battlefield environment awareness.

"Information systems have been widely applied in logistics and equipment support.

"A preliminary level has been achieved in <u>interoperability</u> among command and control systems, combat forces, and support systems, making order transmission, intelligence distribution, command and guidance more efficient and rapid...

"Notable achievements have been made in the training of commanding officers for joint operations, management personnel for informationization, personnel specialized in information technology (IT), and personnel for the operation and maintenance of new equipment.

"The complement of new-mode and high-caliber military personnel who can meet the needs of informationization has been steadily advanced.

<u>Building Joint Operation Systems</u>

"The PLA takes the building of joint operation systems as the focal point of its modernization and preparation for military struggle (PMS), and strives to enhance its fighting capabilities based on information systems..."

On China's building an informationized military, the Pentagon reported to Congress in April 2014: "Chinese military writings describe informationized warfare as an <u>asymmetric form of warfare to defeat a technologically superior, information-dependent adversary</u> **through dominance of the battlefield's information space...**" (7)   2,312 words 28.10.2016 02:18

The **2015 White Paper on China's Military Strategy** has described cyberspace (CS) as "a new pillar of economic and social development, and a new domain of national security..."

With international strategic competition in cyberspace "turning increasingly fiercer, quite a few countries are developing their cyber military forces..."

The White Paper says: "As cyberspace (CS) weighs more in military security, China will expedite the development of a cyber force (following the US pathfinder and pioneer), and enhance its capabilities of cyber space awareness, cyber defense, support for the country's endeavours in cyberspace..."

In April 2016, the Pentagon reiterated to Congress what it had reported a couple of years back: "The development of cyber capabilities is consistent with authoritative writings which identify information operations (IO) as integral to **achieving information superiority and as an effective means for countering a stronger foe...**" (8)   2,705 words 29.10.2016

According to the August 2018 Report of the Department of Defense (p.73), China fields advanced automated command systems, such as the Integrated Command Platform (ICP), to enable joint operations across the 6-D domains of land, sea, air, space, counterspace and the electromagnetic spectrum.

China continues to prioritize C4I (Command, Control, Communications, Computer, and Intelligence) modernization in response to trends in modern warfare that stress rapid information-sharing, processing, and decision-making.

The PLA considers information operations (IOs), including cyber, electronic, and psychological warfare, integral to waging modern warfare.

President Xi's speeches at the PLA's 90th anniversary in July 2017 and the 19th Party Congress in October 2017 highlighted recent progress in "accelerating toward informatization" to provide the Chinese military with a "great rise in strategic capability".

In its 2018 Report to Congress, the U.S.-China Economic and Security Review Commission has highlighted the role of the recently-constituted PLA Strategic Support Force (SSF).

In No. 4 of its 9 key findings, the Commission has reported (p. 11):

"The PLA Strategic Support Force -- whose organization and operations reflect the importance Beijing places on information warfare -- poses a fundamental challenge to the United States' ability to operate effectively in space, cyberspace, and the electromagnetic spectrum. The new force signals Beijing's intent to build a military capable of dominating these domains of warfare..."

Further on, the Commission has elaborated (p. 238): "The PLA established the SSF on 31 December 2015 (in tandem with PLA reogranization) to oversee PLA space and cyber capabilities and conduct operations in space, counterspace, and the electromagnetic spectrum as its primary warfighting domains..."   31.03.2019 18:57

APPENDIX (A): The US Perspective on Information Warfare (IW)

Lieutenant General Cerjan, former President of US National Defense University wrote in **Army** magazine (1994): "Information warfare is a means of armed struggle **aimed at seizing the decisive military superiority and focused on the control and use of information**..." (9)

In a two-part article published in **Liberation Army Daily** June 1995, Senior Colonel Wang Baocun and Li Fei of the Academy of Military Science, Beijing, wrote on Information Warfare (IW) from the American military perspective.

"Information warfare in the broad sense refers to warfare dominated by information in which digitized units use information (smart) equipment. While warfare has always been tied to information, it is only when warfare is dominated by information that it becomes authentic information warfare," Wang and Li have written.

"Information warfare in the broad sense has many manifestations, as follows:

- **Computer virus warfare**. Sharven (as translated) claims that: While the major 20th century weapons were tanks, <u>the key 21st century weapon will be the computer</u>. In future wars, operations against military computers will become a key type of information warfare. That will mean computer virus warfare.

  Computer viruses are special software programs that can alter or destroy a computer's normal operating programs.

  They are characterized by detection difficulty, rapid contagion, longstanding potency, and active and continuous encroachment, and can severely disrupt the C3I (command, control, communications and intelligence) system, smart weapons, and combat potential.

  Some countries are now considering the organization and establishment of computer virus warfare platoons.

- **Precision warfare**. The advent of smart weapons was bound to cause the appearance of precision warfare. Precision warfare means precision in reconnaissance (spying) and advance warning, in information transmission, in command coordination, in mobile positioning, in target strikes, and in damage extent.

  Precision warfare is characterized by less destruction and fewer casualties, less "combat fog" and fewer troops, less logistics support, and better troop mobility.

- **Stealth warfare.** Stealth aircraft, ships, tanks, and missiles will flood future battlefields. In future wars, as target detection will mean immediate elimination, future warfare will be a confrontation between the "stealthy" and the "detractors." So stealth and counter-stealth warfare will not only arrive in the battle arena as an independent and crucial type of warfare, but will also be conducted very intensely...

To conduct and win information warfare, two major supports are needed: (1) a digitized battlefield, and (2) an informationized military.

In 1994-95, the US Army, Navy and Air Force started to study and design the technology and software needed for their battlefield digitization.

It's reckoned that it will probably take about three decades (one human generation) to fully informationize the American military.

"By about 2040, once all services are informationized, it will still take more than a decade to get the entire military into a digitized joint network," Senior Colonel Wang Baocun and Li Fei wrote in 1995.

"So it is obvious that by mid-century, the United States probably will have built the world's first completely smart military..." (9)

Notes CHINA B(1) WAGING INFORMATION WARFARE

1. Gen Wang on cultivating talent through study and training: "... The main methods of cultivating talent are study and training. In addition to conducting training in politics, ethics, and psychology, there must also be study of high-tech knowledge

and the fundamental knowledge of warfare techniques related to information warfare.

"If conditions permit, we want to create as much as possible the conditions necessary for implementing simulation training. We can first consider creating simulated battlefields with information in key areas of the army, navy, air force, and artillery, and, second. conducting rotational training of cadre and key troops.

"Colleges and universities should also establish curriculae in information warfare. Scientific research institutions should also engage in research on information warfare..."

Gen Wang's keynote essay on IW is also published in **CHINESE VIEWS OF FUTURE WARFARE**, edited by Michael Pillsbury, Institute for National Strategic Studies, 2004 (Revised Edition).
au.af.mil

2. According to Major General Zheng Shenxia, President of the Air Force Command College in Beijing, and his colleague Senior Colonel Zhang Changzhi, US Secretary of Defense William Perry proposed the concept of the new military revolution in 1994.

    "After the (1991) Gulf War, the U.S. military gradually increased research centered on information combat," Gen Zheng and Senior Col Zhang wrote in their essay published in **China Military Science** (Spring 1996).

    "A special group was organized to conduct research on how the Pentagon can obtain and maintain decisive military superiority within the next two and three decades..." (and develop an

informationized military to prevail in information warfare).
au.af.mil

3. In an article published on 11 March 1996 in **Contemporary Military Affairs**, Ch'en Huan has called it the Third Military Revolution, following the rapid development of information technology, stealth technology, and long-range technology, which were all originally deployed in the 1991 Gulf War, which "opened the curtain in the information war era and marked the sudden appearance of the third military revolution."

According to Ch'en Huan, the first military revolution appeared before the 1930s, in the era of "hot weapons" including airplanes, tanks, and radios.

"From World War II to the 1960s, the development of nuclear technology and the use of guided missile technology on the battlefield brought about the second military revolution," Ch'en wrote, "proclaiming the arrival of the "nuclear-hot weapon" era, followed by the rapid development of nuclear strategy and the theory of nuclear deterrence..." **au.af.mil**

1,423 words 26.10.2016 20:55

4. ANNUAL REPORT TO CONGRESS 2007

Military Power of the People's Republic of China
pp.21-22

5. PLA founded on 1 August 1927, PLA Air Force (PLAAF) 11 November 1949, PLA Navy (PLAN) September 1950, Second Artillery Corps (SAC) 1 July 1966 and changed to PLA Army Rocket Force (PLAARF) on 31 December 2015. According to a report in **Wikipedia**, the PLAARF has 6 brigades, 1,833 ballistic missiles and 350 cruise missiles.

6. As reported by **People's Daily** on 30 September 2004, President Hu Jintao urged the PLA to prepare for a military struggle as well as to "comprehensively revolutionize, modernize and standardise" its development.

7. **ANNUAL REPORT TO CONGRESS 2014** p. 40 **defense.gov**

8. In April 2014, the Department of Defense reported to Congress: "Developing cyber capabilities for warfare is consistent with authoritative PLA military writings... on information warfare (IW) as integral to achieving **information superiority and an effective means for countering a stronger foe...**"   12 pages 3,207 words 29.10.2016 02:12

8 (a) "The importance of cyberspace is growing rapidly as the world becomes increasingly interconnected and networked. National power and security depend on the ability to operate securely in and through cyberspace," Admiral Harry B. Harris, Jr, then U.S. Navy Commander, U.S. Pacific Command, submitted in his 56-page statement before the Senate Armed Services Committee on U.S. Pacific Command Posture, 15 March 2018.

"The two most capable cyber actors worldwide are Russia and China. Both of these countries have incorporated cyber into their joint warfighting doctrine and routinely exercise these capabilities alongside more traditional elements as a force multiplier, In fact, China values cyber so highly it created the Strategic Support Force (SSF) to integrate and synchronize cyber operations..." **armed-services.senate.gov 03-15-18.pdf**   22.08.2018 18:45

9. Extract from articles in **Liberation Army Daily** June 13 and 20, 1995.

Published in **CHINESE VIEWS OF FUTURE WARFARE**, edited by Michael Pillsbury, Institute for National Strategic Studies, 2004.

Both Senior Colonel Wang Baocun and Li Fei work at the Academy of Military Science, Beijing.

9 (a)"We are on the eve of a new era in the business of warfighting and combined arms," Gen. Dave Goldfein, chief of the US Air Force posted on 17 November 2016 for the Defense One Summit held in Washington, D.C. a commentary on his speed-infused vision of combined arms across all the domains of the land, sea, air, space, and cyberspace.

"The primary warfighting attributes will be decision speed and operational agility.

"In short, <u>our asymmetrical advantage in future battles depends on harnessing the vast amount of information our sensors can generate,</u> **fusing it quickly into decision-quality information, and creating effects simultaneously from all domains and all functional components anywhere in the world**..."

Above extracted from **CRISIS, CONFLICTS & CONTINUITY News and Commentary from the 2016 Defense One Summit,** held on 17 November 2016 in Washington, D.C. page 3.

03.12.2016 07:03 13 pages 3,677 words 03.12.2016 07:05 22.08.2018 18:52

APPENDIX (B): Future Cyberwarfare

"… The benefits to an attacker using cyber exploits are potentially spectacular. Should the United States find itself in a full-scale conflict with a peer adversary, attacks would be expected to include denial of service, data corruption, supply chain corruption, traitorous insiders, kinetic, and related non-kinetic attacks at all altitudes from underwater to space," the 2013 Defense Science Board report warned.

(As quoted in James N. Miller Jr. And Richard Fontaine, NEW ERA IN U.S>-RUSSIAN STRATEGIC STABILITY, Harvard Kennedy School, BELFER CENTER for Science and International Affairs, 2017, p. 16)

In response, the US Department of Defense has stated in CYBER STRATEGY 2018 (**media.defense.gov**/2018/Sep/18):

"... We are engaged in a long-term strategic competition with China and Russia. These States have expanded that competition to include persistent campaigns in and through cyberspace that pose long-term strategic risk to the Nation as well as to our allies and partners.

"China is eroding U.S. military overmatch and the Nation's economic vitality by persistently exfiltrating sensitive information from U.S. public and private sector institutions.

"Russia has used cyber-enabled information operations to influence our population and challenge our democratic processes...

"The Department (DoD) must take action in cyberspace during day-to-day competition to preserve U.S. military advantages and to defend U.S. interests.

"Our focus will be on the States that can pose strategic threats to U.S. prosperity and security, particularly China and Russia.

"We will conduct cyberspace operations to collect intelligence and prepare military cyber capabilities to be used in the event of crisis or conflict... (p.1)

(p.2) "The United States cannot afford inaction: our values, economic competitiveness, and military edge are exposed to threats that can grow more dangerous every day...

(Strategic Competition in Cyberspace): "First, we must ensure the U.S. military's ability to fight and win wars in any domain, including cyberspace. This is a foundational requirement for U.S. national security, and a key to ensuring that we deter aggression, including cyber attacks that constitute a use of force, against the United States, our allies, and our partners..."

According to the August 2018 Report by the US Department of Defense to Congress, China fields advanced automated command systems, such as the Integrated Command Platform (ICP), to enable joint military operations across the 6-D domains of land, sea, air, space, cyberspace, and the electromagnetic (EMG) spectrum.

According to the DOD, China has established its Strategic Support Force, probably in 2015, to centralize the military's space, cyber, and EW (Electronic Warfare) missions for seizing and maintaining battlefield information control.

Like the US Cyber Command, China's SSF "may represent the first step in developing a cyber force that creates efficiencies by combining cyber reconnaissance, attack, and defense capabilities into one organization..."

According to David Ochmanek, DoD has not moved quickly enough to provide the capabilities and basing posture called for to meet the manifold challenges posed by China's rapidly modernizing armed forces.   04.05.2019 09:10

"Recognizing the critical importance of accurate, timely information and agile command and control in modern military operations, U.S. adversaries (principally China and Russia) are investing heavily in capabilities intended to improve their understanding of the battlefield and to deny the United States the same," David Ochmanek of The RAND Coporation said In testimony before the Committee on Armed Services United States Senate, Nov 30, 2017, and recommended necessary capability development for the US to win the fight for information superiority and to operate effectively in disrupted "low band width" environments.

In **CYBERSECURITY READINESS REVIEW March 2019** presented to the US Secretary of the Navy, the review team has clearly and strongly stated in the Forward (p. 1):

"In prior eras, for good or ill, navies shifted their definition from wood to steel to wing, or from sail to steam and beyond.

"This time **technology** (emphasis added), not the naval service, or its opponents, have imposed a definition of what navies must be for the rest of the 21st Century. Nothing the Navy or Marine Corp does, or will do, can exist without it. It is the keystone of capability and survival.

"Navies must become information enterprises who happen to operate on, over, under, and from the sea; a vast difference from a 355 ship mindset.

"Today, knowing and living what business the Department of the Navy is in, is essential…"

The Pentagon's password is **lethal**.

04.05.2019 09:39

17 pages 4729 words 17.10.2018 19:45 20:07 12.12.2018 04:23 31.03.2019 19:02 04.06.2019 09:41

NEW CHINA B(2)
ASAT & SPACE WAR (UPDATED COPY)

Commanding the new high ground:
The Dragon ascending deep space

In **Countdown to space war** the 1984 publication of Stockholm International Peace Research Institute (Sipri), the authors Bhupendra Jasani and Christopher Lee have written (p. vii):

"... Earth orbiting satellites are invaluable in the enhanced performance of armed forces and weapons. From 1958 to 1983 2114 military orientated satellites were launched.

"Seventy five per cent of all satellites have some direct military use. Their missions range from navigation, communications, meteorology and geodesy to surveillance.

"Once the superpowers (the United States and the Soviet Union) recognized the military value of satellites they immediately went about developing *anti*-satellite (ASAT) weapons..."

That crucial move paved the way for the militarisation of space.

"Space is the new high ground," Jasani and Lee have declared (p. 5). (1)

Though the US was the first country to develop anti-satellite (ASAT) weapons in the late 1950s, it currently has no known weapons dedicated to that mission. The last American test of an ASAT weapon was conducted by the US Navy on 14 February 2008.

Russia reportedly carried out a couple of tests of its direct ascent anti-satellite (ASAT) missile, known as Nudol, on 18 November 2015 and then in May 2016.

From mid-2005 to early 2013, China conducted five tests in space of the direct ascent SC-19 ASAT weapon system: (1) 7/5/2005, (2) 2/6/2006, (3) 1/12/2007 successful intercept and destruction of orbital target, a defunct FY-1C weather satellite, (4) 1/11/2010 successful intercept and destruction of a suborbital target, CSS-X-11 ballistic missile, and (5) 1/27/2013 successful intercept and destruction of an unknown suborbital ballistic target. (2)

While the Chinese Academy of Sciences claimed that the May 2013 test was a high-altitude scientific research mission, it was to wake up the US military which saw it as a test of a new ballistic missile in deep space (up to 30,000 km/18,600 miles) related to China's anti-satellite (ASAT) program.

In **The Washington Post Online** (May 9, 2016), Christian Davenport wrote "only after the 2013 launch by the Chinese that the Pentagon acted with a sense of urgency" and made space a priority.

Air Force General John Hyten, commander of the Air Force Space Command, said, "Every military operation that takes place in the world today is critically dependent on space in one way or another..."

Brian Weeden, Technical Advisor of NGO Secure World Foundation, has commented: "While there is no conclusive proof, the available evidence strongly suggests that China's May 2013 launch was the test of the rocket component of a new direct ascent ASAT weapons system derived from a road-mobile missile.

"The system appears to be designed to place a kinetic kill vehicle (KKV) on a trajectory to deep space that could reach medium earth orbit (MEO), highly elliptical orbit (HEO), and geostationary Earth orbit (GEO).

"If true, this would represent a significant development in China's ASAT capabilities. But it would not be the first instance of an ASAT weapons system designed to attack satellites in deep space, as the Russians developed at least the components of such a system in the 1990s…" (3)

According to Weeden, satellites in GEO are the most vulnerable to a hit-to-kill (HTK) direct ascent ASAT weapon system

US satellites in GEO include reconnaissance, early warning, meteorological and communications satellites, also satellites for nuclear explosion detection (beyond the range of solid-fuel ICBMs), and the US military's Advanced Extremely High Frequency (AEHF) communications satellites over the Equator.

Weeden wrote that no other country had tested a direct ascent ASAT weapon with the potential to reach deep space satellites in MEO, HEO, and GEO.

"China is working on, and plans to field, ASAT systems. Beijing has and will continue to enhance its satellite tracking and identification network – the first step in establishing a credible ASAT capability," the US Secretary of Defense reported to Congress in 2005. (4)

"China can currently destroy or disable satellites only by launching a ballistic missile or space-launch vehicle armed with a nuclear weapon…

"China is also conducting research to develop ground-based laser ASAT weapons. Based on the level of Chinese interest in this field, the Defense Intelligence Agency believes Beijing eventually could develop a laser weapon capable of damaging or destroying satellites.

"At lower power thresholds, Chinese researchers may believe that low-energy lasers can "blind" sensors on low-Earth-orbiting (LEO) satellites; whether Beijing has tested such a capability is unclear…"

In 2007, the Defense Secretary reported to Congress (5):

"… In January 2007, China successfully tested a direct ascent ASAT missile attack against a Chinese weather satellite, demonstrating its ability to attack satellites operating in low-Earth-orbit (LEO).

"The direct ascent ASAT system is one component of a multi-dimensional program to generate the capability to deny others access to outer space…

"China's nuclear arsenal has long provided Beijing with an inherent ASAT capability.

"However, in recent years Beijing has pursued a robust, multidimensional counterspace program.

"UHF-band satellite communications jammers acquired from Ukraine in the late 1990s and probable indigenous systems give China today the capacity to jam common satellite communications bands and GPS receivers.

"In addition to the direct ascent ASAT program demonstrated in January 2007, China is also developing other technologies and concepts for kinetic (hit-to-kill) weapons and directed energy (e.g. lasers and radio frequency) weapons for ASAT missions.

"Citing the requirements of its manned and lunar space programs, China is improving its ability to track and identify satellites – a prerequisite for effective, precise physical attacks..."

As published in **BBC News (bbc.com)** 11 January 2011, Alexander Neil, head of Asia Security Programme at the Royal United Services Institute:

"... The PLA is rapidly developing asymmetric warfare techniques against US command, control, communications, computers, intelligence, surveillance and reconnaissance infrastructure, known as "C4ISR" in military parlance.

"For China, with its inferior conventional military capabilities, the key to gaining the upper hand in a conflict with the US is **to gain dominance of the space theatre** and to damage its digital nerve system.

"China views space as a corner-stone of its future prosperity: a mandate from heaven for China's growth and military strength. For this reason, China is working hard to counter the Pentagon's monopoly in space and to build its own **space-based deterrent**.

"The PLA's doctrine of "pressure point warfare" (**"dim mak" attack strategy**), a multi-layered approach using space, cyberspace and information operations alongside conventional capabilities is designed to cripple an adversary in one swift stroke.

"This fast-paced and high-tech military modernisation has led to the emergence of weapons systems and technology which on certain theatres has closed the military capability gap with the US considerably.

"These include directed energy, jamming and cyber attack technologies, designed to paralyse the US military machine.

"The PLA has recently developed and successfully tested advanced anti-satellite (ASAT) weapon systems, demonstrating it can destroy or manoeuvre close to enemy satellites in space.

"ASAT weapons are part of a new genre of "assassin's mace" or surprise weapons aimed at the Pentagon's Achilles Heel in space and cyberspace.

"All of these capabilities require state of the art signals processing and communications systems, technology which China has been developing indigenously to create its own command and control architecture..."

Jiang Lianju and Wang Liweh have written in their 2013 Study of Space Operations: "... Whoever is the strongman of military space will be the ruler of the battlefield; whoever has the advantage of space has the power of the initiative; having 'space' support enables victory, lacking 'space' (support) ensures defeat..." 17.10.2018 20:28

In November 2014, the US-China Economic and Security Review Commission reported to Congress: "... Based on the number and diversity of China's existing and developmental counterspace capabilities, China probably will be able to hold at risk U.S. national security satellites in every orbital regime in the next five to ten years (2020-2025)..." (6)

On 28 October 2015, the Congressional Commission (ESRC) reported: "... China is pursuing a broad and robust array of counterspace capabilities, which includes direct-ascent anti-satellite (ASAT) missiles, co-orbital anti-satellite (ASAT)systems, computer network operations (CNO), ground-based jammers and directed energy systems..."

US Air Force Maj. Gen. Nina Armagni said in mid-October 2016, "Russia and China, by the year 2025, will be able to hold at risk every one of our satellites in any orbit..." (7)

In an interview with **Spuknit China** late October 2016, military expert Vasily Kashin says future satellites should be built with advanced electronic warfare systems as existing satellites are defenceless against interceptor missiles.

According to US Air Force General John Hyten, Commander, US Strategic Command (USSTRATCOM), Russia and China are developing their anti-satellite (ASAT) capabilities which will soon pose a threat to the US in space.

"In the not-too-distant future, they will be able to use that (ASAT) capability to threaten every spacecraft we have in space," Hyten said. The Stratcom chief repeated his message when he spoke about a fortnight later at Stanford University in California.

"We have to prevent that (threat in space), and the best way to prevent war is to be prepared for war. So the United States is going to do that, and we're going to make sure that everybody knows we're prepared for war..."

Speaking on Stratcom's perspectives on 21st century deterrence in space at the Center for Security and Cooperation, Stanford University, 13 February 2017, Hyten said space capabilities have created a revolution in military affairs.

As reported by Cheryl Pellerin, **DoD News (usapatriotism. org)**, Hyten said major military operations critically depend on space capabilities.

The most important element of space is the geosynchronous (GEO) orbit 22,300 miles above Earth (as mathematically determined in 1947 by Arthur C. Clark, internationally celebrated British science fiction writer, futurist and inventor).

Preventing potential aggression in space requires deterrence, Hyten said.

China tested its low earth orbit (LEO) capability in 2007.

"In the not-too-distant future, they (the Chinese military) will be able to use that capability to threaten every spacecraft we have in space," the Stratcom commander warned again.

According to him, China and Russia are building weapons to deploy in low earth orbit and GEO.

To make sure war never happens in space, the general said, the US has been working since after the 1990-91 Gulf War to bolster and build new space capabilities. (8)   25.02.2017 15:51

According to the August 2018 Report by the Department of Defense to Congress, the PLA is acquiring a range of technologies to improve China's counterspace capabilities. In addition to the development of directed-energy (DE) weapons and satellite jammers, China is also developing direct-ascent (DA) and co-orbital kinetic kill capabilities, and has probably made progress on the anti-satellite missile (ASM) system which it tested in July 2014.

According to DoD, China is employing more sophisticated satellite operations and is probably testing dual-use technologies in space that could be applied to counterspace missions.   17.10.2018 20:48

China is reportedly on track to develop "a global, 24-hour, all-weather earth remote sensing system" by 2020, including satellites with EO (electrro-optical), SAR (synthetic aperture radar) and ELINT (electronic intelligence) payloads.

BeiDou will also go global in 2020.

"Russia and China continue to launch 'experimental' satellites that conduct sophisticated on-orbit activities, at least some of which are intended to advance counterspace capabilities," the Office of the Director of Intelligence reported on February 2018.

Speaking at the Defense One Technology Summit in Washington, DC, 24 July 2018, Lt. Gen. Robert Asley, head of Defense Intelligence Agency (DIA) said Russia and China are developing new space-based weapons for use "in the near future..."   17.10.2018 21:29 12.12.2018 05:00

Notes NEW CHINA B(2) Commanding the new high ground

1. The authors have listed the various earth-orbiting satellites (EOS) used by the military to enhance the performance of Earth-based armed forces and their weapons (pp. 83-86):

    (1) <u>Photographic reconnaissance satellites</u> to detect, identify and pin-point military targets.

(2) <u>Electronic reconnaissance satellites</u> (the 'ears' in space) to detect and monitor radio signals generated by the opponent's military activities. According to a **Pravda** report 20.07.2016, Russia is developing an advanced system of sonar detection, interconnecting space satellites sensors and ground facilities to detect underwater objects, particularly alien submarines.

(3) <u>Ocean-surveillance and oceanographic satellites</u> to detect and track naval ships, including submarines lurking beneath the surface.

(4) <u>Early warning satellites (EWS)</u> to give warning of a surprise attack by ballistic missiles.

(5) <u>Communications satellites</u> to meet military demand for rapid and efficient communications, generation and transmission of data and information for military uses.

(6) <u>Navigation satellites</u> for the armed forces to plot their own positions with a high degree of accuracy.

(7) <u>Nuclear explosion detection satellites</u> to detect nuclear explosions in the atmosphere and in outer space as well as to provide data and information for waging a nuclear war.

(8) <u>Meteorological and geodetic satellites</u> to provide needed information for the military to launch their missiles with well-informed and guided accuracy.

2. **The Space Review thespacereview.com** Report by Brian Weeden March 17, 2014.

A former US Air Force space analyst, B. Weeden is Technical Advisor for Secure World Foundation, a non-profit organisation dedicated to long-term sustainable use of space for benefits on Earth.

3. Ibid.

4. **ANNUAL REPORT TO CONGRESS**
The Military Power of the People's Republic of China 2005 p. 36

5. **ANNUAL REPORT TO CONGRESS**
    The Military Power of the People's Republic of China 2007 p.21

According to the Pentagon, the Soviets had since the late 1960s explored the use of particle beam and kinetic energy weapons for anti-satellite (ASAT) and ballistic missile defense missions.

"The USSR has also conducted research in the use of radio-frequency weapons to interfere with or destroy the electronic components of ballistic missile warheads or satellites. A ground-based version of such a weapon could be tested in the 1990s," Secretary of Defense Frank C. Carlucci reported in April 1988 **SOVIET MILITARY POWER:** AN ASSESSMENT OF THE THREAT **1988** p. 59.

"Free-electron lasers, which generate intense microwave and millimetre-wave pulses, have been developed by the Soviets, possibly for use in radio-frequency weapons..."

6. **uscc.gov** PDF Commission's Report to Congress p. 28
7. Cheyenne MacDonald **DAILYMAIL.COM** 27 October 2016

On 12 January 2007 China tested its Dong Neng (DN)-1 ASAT missile against an old orbiting weather satellite.

According to a report by Kyle Mizokami in **NATIONAL INTEREST**, a SC-19 missile (based on the DF-21, China's first two-stage solid-propellant single-warhead medium-range ballistic missile (MRBM) deployed in 1991) was used with a KT-2 kinetic kill vehicle (KKV). According to Mizokami, the SC-19 is operational.

The direct ascent KKV destroyed an old FY-1 meteorological satellite in low Earth orbit, resulting in an outburst of some 3,400 pieces of debris.

"Due to high-impact speed in space, even sub-millimeter debris poses a realistic threat to human spacecraft and robotic missions," Frank Rose, US assistant secretary for arms control, said in Beijing on 30 Nov 2015.

In June 2016, China launched an Aolong-1 space debris satellite with a robotic arm to test its space debris removal capability.

On 27 September 2008 two astronauts onboard the Shenzhou spacecraft deployed a BX in the Low Earth Orbit (LEO) to demonstrate China's ability to develop and deploy a micro-satellite with ASAT capabilities.

On 13 May 2013 China tested its DN-2 ASAT interceptor at a high –sub orbit attitude of over 18,600 miles.

"No other country has tested a direct ascent ASAT weapon system that has the potential to reach deep space satellites in medium earth orbit (MEO), highly elliptical orbit (HEO) or geostationary orbit (GEO)," commented Brian Weedon, a former US Air Force space analyst, now a technical adviser for Secure World Foundation (SWF), a Colorado-based NGO focused on secure and peaceful uses of outer space.

According to Gen. William Shelton, Commander of the US Air Force Space Command (as reported in **RT it.com** 9 January 2014), American satellites are defenceless against a possible attack in space and their destruction would "create a huge hole" in America's capabilities for high-tech warfare.

According to a draft of the late 2015 report of the U.S.-China Economic and Security Review Commission, China may deploy the DN-2 as early as 2020.

According to the ESRC report, the Chinese military also plan to attack the US through kinetic, electronic and cyber means to disable satellites and ground support structures in a conflict. The PLA believes that these weapons are more effective in deterring adversaries than nuclear arms.

"The PLA assesses US satellites are critical to the United States' ability to sustain combat operations globally," the draft report says. "PLA analysis of US military operations states that 'destroying or capturing satellites and other sensors will deprive an opponent of <u>initiative</u> on the battlefield and (make it difficult) for them to bring their precision-guided weapons into full play'..." (as reported in **MISSILE THREAT/Spike Daily** 2015/10/28).

On 9 November 2015 the DN-3 direct ascent missile satellite-killer was tested, as first reported by Bill Gertz in **Free Beacon Washington** and subsequently confirmed in a Chinese article in the official publication **Science and Technology Daily** on 7 December 2015.

According to Gertz, China conducted another flight test of the DN-3 early December 2016. **freebeacon.com** December 21, 2016

Gertz has also reported that Russia successfully tested its PL-19 Nudol (A-235) ASAT missile in the fifth test of this counterspace weapon, and its third successful flight.

"Russia views U.S. dependency on space as an exploitable vulnerability, and they are taking deliberate actions to strengthen their counterspace capabilities," Air Force Lt. Gen. David J. Buck, Joint Functional Component Command for Space, said in House testimony on March 2016.

According to US defense and intelligence officials, as few as two dozen strikes could cripple the critical satellites used for communications, navigation, targeting and other strategic military functions.

Small manoeuvring satellites have also been tested, capable of grabbing and crushing orbiting satellites.

According to Fraser Cain, publisher of **Universe Today (universetoday.com)** 23 December 2015, there are 1071 operational satellites orbiting Earth, half of them launched by the US: Slightly over 500 of them (50%) are in Low-Earth Orbit (LEO), from about 200 km to 20,000 km above Earth; about 50 Medium-Earth Orbit (MEO) satellites, above 20,000 km up, generally global positioning satellites (GPS) used for navigation, and a handful in elliptical orbits; and about 500 in geostationary orbit (GEO) about 36,000 km above Earth.

According to the Union of Concerned Scientists (UCS), there are over 1,300 orbiting satellites, of which 549 American, 142 Chinese, 113 Russian, etc. **wikipedia.org** last modified on 4 March 2017

On 15 August 2016, China launched the world's first "hack-proof" quantum communications satellite.

According to Pan Jianwei, chief scientist of the US$100million project, a global quantum communication network could be set up around 2030.

Xinhua August 16, 2016

On November 2016 China launched a XPNAV-1 satellite to test pulsar navigation technologies in deep space. Satellites using pulsar navigation can operate independently in space to further improve the accuracy of satellite navigation signals, and thus to enhance the precision of guided munitions and military navigation.   17.10.2018 21:33

On February 2017, scientists from the **Chinese Optics** journal were reported as saying that China had successfully tested a 50-100 kilowatt ground laser weapon system (LaWS) capable of destroying in-orbit satellites. **sputniknews.com** 19.03.2017

From the time of President Reagan's SDI development in the mid-1980s, space has fired the imagination of the world's militaries, and space has recently emerged in the consciousness of the world's military to become the new high ground of military operations, despite all the self-serving denials of the militarization of space.

Command and control of space equates space superiority, which is highly valued as vital to waging and winning modern war.

With launching on 7 Oct 2015 of the Jilin-1 mission with four satellites for remote sensing, the PLA plans to put 138 Jilin satellites in orbit by 2030.

In the testimony by Kevin Pollpeter, Research Scientist, CNA, on 23 February 2017 for the U.S.-China Economic and Security Review Commission (**uscc.gov**), China plans to establish by 2020 a "high resolution Earth observation system" through a network of 60 Jilin satellites.

Counterspace capability forms the second component of the PLA's goal of achieving space superiority.

And, to quote Kevin Pollpeter: "Chinese analysts assess that the United States relies on space for 70-90 percent of its intelligence and 80 percent of its communication. Based on this assessment, Chinese analysts surmise that the loss of critical sensor and communication capabilities could imperil the U.S. military's ability to achieve victory or to achieve victory with minimal casualties.

"According to the U.S. defense department, China is developing a wide range of counterspace technologies intended to threaten an adversary's space capabilities from the ground to high Earth orbit (HEO)..."

At the Reagan National Defense Forum in California on 3 December 2017, US Air Force Gen. John Hyten said: "... The Chinese and the Russians, in particular, for the last twenty years (since the first Gulf War in 1991) have been watching what we have been doing and developing capabilities and they have not been secret about it.

"They have been... testing weapons, building weapons to operate from the earth in space -- jamming weapons, laser weapons, and they have not kept it secret..."

According to Hyten, Moscow and Beijing are building those capabilities to challenge the US and its allies as well as to "change the balance of power in the world..."

On 10 January 2018 the US Defense Advanced Research Projects Agency (DARPA) issued a press statement in Washington to re-affirm the US military's stance in space operations.

"To help ensure future US technological and strategic superiority, DARPA's Hallmark program seeks to develop revolutionary tools and technologies to plan, assess, and execute US military operations in space," the release stated. DARPA has awarded Phase I contracts to 11 organizations (not specified), which "both augment existing commercial technologies and pursue entirely new capabilities."

8. "... China and Russia, our strategic competitors, are explicitly pursuing space warfighting capabilities to neutralize US space capabilities during a time of conflict," the Pentagon asserted in its new space report released in Washington on 9 August. **sputniknews.com** 19.27 o9.08.2018

The Trump administration will establish the US Space Force by 2020 as the sixth branch of the US Armed Forces. Trump said at the meeting of the National Space Council on 18 June 2018 that "we must have American dominance in space, so important…"   22.08.2018 19:

12 pages 3,139 words 02.11.2016 08:03 26.03.2017 20:26 14.06.2017 17:22 18.07.2017 07:02

APPENDIX (A): Militarization of Space

According to a background report in **Sputnik News (spukniknews. com** 19:02 14.05.2017), the Soviet Union began working on space-based systems for military use in the 1960s, starting conceptually with ASAT (anti-satellite). In its debut, the Polet-1 was first tested in 1963, followed five years later by the first successful interception of a dummy satellite on 1 November 1968.

Between 1973 and 1976, under the secretive Almaz program, the SU launched three manned dual-use civilian and military reconnaissance stations into orbit. Dozens of tests were also conducted in improving ASAT systems.

In massive strategic drills carried out June-September 1982 (later dubbed by NATO as the "seven-hour nuclear war"), the SU and allies conducted exercises that included launching ground- and air-based ballistic missiles, testing anti-missile missiles (AMMs), and exercises involving military satellites.

According to Alexander Khrolenko, Russian military observer and journalist, the Energia Space Corporation was also engaged in creating space-based strike weapons. In the late 1970s, Energia created two prospective combat spacecraft: (1) the 17F111 Kaskad with space-based missile weapons to target enemy systems in low-earth orbit (LEO) up to 300 km, and (2) the 17F19 Skif armed with lasers against enemy satellites in medium earth orbit (MEO) and geostationary orbit (GEO).

The Kaskad project included an interceptor missile designed to intercept re-entry vehicle warheads of enemy ICBMs during the passive stage of their flight in outer space.

To destroy key military installations on the ground, Soviet engineers developed the concept of a heavy space station known as the 17K DOS, and autonomous vehicles of the Buran spaceship type, with up to 15-20 nuclear warheads per module. In the event of war, the modules would separate from their carriers, position themselves and begin their descent to hit their targets with a high degree of precision.

According to Khrolenko, the US lagged behind the USSR in developing space-based military.

President Ronald Reagan ordered development of an American ASAT system in 1982 and announced his Strategic Defense Initiative (SDI) in March 1983 to R&D a missile defence system to make nuclear weapons "impotent and obsolete".

When President Mikhail Gorbachev visited the Baikonur Cosmodrom in Kazakhstan on 11-13 May 1987, according to this **Spuknik News** report, he ordered closure of the Soviet military space program to demilitarize space, stopping all work on Energia heavy rocket and Buran spacecraft.

By his own account, however, Gorbachev wrote in his **MEMOIRS** (Bantam edition published 1997, p. 295): "... I went down to Baikonur in Kazakhstan for a few days to inspect work on developing and launching the Buran space shuttle by a powerful rocket system. Once again I could see the enormous potential of our science and technology and the prospects that lay before us if they were supported with a strong economy..."

(Earlier at their two-day summit meeting on 11-12 October 1986 at Reykjavik in Iceland, Gorbachev and Reagan had come very close to a historic agreement on a 10-year programme (1986-96) programme for total nuclear disarmament, which the then airy fairy SDI had spiked and spoiled at the last minute.)

Following the dissolution of the Soviet Union at the end of 1991, the SDI was formally disbanded in 1993, however, without abandoning the arms race in space.

On 7 May 2017 the US brought back its X-37B Orbital Test Vehicle-4 after it had been in space on a secret mission for nearly two years. Russian experts call the X-37B a military space-based interceptor, a descendent of the Reagan era orbital strike weapons system.

"'Star Wars' (SDI) remains a reality in the 21st century," Khrolenko has observed. "Russia will have to catch up in the field of military space, create a new heavy-class rocket and a dependable hardware base."

According to Khrolenko, out of about 1,380 satellites presently in orbit, 149 are US military and dual-use devices. Russia has 75 military satellites, China 35, Israel 9, France 8, UK 7, and Germany 7.

"All major powers are currently at work developing military technology for use in space," Khrolenko wrote in **RIA Novosti** to commemorate the 30th anniversary of Gorbachev's decision on May 1987 to close down (destroy) the Soviet military space program.

"Near-Earth (NE) space is becoming more and more militarized..."

The Office of the Director of Intelligence reported on February 2018:

"Russia and China continue to launch 'experimental' satellites that conduct sophisticated on-orbit activities, at least some of which are intended to advance counterspace capabilities.

"Some technologies with peaceful applications -- such as satellite inspection, refueling, and repair -- can also be used against adversary spacecraft..."

Russia and China are developing new space-based weapons to interdict satellites from the ground and in space, which will become operational "in the near future" according to Lt.Gen. Robert Ashley, head of the Defense Intelligence Agency (DIA), speaking on 27 June 2018 at the Defense One Technology Summit in Washington.

-- Report by Patrick Tucker, Technology Editor, June 27, 2018

Defense One defenseone.com   08.09.2018 23:09

Directed-energy (DE) Weapons in Space

"China's military is developing powerful lasers, electromagnetic railguns and high-power microwave weapons for use in a future "light war" involving space-based attacks on satellites.

"Beijing's push to produce so-called directed-energy (DE) weapons aims to neutralize America's key strategic advantage: the web of intelligence, communication and navigation satellites enabling military strikes of unparalleled precision expeditionary warfare far from US shores," Bill Gertz wrote on March 10, 2017 in **THE NATIONAL INTEREST**.

"Developing dedicated space combat systems is in line with China's long-term goal of achieving global strategic ascendency...

"China has been working on developing laser weapons since the 1960s, and the People's Liberation Army (PLA) in 2015 published the book **Light War** that gives a central role to fighting a future war using lasers.

"The book argues that future warfare will be dominated by combining Big Data analytics, a specialty of Chinese military cyber warriors with artificial intelligence (AI) and directed energy (DE) weapons.

"According to **Light War**, deploying robot laser weapons is needed since directed energy (DE) will dominate the battlefields in 30 years..."

According to Bill Gertz, the Pentagon in the past developed an airborne laser for use in missile defences and railguns are expected to be deployed in the early 2020s. High-powered compact laser guns are slated for the 2030s.

24.07.2017 09:03

Postscript: Electromagnetic Pulse (EMP) Attack

In an article published in **38 North** 02 June 2017, William R. Graham has written on the possibility of a North Korean EMP (Electromagnetic Pulse) attack on the US, even with a primitive and low-yield nuclear weapon (10 KT), to inflict massive damage on the electric grid and cause an extensive and protracted blackout with disastrous consequences.

Graham has pointed out that such an EMP attack could be made by a North Korean satellite with a small and lightweight nuclear weapon, citing North Korea's Kwangmyongsang-3 (KMS-3) and KMS-4 presently orbiting the Earth, on their south polar trajectory evading US Ballistic Missile Early Warning Radars and National Missile Defenses.

On its 6th nuclear test conducted at high noon of Sunday 3 September 2017, North Korea said it detonated "a multi-functional thermonuclear nuke with great destructive power which can be detonated even at high altitudes for super-powerful EMP attack according to strategic goals..."

FOX NEWS September 3, 2017

4,239 words 15 pages 14.06.20:12 18.07.2017 07:03 24.07.2017 09:05 05.09.2017 11:11 27.12.2017 21:21

APPENDIX (B) AN UDATE

From the 148-page report released on 11 April 2018 **Global Counterspace Capabilities: An Open Source Assessment**, edited by Dr Brian Weeden, Director of Program Planning, Secure World Foundation, and Ms. Victoria Samson, Washington Office Director, Secure World Foundation (SWF), a private operation foundation headquartered in Broomfield, Colorado, and dedicated to the secure and sustainable use of space for the benefit of Earth and all its peoples.

: **China** has at least one, and possibly as many as three, programs under way to develop direct ascent anti-satellite (DA-ASAT) capabilities, either as dedicated counterspace systems or as midcourse missile defense systems that could provide counterforce capabilities. China has engaged in multiple, progressive tests of these capabilities since 2005, indicating a serious organizational effort. (p, 10)

Chinese DA-ASAT capability against LEO (Low Earth Orbit) targets is likely mature and may be operationally fielded on mobile launchers within the next few years.

Chinese DA-ASAT capability against deep space targets -- both medium Earth Orbit (MEO) and GEO (Geostationary Earth Orbit) -- is likely still in the (p. 11) experimental or development phase, and there is not sufficient evidence to conclude whether it will become an operational capability in the near future.

: **The United States** has conducted multiple tests of technologies for close approach and rendezvous in both LEO and GEO, along with tracking, targeting, and intercept technologies that could lead to a co-orbital ASAT capability (in a short period of time if it chooses to)… (p.12)

The United States has developed dedicated DA-ASATs in the past, both conventional and nuclear-tipped, and likely possesses the ability to do so in the near future should it choose to. 22.08.2018 20:15

In its new space report released on 9 August 2018, the Pentagon stated:

"… China and Russia, our strategic competitors, are explicitly pursuing space warfighting capabilities to neutralize US space capabilities during a time of conflict…"

In "Challenges to Security in Space" published on 11 February 2019, the Defense Intelligence Agency (DIA) has reported: "China likely will field a ground-based laser weapon that can counter low-orbit (LO) space-based sensors by 2020, and by the mid-to-late 2020s, it may field higher power systems that extend the threat to the structures of non-optical satellites…"

In addition to directed-energy lasers, the DIA warns that China has an operational missile capable of hitting satellites in low-earth orbit (LEO) while Russia is in the process of developing one of its own. China has also formed military units that have begun training with anti-satellite missiles;

Report by Ryan Browne, **CNN** Feb 12, 2019   01.04.2019 18:00 18:05

20 pages 5,601 words 22.08.2018 22:25 08.09.2018 23:16 17.10.2018 21L52 21:57 12.12.2018 05:23

NEW CHINA B(3)
AIRCRAFT CARRIERS

Aircraft carriers for China's naval strength and security

According to an article in **Wikipedia** (1), there are 37 active aircraft carriers in the world. They belong to a dozen national navies.

The US has the most, with 10 Nimitz-class nuclear powered supercarriers (CVNs), each capable of carrying up to 90 aircraft, and they're by far the most powerful lot in the oceans.

At the time of the **Wikipedia** entry, last modified on 3 November 2016, China had only one. In 2018 China's second flattop, designed and developed domestically, is undergoing sea trials and will be commissioned in 2019 or 2020, and its third carrier is under construction.

China's first aircraft carrier <u>Liaoning</u> (001/CV-16) was commissioned on 25 September 2012. That's nine decades after America's first carrier, <u>USS Langley</u> (CV-1), commissioned on 20 March 1922 (shortly after the founding of the Communist Party of China July 1921).

China has for long wanted to build an aircraft carrier, according to Richard D. Fisher, Jr., veteran China military expert. (2) Premier Zhou En Lai was reported to have said in 1973 (towards the tail end of the Cultural Revolution): "I am not satisfied with the fact that China does not have an aircraft carrier..."

But, why?

"All of the great nations in the world own aircraft carriers – they are symbols of a great power," said Qi Jianquo, assistant chief of the PLA's general staff. (3)

"An aircraft carrier is a symbol of the power of your navy," said retired General Xu Guangyu, who had served in the PLA's HQ. (4)

"It's also a symbol of **deterrence**..."

TIME magazine was probably the first media in the West to report on the construction of China's second aircraft carrier, with a good copy by Mark Thompson on January 20, 2014.

According to a report in mid-February 2017 in the **South China Morning Post**, citing Chinese online news reports, China started construction of its first indigenous aircraft carrier at the port city of Dalian for possible completion by 2018. The PLA Navy wants a flotilla of four carriers by 2020. (5)

To quote Mark Thompson:

"The push to build carriers – the bluest of ships in a so-called blue-water fleet, designed to operate in mid-ocean – comes as China is expanding its territorial reach off its coast and developing the weapons needed to make such claims stick...

"The Chinese strategy is twin-pronged. First, a fleet of aircraft carriers is a mark of a major military power and gives its owner the ability to attack targets far from the homeland. But building such ships is complicated and operating them is even more so. It helps to think of carriers as being like nuclear weapons – as daunting as they are to build, deploying them and using them in a militarily significant way is even more challenging..."

On the second prong of China's strategy, which Thompson has described as vital, and what other analysts have seen as possibly game-changing:

"Instead of only challenging U.S. carriers on the high seas with similar warships, it's developing land-based **DF-21D missiles** with maneuverable warheads, designed **to reach out and kill U.S. carriers from at least 930 miles away**...

"While its accuracy is questionable (then), "large salvo attacks" could make up for that...

"Pentagon officials, speaking privately, are more concerned with the new missiles than the new warships..."

The 2015 White Paper on **China's Military Strategy** has stated:

"... Building a strong national defense and powerful armed forces is a strategic task of China's modernization drive and a security guarantee for China's peaceful development..."

On the role of the PLA Navy: "In line with the strategic requirement of offshore waters defense and open seas protection, the PLA Navy (PLAN) will gradually shift its focus from "offshore waters defense" to the combination of "offshore waters defense" with "open seas protection", and build a combined, multi-functional and efficient marine combat force structure.

"The PLAN will enhance its capabilities for strategic deterrence and counterattack, maritime manoeuvres, joint operations at sea, comprehensive defense and comprehensive support..."

In 2015 Pentagon reported to Congress: "... Whereas "near seas" defense remains the PLA Navy's primary focus, China's gradual shift to the "far seas" has necessitated that its Navy support operational tasks outside the first island chain (comprising Japan, South Korea, the Philippines, Indonesia) with multi-mission, long-range, sustainable naval platforms with robust self-defense capabilitites..."

Rick Fisher, a senior analyst at the International Assessment and Strategy Center, a think-tank in Virginia, USA, who has spent over 20 years studying China's military strategy, has commented on the rapidly rising nation's big ambitions:

"By the 2020s, China wants a military that will be globally deployable and will be able to challenge American interests where they need to be challenged..." (6)

According to the US Naval Institute on 22 September 2016, China is developing its Catapult- Assisted Take-Off But Arrested Recovery (CATOBAR) technology for aircraft carriers.

Using the enhanced CATOBAR system, China's future carriers will support the operation of a well-rounded carrier air wing with heavier and more efficient aircraft. (7)

According to the 2018 Report by the US Department of Defense released on 16 August 2018, China is expected to begin constructing its first catapult-capable carrier in 2018, which will enable additional fighter aircraft, fixed-wing early-warning aircraft, and more rapid flight operations' Launched in 2017, China's first domestic aircraft carrier will likely join the fleet by 2019.

According to Brian Wong's report on March 16, 2018 **nextbigfuture. com**, China Shipbuilding Industry Corporation (CSIC) will build China's first nuclear-powered aircraft carrier Type 095 SSN at its Bohai Shipyard, China's sole nuclear submarine shipyard. It will have a displacement of 90,000-100,000 tons and electromagnetically assisted launch system (EMALS) catapults. For launching in the late 2020s.   18.10.2018 20:43

According to Pentagon, Beijing expects to operate by 2030 four to six aircraft carrier groups in the East China Sea and the South China Sea. (8)

Three days after the 68th anniversary of the founding of the PLA Navy (PLAN), China launched its first domestically built aircraft carrier on 26 April 2017. Construction of the Type 001A began in November 2013 at the Dalian shipyard of the China Shipbuilding Industry Corp in Dalian, northeast China's Liaoning Province. China's second aircraft carrier is expected to be commissioned before 2020, after equipment debugging, outfitting and comprehensive mooring trials.

A third carrier the Type 002 is under construction in Shanghai.

According to Xu Guangyu, a former PLA rear admiral, and senior adviser to the China Arms Control and Disarmament Association, the PLAN will have 6 carriers.

Senior correspondent and chief commentator of the German newspaper **Die Welt**, Torsten Kranel posted on 27.04.2017:

"... Beijing sends the message: We want to become (a) world power...

"The desire to equalize with America plays a part in the project (to build a core of carrier combat groups like the US Navy). But it is by no means the only motive. Beijing's leadership has not forgotten why Europeans and Japan were able to share ("slice" like a melon) China among themselves 150 years ago...

"Donald Trump's threat to start a war in East Asia when China does not do what it (the US) wants in North Korea certainly strengthens the Chinese Politburo.

"If everything goes according to Beijing's plan, there are two countries that can demonstrate their power before every coast on earth. Having military means in hand strengthens nationalist instincts..."

China has a long coastline of about 16,000 km and territorial waters covering a total area of some 3 million sq km (about one-third of China's land mass).

Back in December 1986 Yang Shangkun, a vice-chairman of the military commission, thought that China would approach the level of the world's "first-class powers" by 2050 when the PLAN would operate a blue-water navy (*yuanyang haijun*). (9)

In a white paper on The Future Navy authored by Admiral John Richardson and published on 17 May 2017, the Chief of US Naval Operations concludes: "The pace at which potential competitors (potential adversaries like China and Russia) are moving demands that we in our turn must increase the speed at which we act. Our advantage (US military superiority/supremacy) is shrinking – we must reverse this trend... Most importantly, the future fleet (of about 355 ships including 12 aircraft carriers, deployable in 5-6 carrier strike groups) must be in station ASAP (AS Soon As Possible)! We need this more powerful fleet in the 2020s, not the 2040s..." (10)

In testifying before the Senate Armed Services Committee in Washington on 23 May 2017, Marine Corps Lt. Gen. Vincent R. Stewart said that China is in the third decade of an unprecedented military modernization program involving weapons systems, doctrine, tactics and training, and space and cyber operations.

According to the director of the US Defense Intelligence Agency (USDIA), China now stands firmly as a near-peer U.S. competitor; "its navy remains on a course for 350 ships by the year 2020 and (its) anti-access anti-denial (AA/AD) capabilities continue to improve..." (11)

1,888 words 15.06.2017 21:00 16.06.2017 19:00

Notes NEW CHINA B(3) Aircraft Carriers for China

1. **wikipedia.org** last modified on 3 Nov 2016 at 00:03
    The nonpareil and colossus in the top-notch CVN category (of nuclear powered as well as nuclear armed aircraft carriers), the US Navy has for long dominated and maintained its carrier superiority, not only as a shining symbol of its predominant naval strength, but also as a highly visible platform of its global power projection.

    As explained clearly by Tom Harris in **science. howstuffworks.com**:

    "While the ship itself isn't especially useful as a weapon, the **air power** it transports can make the difference between victory and defeat...

    "The US military can move a carrier battle group (aircraft carrier escorted by 6-8 other warships) all over the world...

    "Carriers can move in excess of 35 knots (40 mph/64 kmh), which gives them the ability to get anywhere in the ocean in a few weeks.

    "The USN currently has six carrier groups, stationed around the world, ready to move into action at a moment's notice..."

    In his 1971 book **Gunboat Diplomacy**, Sir James Cable has written (p. 21) that unrivalled and unique capability has endowed the US Navy with the full spectrum of <u>gunboat diplomacy</u>, from exerting gentle influence ("by sailing a single escort ship within sight of a foreign port") to "very rapidly transition to the far extreme of the spectrum and apply large amounts of high-tech ordnance with great accuracy..." **globalsecurity.org**

2. **THE JAMESTOWN FOUNDATION** China Brief March 14, 2002
3. **BBC News** 8 June 2011
4. **BBC News** 8 June 2011
5. **swampland.time.com**
   5 (a) On July 2011, China announced its construction of two indigenous aircraft carriers at the Jianguan Shipyard in Shanghai.

China's second aircraft carrier Type 001A class, also reported to be named as the Shangdong, will be launched in 2017, begin sea trials by early 2019, and enter service in 2020. With a "ski-jump" fight deck similar to the Lioaning's short-take-off but arrested recovery (Stobar) configuration, the second carrier has a similar displacement of 50-55,000 tonnes.

Construction of China's third carrier, the Type 002, started in March 2015, and is expected to be launched by 2021, according to Hong Kong-based military expert Liang Guoliang.

85,000 tonnes, the PLAN's third carrier will have the more sophisticated catapult-assisted take-off but with arrested (Catobar) flight deck configuration similar to the more advanced system incorporated in all the 10 nuclear-powered supercarriers (CVNs) of the US Navy. **todayonline** 14 February 2017

As reported by Mike Yeo Nov 9, 2017 in **Defense News**, China has made a breakthrough in developing a medium-voltage direct current (DC) power propulsion system to operate an Electromagnetic Aircraft Launch System (EMALS) for the PLA Navy's new aircraft carrier.

According to reputed website author Brian Wong, the third carrier will use electromagnetic launch system (EMALS), powered by an indigenously developed and highly innovative, integrated propulsion system (IPS) without resort to nuclear power. **nextbigfuture.com** Nov 24, 2017

6. **BBC News** report by Damian Grammaticas 8 June 2011
7. **sputniknews.com** 24.09.2016
8. **sputnitnews.com** 08.08.2015

Four and a half years after the start of its construction on November 2013, China's new medium-class aircraft carrier left Dalian Shipbuilding Industry's shipyard in Liaoning province at about 7 am on Sunday 13 May 2018 for its maiden sea trial to demonstrate reliability and capability of its propulsion systems before delivery to the PLA Navy, **China Daily** reported 14 May 2018.

According to the report by Jeffrey Lin and P.W. Singer in **POPULAR SCIENCE** April 27, 2018, after the Type 001A and the Type 002 carriers, the Type 003 will follow in the late 2020s, which will be a nuclear-powered 90-100,000 supercarrier, the most powerful non-American aircraft carrier in the world.

"Perhaps more than any other warship, China's aircraft carriers are representative of its modernization and upcoming superpower status," Lin and Singer commented.   08.09.2018 23:59

According to Yin Zhuo, a senior researcher at the PLA Navy Equipment Center, China needs two carrier strike groups in the West Pacific and two in the Indian Ocean, to protect Chinese territories and overseas interests. "So we need at least five to six carriers," he said to Yang Seng of **Global Times**.2017/2/21

Global Times reported 28 Feb 2018 the announcement by the China Shipbuilding Industry of its priorities in weaponry and technical developments for the PLA Navy by 2025, to "speed up the process of making technological breakthroughs in nuclear-powered aircraft carriers, new-type nuclear submarines, quiet submarines, maritime unmanned intelligent confrontation systems, maritime three-dimensional (3D) offensive and defensive systems and naval warfare comprehensive electronic information systems…"

Iterating the **GT** report, **Sputnik News International (sputniknews.com** 22.08 28.02,2018**)** added that China's ambition is to have four carrier groups by 2030.   09.09.2018 00:12

9. John Wilson Lewis and Xue Litai, **China's Strategic SEAPOWER,** Stanford University Press, Stanford, California, 1994, pp. 229-230.
10. Bradley Peniston May 17, 2017 **defenseone.com**
11. Report by Cheryl Pellerin, DoD News May 23, 2017 **globalsecurity.org**

9 pages 2478 words 07.11.2016 03:59 27.02.2017 09:21 15.06.2017 20:59 21:02 16.06.1017 19:02 12.12.2017 12:48 09.09.2018 00:18 18.10.2018 20:55 12.12.2018 17:29
01.04.2019 18:23

NEW CHINA B(4)
CHINA'S STEALTH BOMBERS

China's strategic stealth bombers and fighters

By way of Stealth

"...**Stealth technology** is part of high technology; **stealth weaponry** is extremely important in modern warfare," Cao Benyi wrote in an article published by the Commission of Science, Technology and Industry, **Modern Weaponry**, no. 11 (8 November 1992).

"Several countries have by now developed various kinds of highly efficient stealth weaponry, such as stealth planes, stealth missiles, stealth naval vessels, stealth tanks, etc. Some have indeed already been transferred for use by the armed forces and successfully tried out in actual combat..." (1)

Cao cited the use of the French-made Exocet guided missile to sink the British destroyer Sheffield in the 1982 Falkland War. On the opening day of the Gulf War on 17 January 1991, American F-117A stealth fighters led the main formation in the Allied attacking air force, and dropped laser-guided bombs with unerring precision to destroy key targets in Baghdad, including the communications centre of the Iraqi military and the air force HQ.

"The great importance of stealth weaponry in modern warfare has gradually been realized by China's scientific and military experts. China has vast territories, vast territorial skies and waters, and long shorelines," Cao wrote.

"To protect its territorial rights over its land, air, and sea against any future aggression, it is necessary for China to make every effort to develop stealth technology, to develop stealth weaponry, and to do what is necessary to enable China's stealth technology to catch up with the world's most advanced level of such technology in a short time."

Cao added: "In China, research on stealth weaponry was started in the 1980s, and great progress has been achieved, particularly in aspects of theoretical research on active and exterior stealth applications for entire aircraft and for components..."

However, he urged stringency in view of the extremely high costs of stealth weaponry: "China's economy is still very backward, and its financial and material resources are extremely limited, which makes it even more necessary to reduce the costs of developing stealth weaponry and make its production more acceptable."

In 1992 when Cao composed his concise but consequential article advocating research on both stealth weaponry and anti-stealth technology, China's GDP was well below half a trillion dollars (USD); subsequently, it exceeded its first trillion dollars in 1998, and then topped US$10 trillion in 2014.

Development of the Chinese warplanes

"The first generation aircraft were jet-propelled and pursued supersonic speed; the second generation could reach bi-sonic speed and a height of over 20,000 meters.

"On this basis, information equipment on board second generation aircraft began to hold an important position. Fire-control radars were generally used in second generation aircraft," Colonel Ming Zengfu of the Air Force Command Institute, Beijing, wrote in a paper on "New Changes in Air Defense Operations", published in **Chinese Military Science** (Spring 1995). This article appeared several years after the 1991

Gulf War in which the application of high-tech air power triggered the new military revolution. (2)

"Information equipment in third-generation aircraft holds a more important position. What are generally used on board include pulse Doppler radar, forward-looking infrared devices, night vision devices, low-light TV, navigational and digital headsup display, etc.

"Equalling 50 to 60 percent of the total cost of common aircraft (or over 60% of the total cost of a stealth plane), information equipment aboard fourth-generation aircraft holds a far more outstanding position. For example, there are more than 700 computers on a B-2 (the US premier bomber and the world's leading and most expensive battle plane, costing a bomb of half a billion American dollars or more).

"For this reason fourth-generation aircraft have become intellectualized operational platforms, which have three apparent advantages: they can extensively collect information; they can deal with all kinds of information; and they can carry all kinds of ammunition. With the help of the fire-control system, they can automatically distribute targets and control a number of warheads to attack simultaneously.

"Their electronic warfare (EW) system can authoritatively judge the threatening sources and provide the pilot with conduct methods for him to select. Additionally, their operations assisting system can help drive the aircraft.

"Nowadays, modern aircraft has become an **information-dominated (informationized) weapon.** Compared with that of WWII, the efficiency of the battle aircraft of the 21st century will increase more than 100 times..."

In an essay published in **China Military Science** (Spring 1996), Major General Zheng Shenxia, President of the Air Force Command College, Beijing, and his colleague Senior Colonel Zhang Changzhi, Assistant Professor at the College, have written on seven aspects of the development of modern air weapons (many of them used for the first time in Operation Desert Storm aka 1991 Gulf War):

1. <u>Higher precision</u>. Precision-guided weapon technology helps to produce space weapons that can attack various objects

thousands of kilometres away around the clock. The deviation (CEP/margin of error) of cruise missiles is only around a dozen meters, and that of various tactical missiles is 1 meter. The percentage of hits can amount to 98 percent.

2. <u>Increased stealth</u>. The development of **stealth aircraft** reduces radar determining range from a few hundred kilometres to a bit more than a dozen kilometres. Further advances in stealth aerospace weapons will make sudden attacks realistic and disable the air-defense warning system and entire air-defense systems.

3. <u>Improved night vision</u>. The infrared observation system installed in aircraft makes it possible that a pilot can position at night, discover and destroy targets.

4. <u>Increased long-range attack ability</u>. Advanced aviation power, impetus technology, and new materials have greatly improved the mobility of aircraft. Accompanied with in-flight refuelling and space technology, an air force can realize the legend of combat at the global range. (Global reach and global strike capability.)

5. <u>Increased destructive power</u>. High-tech equipped weapons have more power to attack and destroy targets. Ordinary aircraft, when equipped with new weapon systems, are doubled and redoubled in combat ability. An operational assignment that needed 230 B-17 bombers during World War II can now be accomplished by 8 F-16 fighters. (3)

6. <u>Increased command and control capacity</u>. Infrared, laser, telemetry, and remote-sensing technologies have greatly improved the function of air and space reconnaissance systems. The side with technical advantages will take the <u>initiative</u> of the war <u>by controlling information</u>, and use the highly automatic CI to control air operations effectively. The pre-warning command aircraft can improve the combat effectiveness by a few dozen times.

7. <u>Increased electromagnetic confrontation capacity</u>. Electron confrontation technology provides air electromagnetic combat with high efficiency, complete coverage, and strong power...

The 2010 White Paper on **China's National Defense** has highlighted the modernization and informationization of the PLA Air Force (PLAAF):

"To satisfy the strategic requirements of conducting both offensive and defensive operations, the modernization and transformation of the PLA Air Force (PLAAF) follows a carefully-structured plan.

"It strengthens and improves the PLAAF development and personnel development strategies, and enhances its research into the operation and transformation of air forces in conditions of informationization.

"The PLAAF is working to ensure the development of a combat force structure that focuses air strikes, air and missile defences, and strategic projection, to improve its leadership and command system and build up an informationized, networked base system..." (4)

In a monograph prepared for the US Air Force in 2011, RAND Corporation reported: "China's air force is in the midst of a transformation. A decade ago, it was an antiquated service equipped almost exclusively with weapons based on 1950s-era Soviet designs and operated by personnel with questionable training according to outdated employment concepts.

"Today, the People's Liberation Army Air Force (PLAAF) appears to be on its way to becoming a modern, highly capable air force for the 21st century..." (5)

In its August 2018 Report to Congress, the US Department of Defense has written: "... The PLAAF is the largest air force in the region and the third largest in the world, with more than 2,700 total aircraft (not including UAVs) and 2,000 combat aircraft (including 1,490 fighters and 530 strategic and tactical bombers and attack aircraft).

"In 2017, Lieutenant General Ding Laihong assumed the post of PLAAF commander, and exhorted the service to build a truly "strategic" air force capable of projecting air power at a long range.

"The PLAAF continues to modernize and is closing the gap with the U.S. Air Force (USAF) across a broad spectrum of capabilities, gradually eroding the United States' longstanding significant technical advantage..."

The PLAAF continues to modernize with delivery of indigenous manned aircraft and a wide range of UAVs (unmanned aerial vehicles). It is working, the DoD states, to become a "strategic" air force capable of long-range power projection.   18.10.2018 21:24

Xian H (Hong)-6 Bombers

China's bomber has been developed from the Soviet-era Tu (Tupolev)-16 twin-engine jet bomber (code-named by NATO as "Badger-A"), which had first entered service in 1954. (6)

The Tu-16 was first delivered to China in 1958, and Xian Aircraft Industrial Corporation produced it manufactured it under license as Xian Hong (H)-6 in the late 1950s. (7)

The first domestically produced H-6 took to the skies in 1968. The PLAAF has reportedly developed and fielded 13 variants of the H-6. Over 120 H-6 bombers are said to remain in service presently.

"In line with the strategic requirement of building air-space capabilities and conducting offensive and defensive operations, the PLA Air Force (PLAAF) will endeavour to shift its focus from territorial air defense to both defense and offense, and build an air-space defense force structure that can meet the requirements of informationized operations," states the May 2015 White Paper on **China's Military Strategy**.

"The PLAAF will boost its capabilities for strategic early warning, air strike, air and missile defense, information countermeasures, airborne operations, **strategic projection and comprehensive support**..."

The H-6 bomber has very recently been heavily re-designed to carry air-launched cruise missiles, to give the PLAAF "a long range standoff offensive air capability with precision guided missiles" (to quote from the 2016 Report by the Secretary of Defense to Congress).

The H-6 bombers are to be further armed with the new YJ-12 Anti-ship Cruise Missiles (ASCMs) with their long striking range of 400 km and supersonic speed to increase threat to naval assets.

"Crucially at 400 kilometers, Chinese attack aircraft will be able to launch the YJ-12 beyond the engagement range of the U.S. Navy's Aegis Combat System and the SM-2 surface-to-air missiles (SAMs) that protect U.S. aircraft carrier strike groups," Robert Haddick, an independent consultant, has commented. (8)

Military Today has listed the Xian H-6K as no 7 among the top 7 bombers in the world, led by Northrop Grumman B-2 Spirit and Russia's Tu-160 Blackjack.

The latest H-6K has recently evolved into a long-range strategic bomber, armed with air-launched cruise missiles (ALCMs) capable of attacking US carrier battle groups. The Chinese bomber is also nuclear-capable. (9)

In one of the series of articles published June 2015 in the Chinese defense technology magazine **Aerospace Knowledge**, China's need for a **long-range stealth bomber** has been highlighted. The PLAAF "does need an intercontinental strategic bomber capable of penetrating an enemy's air defences..."

According to the 2016 DoD Report to Congress, China is developing long-range bombers, including some "capable of performing strategic deterrence" (a role and mission reportedly assigned to the PLAAF in 2012). China may also build a "strategic" stealth bomber "to improve survivability and strategic deterrence..."

Following the US and Russia, China is also developing the third arm of its strategic nuclear triad (together with land-based intercontinental ballistic missiles (ICBMs) and submarine-launched ballistic missiles).

"We are now developing a next-generation long-range strike bomber that you will see sometime in the future," General Ma Xiaotian, top commander of the PLAAF told reporters in Changchun, Jilin province, on 2 September 2016.

According to report dated 21 September 2016 in **wikipedia.org**, China is developing the Xian H-20 /Xian H-X subsonic stealth bomber with a wing design similar to that of the US B-2 Spirit, which may enter service by 2025.

"The new (H-X) bomber will carry air-to-ground missiles (AGMs), particularly anti-ship cruise missiles (ASCMs) to attack aircraft carriers and their escorts," Kyle Mizokami wrote several days after General Ma's disclosure.

"China will use them in conjunction with its "carrier-killer" ballistic missiles (probably referring to the DF-21D anti-ship ballistic missiles and the DF-26 ballistic missiles) and attack submarines to create a triple threat that would overwhelm a carrier battle group's defences..." (10)

On 20 February 2017, **DEFENSE WORLD.NET** reported that China's new nuclear capable Long Range Strike Bomber (LRSB) H-20, the "red B-2" (after the US B-2 Spirit stealth warcraft first deployed in 1989), will be developed by 2020.

The next-generation LRSB has an intercontinental flying range of over 10,000 km and combat radius of over 5,000 km. With air refuelling, it can fly and conduct missions around the globe.

That report was based on an earlier one in **China Military** 2017-02-17, a reproduction of an article by Zhang Liyun and Li Wei in **China Youth Daily** February 16, 2017.

Zhang and Li have written on the main features of the H-20 including good stealth performance, ultra long range, large bomb load (about 20 tons), nuclear-regular integration for both nuclear and conventional strikes, strong electronic combat capability including C4ISR. "The new-generation LRSB will considerably improve China's strategic attack capability and make the PLA Air Force a strategic air force in the true sense..."   24.07.2017 10:10

According to the 2018 DoD Report released on 16 Aug 2018, China is developing a stealthy long-range nuclear-capable bomber with an estimated range of at least 8,500 (5,300 miles) that's rated intercontinental, that could debut within a decade, around 2025.

The PLAAF is also developing a refuelable bomber, and upgrading its aircraft with two new air-launched ballistic missiles (ALBMs), one of which may have a nuclear payload.

The extended -range H-6 and future stealth bomber could be nuclear capable.

The Pentagon reported to Congress on 16 August 2018 that "the PLA Air Force has been re-assigned a nuclear mission. The deployment and integration of nuclear-capable bombers would, for the first time, provide China with a nuclear "triad" of delivery systems (intercontinental ballistic missiles (ICBMs), ballistic missile submarines (SSBNs), and strategic bombers) dispersed across land, sea and air..."   18.10.2018 21:54 12.12.2018 17:55

Testifying before House of Representatives Permanent Select Committee on Intelligence 17 May 2018, Richard D. Fisher, Jr, Senior Fellow at International Assessment and Strategy Center, said: "... By the mid-2020s the PLAAF could have its next generation long-range strategic bomber, expected to be a stealthy flying wing design that could perform long-range surveillance and control missions in addition to nuclear and conventional strike missions..."

09.09.2018 21:49

China's Fifth Generation Stealth Fighters

A fifth generation stealth twin-jet fighter, the Chengdu J-20 made its maiden flight on 11 January 2011. According to a report in **Wikipedia**, the J-20 entered service in December 2016. (11)

In the 2011 Report to Congress, the Pentagon described the J-20 as "a platform capable of long range penetrating strikes into complex air defense environments..."

When the fifth generation stealth twin-engine multipurpose medium fighter Shenyang J-31 made its first flight on 31 October 2012, China became the second nation after the US in 1991 to have two stealth fighter prototypes in field testing at the same time. The J-31 is expected to enter service in 2018-19. (12)

The J-31 made its public debut at the biennial Zhuhai Airshow in 2014.

According to a report in **China Daily** 27 December 2016, China tested for the first time the latest version of its most advanced stealth fighter jet the fifth generation J-31 on 23 December 2016. Renamed the FC-31 Gyrfalcon, it's said to be China's answer to the US F-35, the world's most technically advanced fighter.

According to aviation expert Wu Peixin, the new FC-31 has "better stealth capabilities, improved electronic equipment and a larger payload capability" than its earlier sibling the J-31 which made its public debut in October 2012.

The J-20 first appeared publicly at Zhuhai on 1 November 2016 where it did a brief flypast. The J-20 was delivered to People's Liberation Army in 2017.

"Experts say China has been refining designs for the J-20, first glimpsed by plane spotters in 2010, in the hope of narrowing a military technology gap with the US," **Reuters** reported from Zhuhai.

"A key question is whether the new Chinese fighter can match the radar-evading properties of the Lockheed Martin F-22 Raptor air-to-air combat jet, or the latest strike jet in the US arsenal, Lockheed's F-35. The F-22 Raptor, developed for the US Air Force, is the J-20's closest lookalike..."

A veteran China watcher, Bradley Perret of **Aviation Week** said: "It is clearly a big step forward in Chinese combat capability..." (13)

According to Andreas Rupprecht, aviation journalist and author of **Modern Chinese Warplanes**, "the J-20 is a giant leap for the PLAAF both capability-wise and technology-wise alike. Did anyone of us expect a Chinese stealth fighter to be operational before 2020 when asked in, let's say 2010? ... it is a huge step even if it might be well below the F-22's capabilities..." (14)

According to the August 2018 DoD Report, the PLAAF continues to field fourth-generation (4-G) aircraft (now about 600) and probably will become a majority 4-G force within the next several years.

The PLAAF is still developing 5-G fighters including the J-20 and FC-31, and in late 2016 began importing 24 Su-35 advanced 4-G fighters from Russia.

The PLA's 90th anniversary parade in July 2017 featured flybys of its J-20 5-G fighters and introduced its J-16 and J-10C advanced 4-G fighters armed with the latest weapons.

According to the statement issued by Aviation Industry Corporation of China (AICC) on 25 September 2018, China's first-ever large continuous transonic wind tunnel, the 6,620-ton, 17,000-cubic-meter **FL-62** ("a pillar of a great power", a fundamental and strategic facility crucial to China's aviation industry) will be completed "very soon", and will help in developing China's sixth generation (6-G) fighters. FL-62 will also contribute to space research;

Song Zhongping, a military expert and TV commentator, told Liu Xuanzun of **Global Times** 2018/9/26 that China's 6-G fighters will AI, UAVs and directed-energy weapons (DEWs) such as lasers and high-power microwaves.

In the US, the Air Force plans to purchase 351 T-X 6-G aircraft (and eventually up to 475), the first of which is expected to arrive at Joint Base San Antonio-Randolph, Texas, in 2023. The USAF's objective is an initial operational capability (IOC) of its sixth-generation fleet by 2024, and full operational capability (FOC) by 2034, as reported on **GlobalSecurity.org** September 27, 2018.   18.10.2018 22:32

Advanced Missiles for the Fighters

Beyond Visual Range Air-to-Air Missiles (BVRAAMs) are long-range weapons for fighter planes to knock out enemy fighters, bombers, aerial tankers, drones, and other aircraft.

In **POPULAR SCIENCE (popsci.com)** September 22, 2015, Jeffrey Lin and team-mate P.W. Singer reported on the successful maiden flight of a prototype PL-15 on 15 September 2015.

To replace the PL-12 (with a reported range of about 100 km), the PL-15 is reportedly designed with an improved radar, jam-resistant data links, and enhanced propulsion with a dual rocket motor. With a ramjet engine, the striking range of the PL-15 can be extended well beyond 200 km.

In an interview with **Flight Global** magazine, General Hawk Carlisle, Commander of USAF Air Combat Command (ACC) described outmatching the Chinese P-15 as of "exceedingly high priority" for the US.

"The PL-15 and the range of that missile (reported to be up to 400 km), we've got to out-stick that missile," Carlisle stressed (as reported in **sputniknews.com** 27.01.2017).

First delivered in 1994 with a beyond-visual-range capability, America's new generation all-weather AIM-120 is scheduled to remain operational beyond 2020 (as reported in **military.com**). The Advanced Medium-Range Air-to-Air Missile (AMRAAM), the AIM-120D has an operational range of up to 200 km. Russia's R-37 (1989) and K-100 (2010) are designed for up to 400 km.

When deployed, the PL-15 will pose a threat to the F-35 fighters, B-52 and B-2 bombers, aerial tankers and other aircraft in the Asia Pacific. (15)

In **POPULAR SCIENCE** November 23, 2016, Lin and Singer reported on the successful test earlier in November 2016 of a gigantic long-range hypersonic super-manoeuvrable missile, fired from a Chinese J-16 strike fighter.

As reported, the VLRAAM (Very Long Range Air-to-Air Missile) is fitted with a powerful rocket engine to push it to Mach 6 and extend its no escape zone (NEZ), even against supersonic targets like the F-22 fighters.

With lateral thrusters to boost its terminal phase manoeuvrability, the Chinese VLRAAM is also designed to glide in mid-flight from high altitudes and dive-bomb at hypersonic speeds onto stealth fighters and bombers and other high-value targets like aerial tankers and airborne early warning and control (AEW&C) radar aircraft.

Lin and Singer have written that the Chinese VLRAAM will provide the J-20 and other stealth fighters with long range "aerial artillery" to asymmetrically "even the odds" against numerically superior air forces", while extending the operational life of the J-11 and J-16 fighters. For the J-15 carrier fighters, a long range intercept capability. (16)

25.02.2017 13:20 18.07.2017 07:18 24.07.2017 10:19

Notes China B (4) China's stealth bombers

1. **au.af.mil**

   "For the period from 1990 to 2000, the U.S. Defense Department ranks stealth technology second among its 17 technology projects of highest importance. Among the 22 key technology projects for preferential development in 1990, three dealt with antistealth technology," Cao noted. "This makes very obvious that in future warfare stealth technology as well as antistealth technology will both be indispensable."

2. **au.af.mil**

3. On 9 March 1945, 334 B-29s took six hours to fire-bomb Tokyo, dropping 2,000 tons of incendiaries and killing 100,000 people. A solitary B-29 could do the awful mass massacre with a single atomic bomb. That's . why all existing nuclear weapons must be banned and destroyed!

4. March 2011 **scio.gov.cn/english-gov.cn**

5. **rand.org** Preface in **Shaking the heavens and Splitting the Earth Chinese Air Force Employment Concepts in the 21ˢᵗ Century**

   By Roger Cliff et al   6 pages 1,432 words 19.11.2016 15:03

6. Tu-16 has been credited with a maximum speed of 1,050 km/h (652 mph), range of 7,200 km (4,470 mi), high altitude service ceiling of 12,800 m (41,995 feet), and payload of 9,000 kg (20,000 lb/10 tons) of free-fall bombs, 6-7 cannons, and 5 Air-to-Surface Missiles (ASMs).

   wikipedia.org last modified on 28 September 2016 at 18:52.

7. The PLAAF also used the H-6 bomber to conduct a good number of China's nuclear tests, including its second atomic

bomb (20-40 KT) on 14 May 1965, its first H-bomb (3.3 MT) on 17 June 1967 (its 6th test) at the height of the Cultural Revolution, and its seventh thermonuclear (4 MT) on 17 November 1976 (its 21st test) at the Lop Nur test site.

John Wilson Lewis and Xue Litai, **China Builds the Bomb**, Stanford University Press, California, 1988, pp. 244-245.

8. **warontherocks.com**
9. **military-today.com info@defence.aviation.com**

The nuclear-capable H-6K long-range heavy bomber entered service in 2009, and according to a report in **sputniknews.com** 16.08.2015, at least two regiments of the PLAAF are believed to be operating the H-6Ks.

"The H-6K is Beijing's B-52 – a far flying, fuel efficient heavy bomber combining a single, time-tested airframe (based on the Tupolev Tu-16 twin-engine strategic bomber) with modern electronics and powerful, precision weapons," military expert David Axe has commented.

According to Axe, the H-6k can carry 12 tons of weapons, including up to 6 YJ-12 supersonic anti-ship missiles (ASMs) with a striking range of 250 miles, or CJ-20 subsonic land-attack cruise missiles (LACMs) capable of striking targets 1,500 miles away. Mid-air refuelling can significantly extend its reported combat radius of nearly 2,200 miles. 25.02.2017 13:39

According to a report by Larkins Dsouza posted in **Defence Aviation** on June 20, 2016, the Xian H-8 stealth bomber will succeed the ageing twin-engine H-6 bomber. With four engines, the H-8 can climb 40% faster and with an extended range to 8,000 km (combat radius 5,000 km). More weapons can be carried, including bombs of various sizes from 100 kg to 9 tonnes, up to max 18 tonnes. Nuclear warheads as well as anti-ship and land attack missiles, and 18,000 kg of free fall bombs. Service ceiling is 14,000 meters and max speed of 1,000 km/h.

In **The Diplomat** April 10, 2018, Anki Panda, senior editor, has written that the H-6K strategic bomber has been modified and dubbed as the H6X1/H-6N by the US intelligence community, with a combat radius of nearly 6,000 km (ICBM range), to deliver China's new/ unmanned nuclear-capable air-launched cruise missile (ALCM).

Dubbed the CH-AS-X-13 by US intelligence, the new ALCM has been tested five times, first tested in December 2016, and most recently in late January 2018 on board the new bomber.

The new two-stage, solid-fuel missile with a range of 3,000 km will be able to threaten targets in the contiguous US, Hawaii, and Alaska. According to US intelligence, it will be deployed by 2025.   09.09.2018 20:12

10. **popularmechanics.com** September 6, 2016

According to Rear Admiral Yin Zhuo (as reported in **sputniknews.com** 21.12.2016), the H-20 bomber is well on its way to becoming a fully-developed next-generation stealth aircraft, but not operational in the near future.

China has not yet developed an operational heavy-tonnage bomber for long-range strategic missions.

According to **Xinhua**, China is planning to phase out the H-6 bomber with one on par with the US B-2 Spirit – first deployed in 1989, and its designer/manufacturer Northrop Grumman is presently engaged in the next-generation project of Long Range Strike Bombers known as "B-21 Raiders", which are expected to enter service in the mid-2020s.

Moscow is also replacing its Tu-bombers with the new PAK-DA long-range stealth strike bombers, with an expected range of 6,740 nautical miles and capable of carrying 30 tons of weapons, including nuclear and conventional cruise missiles, precision-guided munitions, and eventually hypersonic missiles. First deliveries by 2023. 25.02.2017 14:00

11. **wikipedia.org** quoting a Chinese report in **news.ifeng.com** 2016-12-12

The world's first 5-G fighter aircraft, the US F-22 Raptor entered service in 2005. A 5-G fighter incorporates technologically advanced features such as stealth (anti-radar anti-thermal camouflage), supercruise (supersonic speed without afterburners), operational manoeuvrability and versatility, a compartment for weapons, advanced avionics including a highly integrated computer system and automated guidance, providing positional awareness and capability for full-spectrum offensives.

wikipedia.org sputniknews.com 27.02.2017

12. **wikipedia.org** 14 September 2016
13. **Reuters** report in **NEW STRAITS TIMES** November 2, 2016
14. **THE AVIATIONIST** November 1, 2016

The US Department of Defense recently reported that the PLA Air Force is "rapidly closing the gap with western forces across a broad spectrum of capabilities…"

Other reports have intimated the possibility of China overtaking the US in air superiority by 2030. **BUSINESS INSIDER** Alex Lockie 30.03.2016

Little a year after China's fifth generation fighter the J-20 ('Mighty Dragon') heavy air superiority platform entered service and made the country the second in the world after the US to develop such an aircraft, the PLA unveiled an upcoming next generation platform thought to be the world's very first sixth generation (6G) combat aircraft, **MILITARY WATCH** reported June 08, 2018.

Though well behind its Russian and American counterparts until the mid-2000s, Chinese military aviation has caught up to be on par, and Chinese fifth generation fighters threaten to surpass their foregn equivalents both qualitatively and quantitatively.

Though both Russia and the US have invested heavily in developing a sixth generation air superiority fighter, China appears to have a potential lead and its new generation platform could enter service sooner and with superior technologies as well.

Unveiled as an unmanned combat platform, China's new fighter aircraft has been called **Dark Sword** and is set to enter service in the near future alongside the country's growing fleet of next generation manned combat aircraft including the 4++ generation J-10 C and J-16 and the fifth generation J-20.   09.09.2018 21:02

According to China Academy of Aerospace Aerodynamics (CAAA), Chinese engineers successfully carried out on 2 August 2018 their maiden test of a nuclear capable hypersonic wave-rider aircraft known as Xingkong (Starry Sky), which ascended up to 30 km at a speed of Mach 5-5.6 (17,314 km/h). **China Daily** reported on August 06, 2018.

On 21 September 2018 China tested three scaled-down models of "wide-speed-range" hypersonic aircraft codenamed D18-1S, D18-2S, and D18-3S, according to **CCTV**. Designed with adjustable speeds, they will be nuclear-capable with a precision strike capability.   12.12.2018 18:16

15. "… Raytheon's AMRAAM (Counter-electronics High Power Microwave Advance Missile/CHAMP) is the current go-to-Western weapon for beyond-visual-range air combat, but new long-range missiles being fielded by Russia and China are a significant concern to the Pentagon," James Drew reported on 16 September 2015 in **FLIGHTGLOBAL.COM**,

"(US Air Combat Command Chief Gen. Hawk) Carlisle says outmatching the Chinese **PL-15** air-to-air missile (AAM) in particular is an "exceedingly high priority."

"The PL-15 and the range of that missile, we've got to be able to out-stick that missile," he says.

"The (US) air force is currently exploring a range of next-generation weapon concepts as it also pursues a sixth-generation fighter aircraft."

Douglas Barrie, a veteran defense aerospace journalist and airpower specialist with the International Institute for Strategic Studies (IISS), has written that the Chinese guided-weapons sector in the PLA Air Force (PLAAF) is also developing an even longer-range AAM (reportedly the hypersonic PL-XX VLRAAM with advanced features including active electronically scanned (AESA) radar and a backup sensor with an infrared/electro-optical seeker to zoom in on high-value targets such as aerial tankers and airborne early warning and control radar aircraft.

"… China aims to provide its modern combat aircraft with an array of missiles that can deny any opponent -- starting with the United States -- the luxury of air supremacy.

"Given the obvious geographical friction points between China and the United States, the air and naval domains are of particular importance,

"If China were to deny the United States air superiority in this way, America could only win it back with the commitment of a level of blood and treasure not seriously contemplated by the Pentagon for decades," Douglas Barrie commented on February 21, 2018 (**WARONTHEROCKS.COM**), to mark the IISS release of its annual report The Military Balance 2018.   09.09.2018 22:10

16. In **Defence Aviation** June 20,2016, Larkins Dsouza has also reported on the new Chinese CJ-10 cruise missile.

With the CJ-10 supersonic ground-launched land-attack cruise missile, there is also a subsonic anti-ship missile (ASM) with a range of 800 km and a 500kg payload of conventional or nuclear munitions.

The CJ-10 ASM can be launched by the H-6K bomber and JH-7B fighter-bomber, and can also be fired from the vertical launch system (VLS) of the latest Type 055/DDG-X stealth multi-task guided-missile destroyer.

With its low flight altitude characteristics that enhance its stealthy capabilities against air defence radars, the CJ-10 can also be updated during its flight with new targeting data, allowing it to change targets in mid-flight.

To quote Larkins Dsouza: "The CJ-10's flexibility, large payload and long range make it one of China's most important strategic weapons."

Appendix: Brief Notes from U.S. AIR FORCE WHITE PAPER ON LONG RANGE BOMBERS, March 1999 **fas.org**

The bomber's unique strengths of payload, range, and responsiveness coupled with precision attack are a cornerstone of America's airpower and force projection.

Prior to hostilities, bombers are a strong deterrent. When generated for either conventional or nuclear alert, bombers provide a strong and highly visible deterrent force just over the horizon from the enemy…

Delivering a large quantity and vast array of munitions, our bomber force can attack an enemy's Weapons of Mass Destruction (WMD), Command, Control and Communications (C3) nodes, and advancing forces to greatly reduce their effectiveness…

Should circumstances require, bombers can also provide rapid global response without the need to deploy into theatre before striking…

The current bomber fleet of up to 190 bombers (of which 130 combat-coded) will be operational for the next 35-40 years.

To complement the 21 B-2 bombers (the first "Spirit of Missouri" was delivered on December 1993 to the US Air Force Global Strike Command), the USAF awarded a development contract to Northrop Grumman in October 2015 to build the fifth generation nuclear-capable heavy-payload stealth Long Range Strike Bomber B-21. 80-100 LRS-B21s are envisioned, with IOC in 2025.

wikipedia.org 14 Oct 2016

Released on 14 November 2018, the Report to Congress by the U.S.-China Economic and Security Review Commission has also .among other developments, highlighted the progress made by the PLA Air Force in the construction of long-range bombers and deployment of new heavy-lift aircraft:

Expected to enter service by 2025, the H-20 long-range stealth bomber (with strike nuclear deterrence and A2/AD (Anti-Access/Area-Denial) missions) is China's next-generation bomber which will integrate fifth-generation technologies and be capable of carrying nuclear weapons, according to DoD. To replace the H-6, the H-20 will have a range of at least 5,000 miles (mi).

Operational since 2016, the Y-20 strategic heavy-lift aircraft reportedly has a maximum payload of 66 tons, in the same category as the Russian IL-76 and the US C-17.

To be produced under a China-Ukraine agreement for entry into service in 2019-2020, the AN-225 strategic heavy-lift aircraft is the world's largest transport aircraft with a max payload of 280 tons. 02.04.2019 18:12

19 pages 5,775 words 22.11.2016 07:41 04.2017 09:09 18.07.2017 07:12 09.09.2018 20:16 09.09.2018 22:25 18.10.2018 22:44 12.12.2018 18:18 02.04.2019 18:14 19:37

NEW CHINA B(5) COMBAT DRONES (UPDATED COPY)

Combat Drones for China's Defence

Israel pioneered the military use of Unmanned Aerial Vehicles (UAVs), known simply as the drones, using them for surveillance, electronic warfare, and decoys. Israel deployed combat drones for the first time in the 1973 Yom Kippur War and subsequently in the 1982 Lebanon War. (1)

Impressed by Israel's success, the US quickly acquired the UAVs, and its Hunter and Pioneer systems are reported to be direct derivatives and descendents of original Israeli models. The US first deployed its UAVs in the 1991 Gulf War. The Department of the Navy reported in May 1991: "At least one UAV was used at all times during Desert Storm..."

The US then used its drones in its so-called "war on terror" or assassination campaign against rebel or terrorist leaders, which started with a Predator strike against the Taliban leader Mullah Omar on 7 October 2001 in Kandahar. Afghanistan.

According to a report by Ian Bremmer in **TIME** magazine October 23, 2015, the US has about 7,000 drones in its UAV arsenal, from only about 50 a decade ago.

Over 70 countries, according to one estimate, have robotised their militaries, and there are over 4,000 types of UAVs in the global market. (2)

China has various types of UAVs including particularly the **UCAVs** (Unmanned Combat Aerial Vehicles) such as the Shenyang's Dark Sword (Anjian) and stealth strike UCAV with forward swept wings like the US X-45 called the Warrior Eagle.

According to October 2016 report by the Center for Intelligence Research and Analysis (CIRA), China has made tremendous strides in military robotics since 2009. And, as of July 2016, China has tested or fielded advanced unmanned systems for the various domains covering air, sea (surface and underwater), and land. (3)

According to CIRA, China's commercial and military robotics are rapidly growing in size and quality as the country upgrades its manufacturing sector and modernizes its military capabilities.

China overtook Japan to become the world's largest market for industrial robots in 2013, and will account for a third of the global installation of industrial robots by 2018.

The Chinese military are also fielding more and better unmanned systems in the air, land, and sea domains to reinforce their anti-access/area denial (A2/AD) capabilities.

According to the report released on 11 March 2018 by the Stockholm International Peace Research Institute (SIPRI), China has become the world's leading exporter of armed drones or unmanned combat aerial vehicles, having supplied 153 of them to 13 countries in the past five years. The US, the world's biggest arms exporter, sold only 5 armed drones to Britain over past 10 years. f

For long-range precision strikes, the "Soar Dragon" High Altitude Long Endurance (HALE) UAV is reported ideal for surveillance and could be used to guide the much-vaunted DF-21D anti-ship ballistic missile (ASBM). (4)

Apart from surveillance, Chinese unmanned systems also feature in various applications like intelligence, reconnaissance, military support, border patrol, explosive ordnance disposal.

The PLA Air Force (PLAF) is known to be already working on anti-drone laser weapons and defences against UAVs.

The PLA Navy (PLAN) is pursuing underwater robotics that can enhance its anti-submarine warfare (ASW) capabilities.

With the American X-47B and Global Hawk UCAVs in their cross hairs, China's defence industry and military research institutes focus on "soft-kill" countermeasures that can blind, confuse, or jam unmanned systems.

Technologies for propulsion, autonomous operation, advanced sensors, and data links are considered to be "critical for China to close the technological gap between the U.S. and Chinese unmanned systems..." (5)

China is also known to be investing heavily in emerging industries with transforming multiplier effects on capabilities of the various unmanned systems, such as artificial intelligence (AI) and nanotechnology. (6)

On 21 November 2013 China successfully tested it stealth combat drone named "Sharp Sword". According to **BBC News**, only the US, France, and Great Britain have crossed this military threshold in the field of UAV (Unmanned Aerial Vehicle).

China Daily said on 22 November 2013: "The successful flight shows the nation has again narrowed the air-power disparity between itself and Western nations..."

According to **BBC**'s defence correspondent Jonathan Marcus on 22 November 2013, China is joining a small elite of nations including the US, Israel, France, and UK pushing the boundaries of UAV technology. China has developed a variety of UAVs matching virtually every category deployed by the US.

China's varied inventory ranges from small tactical drones of limited endurance (flying time) to much larger systems akin to, and similarly armed as the US Predator and Reaper models.

Xinhua reported early November 2014 from Beijing that China has developed a highly accurate laser weapon that can shoot down light drones at low altitude. The two-kilometre-range zapper can bring down "various small aircraft" within five seconds of locating its target. (7)

In **POPULAR SCIENCE (popsci.com)** published on May 25, 2015, Jeffrey Lin and P.W. Singer reported on the development of a low observable, high altitude UAV, the world's largest and longest-range stealth drone with special purpose radars, which they considered to be "one of the most important to the future of war".

Dubbed characteristically by its Chinese maker as the "Divine Eagle", its first flight reportedly took place on February 2015.

According to Lin and Singer, Divine Eagle is designed to carry multiple Active Electronically Scanned Array (AESA) radars of three advanced varieties:

(1)   Airborne Moving Target Indicator (AMTI) radars to track airborne targets like the stealth fighter aircraft and cruise missiles,

(2)   Synthetic Aperture Radar (SAR) of high resolution to track slow-moving vehicles and other targets on the ground, and

(3)   Ground Moving Target Indicator (GMTI) radars to identify and track ships such as aircraft carriers, destroyers, etc.

As a High Altitude Long Endurance (HALE) UAV with a long-range anti-stealth capability, Divine Eagle could be deployed both offensively against stealth aircraft like the B-2 bomber and stealth warships like the DDG-1000 destroyer (the first of the three of the US Navy's largest and most technologically advanced destroyers, the USS Zumwalt was commissioned in Baltimore on 16 October 2016), and defensively to detect stealthy enemy military assets in the air, on the waters, and on land.

China Aerospace Science and Industry Corp (CASIC), the nation's largest missile maker, has started to develop stealthy military drones that can evade radar and anti-aircraft weapons.

Within the 13th Five-Year Plan (2016-2020) period, CASIC will develop technologies for long-endurance stealth drones and complete the design of high-speed combat reconnaissance drones for both domestic and international markets.

"As military reforms are drastically changing armed forces around the world, drones have become an indispensable weapon in modern warfare because they can play an important role in high-resolution reconnaissance, long-distance precision strikes, anti-submarine operations and aerial combat," said Wei Yiyin, CASIC deputy general manager and a member of the National Committee of the Chinese People's Political Consultative Conference (CPPCC), China's top political advisory body with over 2,000 members.

Unlike other Chinese drones which resemble fixed-wing planes with landing gear, CASIC drones look like cruise missiles.

The latest stealthy WJ-600 A/D of CASIC's has an ultrafast cruising speed of 700 km/ph, while other Chinese drones can reach a max of only 280 km/ph.

CASIC will also develop near-space drones to operate 20 km to 100 km in the Earth's stratosphere, mesosphere and lower thermosphere. (8)

The 2018 Report by the US Department of Defense refers to claims by Chinese defense industry representatives to development of long-range stealthy and near-space UAVs and imminent delivery of the long-range, high-altitude Xianglang UAV.   18.10.2018 23:22

Early 2016 Beijing unveiled its first stealth combat drone, known as the "Lijian", reportedly resembling the Lockheed Matin RQ-170 Sentinel.

Russian defence analyst Vasily Kashin told **Sputnik News** (14.03.2017) that stealthy long-range drones and anti-ship ballistic missiles (ASBMs) "could present a grave threat" to an adversary's naval forces in the Western Pacific.

Towards the end of May in 2017, the "Caihong" (Raibow), China's largest and most advanced solar-powered unmanned aircraft, made its successful debut when it took off in the morning from an airport in Northwest China and flew back at night.

According to Lo Shi Wen, head of unmanned aircraft development at the China Academy of Aerospace Aerodynamics (CAAA), Caihong flew over 20,000 meters high (above the clouds). The new solar-powered drone will be further improved and tested for several more months or even several years before delivery to go into service. (9)

In **CHINA TOPIX** on 7 June 2017, Arthur Dominic Villasanta reported the CAAA's description of the Caihong X, also referred to as the CH-T4, as an excellent data relay and communication node, and he wrote that "this drone can provide data that will guide ballistic missiles such as the DF-21 to distant targets like U.S. Navy aircraft carriers over a thousand kilometres away…"

Writing in **The National Interest** (June 10, 2017), Zachary Keck has made the point that an operational CH-T4 could increase "the redundancies in China's kill chain" (making it more difficult for Washington to destroy the surveillance step of the kill chain) in nailing an American aircraft carrier.

Although the Jan 2017 Pentagon's report on China's military (released Jan 2017) did not name the CH-T4, Keck wrote that it did note that "the acquisition and development of longer-range unmanned aerial vehicles (UAVs) will increase China's ability to conduct long-range ISR (Intelligence Surveillance Reconnaissance) and strike operations…"

On 26 October 2016 two F/A-18 Hornets, long-serving Navy fighter planes, released a robotic swarm of 103 tiny 6G Perdix drones in a royal demonstration.

"This is the kind of cutting-edge innovation that will keep us a step ahead of our adversaries," said outgoing Secretary of Defense Ash Carter. "This demonstration will advance our development of autonomous systems (designed to overwhelm adversaries)…" (10)

China is also conducting R&D on the **swarming drones** for military applications in offensive and defensive operations as well as support functions like ISR (Intelligence, Surveillance and Reconnaissance).

Presently, the state of the art is limited to small swarms of tens to about a hundred unmanned aircraft.

According to Paul Scharre of the Center for a New American Security, swarming is advantageous in offensive missions because it can overwhelm enemy defense with a large number of targets. In a swarming attack the drones are dispersed, making it difficult and expensive for adversary to defend itself. If 10 drones attack a target simultaneously and 7 of them are shot down, the remaining 3 will be able to complete their mission. (11)

According to **Xinhua** report on 11 June 2017, China Electronics Technology Group Corporation (CETC) tested 119 fixed-wing unmanned aerial vehicles (UAVs), beating its previous record of 67 drones launched in November2016 at the China International Aviation & Aerospace Exhibition in Zhuhai, Guangdong Province (besting the US Navy's display of 50).

25.02.2017 11:39 11:55

According to the 2017 Report by the DOD to US Congress, the Chinese UAV CH-5 (Rainbow 5) is China's most heavily armed combat drone with up to 16 air-to-surface munitions.

The PLA recently unveiled its Gonji-1 armed ISR (intelligence, surveillance, and reconnaissance) UAV.

According to CETC, "swarm intelligence" is regarded as the core of the artificial intelligence of unmanned systems, and it's also their future. According to CETC engineer Zhao Yanjie, intelligent swarms have "changed the rules of the game" since their introduction in robotic systems in 1989.

According to a February 2016 report in the **People's Daily**, China had over 100,000 drones in 2015, multiplying annually. (12)

"... Beijing is now betting that swarms of drones, low-tech hardware knitted together with high-tech artificial intelligence (AI), will become the weapon of the future," **FINANCIAL TIMES** reported from Beijing on 29 August 2017. (12)

"The gamble is that they can be effective both as a lethal and non-lethal weapon. Thousands of cheap 3D-printed drones, for example, could swarm aircraft carriers or fighter jets, which currently have no countermeasures for such attacks.

"They can also be effective, say experts, without being lethal by (not) crossing the line into a shooting war – a valuable form of deterrence, especially for weaker countries (seeking asymmetrical solutions in a conflict with stronger foes)..."

Thomas McMullan of **BBC News** reported on swarming of robotic agents in warfare following his interview with Paul Scharre of the Center for a New American Security:

"... Low-cost, intelligent and inspired by swarms of insects (such as ants, bees, termites, etc), these new machines could revolutionize future conflicts...

"Mr Scharre compares it (the inevitable use of swarm military technology" to the development of precision-guided weapons, tested and refined through the 1970s and 1980s, but only coming into their own during the first Gulf War of the early 1990s.

"That war in many ways set the template for conflicts in the following decades. Self-organising swarms of autonomous machines could well do the same for wars to come."   02.04.2019 19:09

According to China Electronics Technology Group Corporation (CETC), China has made "major breakthroughs" and is now on an even footing with the US in the fast-developing field of drones. (13)
18.07.2017 07:29 22.08.2017 13:11 30.08.2017 10:57

According to a report in **People's Daily Online** September 2017, Caihong (Rainbow) 5 completed a live-fire exercise in September 2017. The latest drone developed by the Chinese Academy of Aerospace and Aerodynamics (CAA), the CH-5 completed its performance flight testing and entered into initial small-scale production.

About 11 meters long and 4 meters high with a wingspan of 21 meters, the CH-5 is China's largest drone for reconnaissance, surveillance, patrols, target positioning, and strike missions.

"China's development of unmanned aerial vehicles (UAVs) and UCAVs (Unmanned Combat Aerial Vehicles) is now approaching the level of the United States," said Richard D. Fisher, Jr., Senior Fellow, International Assessment and Strategy Center, in his testimony on 17

May 2018 before the US House of Representatives Permanent Select Committee on Intelligence.

"China's MQ-1 and MQ-9 class UCAVs produced by the Chengdu Aircraft Corporation and the China Aerospace Science and Technology Corporation are selling well in the Middle East and marketed in Latin America.

"Stealthy turbojet-powered UCAVs could enter PLAAF (PLA Air Force) and PLANAF (PLA Navy Air Force) by early in the next decade, long-range turbofan-powered surveillance UAVs are in PLAAF service and the PLA is developing very high altitude long endurance UAVs and both UAV and anti-ship platforms for Near Space surveillance and electronic missions…" (14)   21.08.2018

China unveiled its new-generation stealth combat aerial vehicle (UAV) known as the CH-7 at the Airshow China 2018 in Zhuhai in south China's Guangdong Province on 6 November. According to Shi Wen, chief engineer and designer of the Caihong/CH or Rainbow UAV series, the CH-7 makes China the second country after the US to produce high-altitude long-endurance stealth capable combat UAVs with advanced penetration capabilities. (15)

"The CH-7 can intercept radar electronics signals, and simultaneously detect, verify and monitor high-value targets, such as hostile command stations, missile launch sites and naval vessels," Shi said to Huweija and Yang Sheng of **Global Times** 2018/11/5. The CH-7 will carry weapons, including air-to-ground or anti-ship missiles as well as long-distance precision-guided bombs.

Notes B(5) Combat Drones

1. **wikipedia.org** 18 November 2016 06:08
2. Pang Hongliang, **The Smart Military Revolution Is Dawning – Interpreting the Track of Military Technology Development from the U.S. "Third Offset Strategy"**, **PLA Daily** January 28, 2016 **mod.gov.cn**

Still undergoing development, the so-named "Third Offset Strategy" emphasizes the role of unmanned systems and robotics among a whole slew of the latest high-tech technologies.

3. **China's Industrial and Military Robotics Development** by Jonathan Rey and six others including Dr James Mulvenon. Research Paper prepared for the U.S.-China Economic and Security Review Commission.

4. Feng Fuzhang, **UAV Industry Is Entering a Period of Rapid Development**, Securities Research Report, China Securities, Sep 15, 2014, p. 14.

According to a recent report in **China Daily (Reuters report in NEW STRAITS TIMES** March 10, 2017), China Aerospace Science and Industry Corp (CASIC), China's largest missile maker, is developing stealthy drones. Said Wei Yiyin, CASIC's deputy general manager, "Drones have become an indispensable weapon in modern warfare in high-resolution reconnaissance, long-distance precision strikes and aerial combat..."

5. **CIRA** Report (Chapter Three) on **China's Military Robotics and Unmanned Systems**, p. 49.

6. Nanotech is expected to spawn its own family of micro-scale weapons.

In an article published in **National Defense** June 15, 1996, Major General Sun Bailin of the Academy of Military Science wrote that "nanotechnological weapons" could well bring about fundamental changes in many aspects of future military affairs. He concluded that "Nanotechnology" "will certainly become a crucial military technology in the 21st century!" **au.af.mil/au**

According to Paul Scharre of the Center for a New American Security, the military could create swarm of millions, perhaps even billions, of tiny, ultra-cheap 3-D printed mini drones.

Irving Lachow **tanddonline.com** 28 Feb 2017

Q: Could an aircraft carrier battle group thwart an attack by "millions of aerial kamikaze explosive drones"?

"Some of the major platforms and strategies upon which U.S. national security currently relies might be rendered obsolete," Greg Allen and Taniel Chan wrote in their July 2017 study report <u>Artificial Intelligence and National Security (p. 22)</u>, published by Harvard Kennedy School, Belfer Center for Science and International Affairs.   21.08.2018 20:05

7. **Xinhua** report in **NEW STRAITS TIMES** November 4, 2014.
8. **thestar.com** Beijing 10 March 2017
9. Report by Zhao Lei **China Daily** 2017-06-02

Article by Zachary Keck, former managing editor of **The National Interest**, THE BUZZ June 10, 2017 **nationalinterest.org**

10. In 2012 then-Deputy Defense Secretary Ash Carter set up the Strategic Capabilities Office (SCO) as part of the Pentagon's Third Offset Strategy to exploit America's technological edge in maintaining US dominance against potential adversaries.

    SCO Director Will Roger said, "You just don't talk about your best abilities..."

    Report by Cheryl Pellerin, DoD News Washington Nov 3, 2016 **defense.gov**

    Kelsey D. Atherton, **POPULAR SCIENCE popsci.com** Jan 11, 2017

11. Scharre, P. 2014. **Robotics on the Battlefield Part II: The Coming Swarm**. Washington, D.C: Center for a New American Security.

Irving Lachow **tandfonline.com** 26 Feb 2017 **Bulletin of the Atomic Scientists** Vol 73, 2017 Issue 2

According to a USAF press release in Washington 24 Feb 2017 (**sputniknews.com** 25.02.2017), the MQ-9 Reaper will replace the 21-year-old MQ-1 Preadator drone which retires on 1 July 2017.

"The MQ-9 is better equipped than the MQ-1 due to its high-definition sensors and increased speed," USAF stated. "The fresh MQ-9 design picked up where the MQ-1 left off, boasting a nearly 4,000-pound payload and the ability to carry missiles and bombs."

The MQ-9 Reaper will be used for close air support for US troops, along with human piloted aircraft, and also for intelligence-gathering and real-time reconnaissance.

12. **FT** report carried online **TODAY todayonline** Singapore 29 August 2017

To quote more from this report: "… China, which is at the center of the commercial drone industry, has some advantages as the era of unmanned systems dawns.

"Manufacturers such as DSI, Zerotech and Ehang dominate the global consumer drone industry and many of these private sector companies have been co-opted to work for the PLA…"

13. **Today online/South China Morning Post** 23 July, 2018 Beijing

According to military researchers and scientists involved in AI-related projects in China, China is developing large, smart and relatively low-cost **unmanned submarines** for a wide range of missions in the world's oceans, from reconnaissance to mine-laying and even suicide attacks against enemy vessels including high-value targets such as nuclear ballistic missile submarines (SSBNs).

The autonomous robotic submarines are expected to be deployed in the early 2020s. The robotic submarine project is part of the government's ambitious plan to boost the country's naval power with AI technologies.

China has built the world's largest testing facility for surface drone boats in Zhuhai, Guangdong Province. Military researchers are also developing an AI-assisted support system for submarine commanders, to help them make faster and more accurate decisions in the heat of conflict.

According to Lin Yang, marine technology equipment director at the Shenyang Institute of Automation (SIA), Chinese Academy of Sciences (CAS), China is developing a series of extra-large unmanned underwater vehicles (XLUUVs).

Lin Yang developed China's first autonomous underwater vehicle with an operational depth beyond 6 km. Now Lin is chief scientist of the 912 Project, a classified program to develop new-generation military underwater robots in time for the centenary of the Chinese Communist Party in 2021.

In 2017 the US military issued contracts for construction of two prototype XLUUVs by 2020 -- Lockheed Martin's Orca system and Boeing's originally developed for commercial uses such as mapping the sea floor.

Russia has reportedly built a large underwater drone, armed with the Status-6 autonomous torpedo capable of delivering a mega monster 100-ton nuclear warhead across large distances at a high speed.

SCMP report by Stephen Chan 23 July, 2018 2:34 PM   21.08.2018 20:41

14. Fisher's 20-page testimony on China's Military Power Projection Challenge to the United States **intelligence.house.gov 5-17-18.pdf**

15. Report by Hu Weija and Yang Sheng 2018/11/5 **globaltimes.cn**

According to the statement by the China Academy of Aerospace Aerodynamics (CAAA), the 10-m-long CH-7 has a 22-m wingspan with a maximum take-off weight of 13,000 kg, a cruise altitude of 10-13 km, a cruising speed of Mach 0.5-0.6, and a flight time of 15 hours.

"The CH-7 can intercept radar electronic signals, and simultaneously detect, verify and monitor high-value targets, such as hostile command stations, missile launch sites and naval vessels," Shi told **Global Times**.

"The CH-7 also has internal weapons bays, so it is capable of launching weapons, like anti-radiation missiles, air-to-ground or anti-ship missiles and long-distance precision-guided bombs…"

Though still behind the other major powers like the US and European countries, Shi said, China is catching up technologically through system integration and optimization. According to Shi, the CH-7 will be test-flown in a year or two.   14.12.2018 00:28 02.04.2019 19:36

9 pages 2,538 words 16.06.2017 23:16 18.07.2017 07:29 22.07.2017 07:50 22.08.2017 13:13 30.08.2017 11:07
13 pages 3,819 words 21.08.2018 20:50 10.09.2018 16:39 18.10.2018 23:59

NEW CHINA B(6) (UPDATED COPY)

Electronic Warfare (EW)

"The level of modernization of our weapons directly corresponds to how sophisticated our electronic technology is and this will have a direct impact on victory or defeat in modern warfare," General Mi Zhenyu, a former Vice President of the Academy of Military Science in Beijing, wrote in a groundbreaking conceptual paper on China's military modernization published in 1988 shortly before the 1991 Gulf War.

"After our forces are equipped with a large quantity of electronic equipment and computers (the nerve centre of modern weapons systems), not only will the electronic command, control, communications and information (C3I) systems within our combat and control become highly automated, and simple platforms and partial electronic equipments of warfare like reconnaissance and anti-reconnaissance, jamming and anti-jamming, destructive and anti-destruction devices be completely transformed for "electronic wars", they will also allow electronic technology to spread and permeate into all of the other weapons systems until it becomes the mainstay of our modern weaponry.

"The energetic development of our country's military use of electronic technology is of utmost importance to upgrading the modernization level of our military weapons and closing the weapons gap with advanced countries..." ((1)

On 22 June 2015, Xu Qiliang, a vice-chairman of the Central Military Commission, called on China to innovate even more.

"Our military's equipment construction is shifting from catch-up research to independent innovations," Xu said. (2)

On the same day, **Reuters** reported from Washington what Deputy Defence Secretary Robert Work spoke to a group of military and civilian aerospace experts.

According to the Pentagon's chief operating officer, China is mounting a serious effort to challenge United States military superiority in the air and space, compelling the US military to seek new technologies and systems to stay ahead of its rapidly developing rival.

Work has said that China is "quickly closing the technological gaps", developing smart radar-evading aircraft, advanced reconnaissance planes, sophisticated missiles and top-notch electronic warfare (EW) equipment. (3)

In the early 1980s Daniel Deudney, a political scientist and senior researcher at the Washington-based Worldwatch Institute, wrote on the "transparency revolution" following advances in information technologies and development of the worldwide military reconnaissance, command, control and communications systems, and subsequent militarisation of the electromagnetic (EM) spectrum, which shifted the emphasis in warfare from the destructive power of weapons to the ability to detect and target the enemy's forces and to "hide and communicate with one's own."

According to Deudney, future warfare will no longer be "a traditional struggle between offensive and defensive military force" but rather "a competition between the visible and the hidden – between transparency and stealth."

Frank Barnaby, formerly a nuclear weapons research physicist and Director of the Stockholm International Peace Research Institute (1971-81) observed: "Does the 'transparency revolution' favour offence or defence? Many experts believe that it favours defence to such an extent that major offensive weapons (battle tanks, long-range combat aircraft and warships) are, or soon will be, obsolete, because of the development of defensive missiles of deadly accuracy..." (4)

On electronic warfare, Barnaby wrote in 1985: "In future warfare, the 'electronic order of battle' will be a crucial factor. The development of new offensive and defensive weapons based on a variety of sensors has stimulated a never-ending electronic arms race for counter-measures, counter-counter-measures, and so on..." (5)

According to Lockheed Martin, a leading American manufacturer of EW systems, electronic warfare (EW) represents the ability to control and use the electromagnetic spectrum – signals such as radio, infrared or radar – to sense, protect, and communicate, as well as to deny an adversary the ability to use or disrupt these signals. Three main areas are involved: (1) electronic attack (EA) for disrupting a signal, for example; (2) electronic protection (EP), preventing a receiver from being jammed; and (3) electronic support (ES), producing the necessary data to disrupt the electromagnetic spectrum. (6)

According to another pioneering EW company Raytheon, electronic warfare uses focused energy, usually radio waves or laser light to confuse or disable an enemy. EW can also involve collecting an enemy's radio signals or sensing the radar of an incoming missile.

Raytheon is developing tactical lasers, directed energy (DE) weapons, high energy lasers against enemy missiles, the next generation jammers (NGJs) to foil enemy sensors with focused radio energy, airborne decoys, anti-radiation missiles to detect and destroy radars, radar-directed artillery systems, etc. (7)

"The PLA identifies electronic warfare (EW) as a way to reduce or eliminate U.S. technological advantages, and considers it an integral component of warfare. The PLA's EW doctrine emphasizes using electromagnetic spectrum weapons to suppress or to deceive enemy electronic equipment. The PLA's strategy focuses on radio, radar, optical, infrared, and microwave frequencies, in addition to adversarial computer and information systems," the US Department of Defense reported to Congress, April 2016. (8)

"China's strategy stresses that EW is a vital fourth dimension to combat, and should be considered equal to traditional ground, sea, and air forces. Effective EW is seen as a decisive aid during military operations and consequently the key to determining the outcome of war.

"The PLA sees EW as an important force multiplier, and would likely employ it in support of all combat arms and services during a conflict..."

According to the DoD in Washington, the PLA's EW units have conducted jamming and anti-jamming operations, testing the military's understanding of EW weapons, equipment, and performance. All this has helped boost the military's confidence in conducting force-on-force, real-equipment confrontation operations in simulateEW environments.

Advances in research and deployment of EW weapons are tested in such exercises, and have proven effective. EW weapons include jamming equipment against multiple communication and radar systems, and the GPS satellite systems. EW systems are also deployed with other sea- and air-based platforms for both offensive and defensive operations.

Speaking to **Voice of America (VOA)** on 6 August 2018, US Chief of Naval Operations Adm. John Richardson spoke of the need to counter jamming devices. Electronic warfare (EW) can "collapse" everything from communications to navigation systems, Geoff Ziezulewicz reported in **Navy Times (navytimes.com)**. Richardson described disruptive EW technologies as "decisive in the future fight, and we've got to make sure that we are investing in those as well…"

According to Bryan Clark, a retired submariner and presently a senior fellow at the Center for Strategic and Budgetary Assessments (CSBA), the US Navy's operating concepts and capabilities "may not be enough to overcome the growing sophistication and capacity of Chinese or Russian missiles and sensors."

Clark said: "The (US) Navy will need to tap into artificial intelligence (AI), networking and unmanned systems for future electronic warfare (EW) operations…"

The following is from the one-para take from the DOD's 2018 China Military Power Report (p. 74):

"The PLA considers EW an integral component of modern warfare. Its EW doctrine emphasizes using electromagnetic spectrum weapons to suppress or to deceive enemy electronic equipment.

"Potential EW victims include adversary systems operating in radio, radar, microwave, infrared, and optical frequency ranges, as well as adversarial computer and information systems.

"China has fielded several types of UAVs (Unmanned Aerial Vehicles) with EW payloads, and showcased several of these during the PLA 90th Anniversary parade in July 2017.

"PLA EW units routinely conduct jamming and anti-jamming operations against multiple communication and radar systems and GPS satellite systems in force-on-force exercises. These not only test operational units' understanding of EW weapons, equipment, and performance, but also help improve confidence in their ability to operate effectively in a complex electromagnetic environment. In addition, the PLA tests and reportedly validates advances in EW weapons research in these exercises."   21.08.2018 18:41

5 pages 1,046 words 13.06.2017 20:12 18.07.2017 07:41

Notes China B(6) Electronic Warfare (EW)

1. China's National Defense Development Concepts, PLA Press, Beijing, 1988
2. **Xinhua/Reuters** report in **New Straits Times** June 24, 2015
3. **Reuters** report in **New Straits Times** June 24, 2015
4. Daniel Deudney was quoted by Frank Barnaby in his essay "The technology of warfare" published in **LIVING IN THE FUTURE**, edited by Isaac Asimov, New English Library, Kent/London, UK, 1985, pp.138-139
5. **LIVING IN THE FUTURE** pp.140-141
6. **lockheedmartin.com**

According to Yang Guanping, chief scientist of the State-owned China Electronics Technology Group Corporation (CETC), China has made remarkable progress in developing passive surveillance radar system, and China's latest YLC-29 radar system has been successfully applied in the military.

Developed by Nanjing Research Institute of Electronic Technology (also known as the No. 14 Institute), under the CETC, the YLC-29 made its public debut at the 52nd International Paris Airshow on 19-25 June 2017.

According to the CETC, the new radar system uses widely distributed civilian radio frequency-modulated signals to detect, locate and track targets moving through the air – including stealth aircraft – without being detected, which greatly improves the system's viability and anti-jamming activity.

Traditional radar detection systems are vulnerable to jamming or attack by anti-radiation weapons, as high-power radar jamming aircraft and anti-radiation missiles are extensively used in modern battlefield.

According to Yang, China is developing a new type of radar system that combines passive and active radars. 22.07.2017 07:32

7. **raytheon.com**
8. ANNUAL REPORT TO CONGRESS CHINA 2016 **freebeacon.com** 2016 April 26

6 pages 1,612 words 18.07.2017 07:41 22.07.2017 07:32 21.08.2018 18:47

NEW CHINA B(7)
BLUE WATER NAVY

Constructing a Blue-Water Naval Force

According to an article written by Dr. Patrick M. Cronin and four other colleagues published May 15, 2017 by the Center for a New American Security (CNAS) in Washington, D.C., China's PLA Navy (PLAN) will build a Blue-Water Naval Power by 2030.

They have written: "China is rapidly transforming itself from a continental power with a focus on its near seas to a great maritime power with a two-ocean focus. The PLAN is looking beyond the *san hai* (three seas) – the Yellow Sea, South China Sea, and East China Sea – and out toward the Pacific and Indian Oceans..." (1)

In Commentary on China's emerging 500-ship Navy published on 3 February by the UK-based Royal United Services Institute (RUSI), Dr Peter Roberts has written that the People's Liberation Army's Navy is growing fast; expect it to grow even faster. It is moving towards "an ambition of 500 warships, including aircraft carriers, amphibious ships and a burgeoning frigate and destroyer force...

"The growth in the PLA(N) force structure has been rapid: indeed it is hard to recall growth at a similar pace in any navy across history.

"Against this, the US Navy – still the world's most powerful naval force (currently with a fleet of about 300 vessels) – has an aspiration of returning to a force design of around 350 units.

"It is even more remarkable given that until the mid-1980s, the PLA had not considered the sea as a domain to be contested, opting instead for a strategy of coastal control, and an element of sea denial – that is, the ability to deny freedom of movement to their adversaries inside their coastline.

"The (sea) change in outlook was stimulated (under) General Liu Huaqing, who was PLA(N) Commander between August 1982 and January 1988, who had a grand design for domination of the Pacific. He first planned to take control of the first island chain (2000-2010, *his timeline*), the second island (2011-2020, *his timeline*), and subsequently the entire Pacific (before 2050).

"His definition of 'control' remains a moot point to many commentators, and is open to wide interpretation. The plan that General – sometimes called Admiral – Liu developed was accepted as doctrine when he became commander of the PLA (N). It was fully funded once he entered the Chinese Politburo Standing Committee in 1992..." (2)

In 1994, on the 100th anniversary of the Sino-Japanese War (1894-1895), General Liu Huaqing, then Vice Chairman of the Central Military Commission, wrote on the need to modernize China's national defense in a paper published in **China Military Science** (Winter 1994):

"... As early as the beginning of the 1950s, Chairman Mao pointed out that China should build a powerful navy. Comrade Deng Xiaoping demanded in the 1970s that our navy forces "must serve our national goals (national development, security, modernization and revitalization).

"On this occasion of 100th anniversary of the Sino-Japanese War, we should build our people's navy even better and make a greater contribution to modernizing our national defense." (3)

Since 2002, the PLAN has constructed 10 nuclear submarines, including 6 nuclear attack submarines (SSNs) and 4 nuclear ballistic missile submarines (SSBNs) armed with CSS-N-14 JL-2 submarine-launched ballistic missiles (SLBMs).

According to Pentagon, the PLAN will probably build its new SHANG class Type 093B guided-missile nuclear attack submarines (SSGNs) over the next decade.

"China's four operational JIN-class SSBNs represent China's first credible, sea-based nuclear deterrent," Pentagon reports.

"China's next generation Type 096 SSBNs will likely begin construction in the early 2020s, and reportedly will be armed with the JL-3, a follow-on SLBM." (4)

To quote from the White Paper on China's Military Strategy May 2015:

"... In line with the strategic requirements of offshore waters defense and open seas protection, the PLA Navy (PLAN) will gradually shift its focus from "offshore waters defense" to the combination of "offshore waters defense" with "open seas protection," and build a combined, multi-functional and efficient marine combat force structure.

"The PLAN will enhance its capabilities for strategic deterrence and counterattack, maritime maneuvers, joint operations at sea, comprehensive defense and comprehensive support." (5)

According to the May 2017 Report by the US Department of Defense to Congress, the PLA Navy (PLAN) has the largest naval fleet in Asia with over 300 surface ships, submarines (63), amphibious vessels, and patrol craft. The PLAN will have 69-78 submarines by 2020.

Following the initial launching of two of China's new-generation guided missile Type 055 destroyers on June 2017 and April 2018, two more of the first batch of home-grown 10,000-ton class missile destroyers were launched on 3 July 2018 at Dalian, a coastal city in northeastern Liaoning Province. (6)

According to Wang Yunfei, a military expert and retired PLAN officer, the Type 055 has multiple roles including aircraft carrier escort, theater missile defense, and sea-to-ground attack. According to Wang, the PLAN will probably have 10 Type 055 warships.

According to Song Zhongping, a military expert cum TV commentator, the Type 055 will also likely be armed with an electromagnetic railgun (EMRG). "The Type 055 is the best fit for

China's future electromagnetic gun, for the all-electric warship could meet the weapon's huge power supply demand," Song said.

According to futurist Brian Wang, a Type 055 destroyer will have a system of 96 MW to deliver and fire shells of a 32 mega-joule EMRG at Mach 7 velocity to targets about 124 nautical miles away. (7)

According to a report in **NAVAL TECHNOLOGY (nanal-technology.com)**,

the Type 055 class stealth destroyer will be powered by a combined gas turbine propulsion system integrating four QC-280 gas turbines (each rated with max output of 28 MW) coupled to two propellers.

Its roles include long-range air defense, anti-surface warfare (AsuW), anti-air warfare (AAW), anti-submarine warfare (ASW), electronic warfare (EW), land and maritime strikes, escort, long-range patrol and surveillance missions (with a standard range of 5,000 nautical miles).

The Type 055 destroyers will be armed with the YJ-18A anti-ship cruise missiles (ASCMs) and YJ-100 long-range ASCMs as well as short-range and long-range surface-to-air missiles (SAMs).

Testifying before the House Permanent Select Committee on Intelligence on 17 May 2018, Captain James Fanell (USN, Ret.) said:

"… As I speak to you today, the PLA Navy consists of over 330 surface ships (including 26 destroyers, 21 of them modern, and 20 modern corvettes) and 66 submarines, nearly 400 combatants. As of 4 May 2018, the U.S. Navy consists of 283 battleforce ships: 211 surface ships and 72 submarines.

"By 2030, it is estimated the PLA Navy will consist of some 550 ships: 450 surface ships (including 34 destroyers, 68 frigates, and 26 corvettes) and 99 submarines (including 12 SSBNs and 12 SSNs).

"As currently debated in the halls of the Congress and Pentagon, it remains unclear if the U.S. Navy of 2030 will even reach a total of 355 ships and submarines. Numbers matter…

"From a technological standpoint, the PRC has quickly achieved parity with U.S. Navy's standards and capacities for warship and submarine production.

"PLA Navy ships and submarines do not have to match U.S. naval capabilities precisely: they just have to be good enough to be able to achieve more hits to win any given battle.

"That said, the quality of PRC warships already presents a credible threat across the Asia-Pacific today…" (8)

Chief of Naval Operations, Adm. John Richardson told Carla Babb of **VOA (Voice of America)** on 6 August 2018 that Chinese military vessels are now operating in the Northern Atlantic and moving into the Mediterranean Sea to create a "new dynamic" (with Russian submarines in those same waters).

Richardson has described the Chinese navy as global, "ready and capable" of operating anywhere Beijing wants.

"They're certainly a pacing competition for us in terms of the naval threat," he told **VOA**. (9)

"... China is now capable of controlling the South China Sea in all scenarios short of war with the United States," Adm Philip S Davidson, now commander of the US Indo-Pacific Command, stated in a written submission during his Senate confirmation process on March 2018.

Davidson has described China as a "peer competitor", gaining on the US, not by matching its forces weapon by weapon, but by building critical "asymmetrical capabilities" including anti-ship missiles (such as the DF-21D and DF-26) and advancing in submarine warfare.

"There is no guarantee that the United States would win a future conflict with China," Adm Davidson concluded. (10)   10.09.2018 19:02

In the National Defense Strategy (NDS), released in mid-January 2018, US Defense Secretary Jim Mattis makes great-power competition with China and Russia as the primary focus of US national security.   21.08.2018 05:55'

Notes CHINA B(7) BLUE WATER NAVY

1. The four co-authors with Dr. Patrick Cronin are Dr. Mira Rapp-Hooper, Harry Krejsa, Alexander Sullivan, and Rush Doshi. **cnas.org**

2. Dr Peter Roberts is Director Military Sciences, RUSI, having been Senior Research Fellow for Sea Power and C4ISR since 2014. **rusi.org**
3. **au.af.mi** 11/2/2004
4. **defense.org** Department of Defense **ANNUAL REPORT TO CONGRESS Military and Security Developments Involving the People's Republic of China 2017** generated 2017 May 15
5. **globalsecurity.org Xinhua**/Beijing May 26, 2016

According to the 2017 DOD Report to Congress, China's conventionally armed CSS-5 Mod 5 DF-21D ASBM "gives the PLA the capability to attack ships, including aircraft carriers in the western Pacific Ocean..."

In 2016 China began fielding the DF-26 IRBM "which is capable of conducting conventional and nuclear precision strikes against ground targets and conventional strikes against naval targets in the Western Pacific Ocean..."

According to Chinese media reports in August 2017, China is developing the JL-3 sea-based ICBM for the advanced nuclear-powered submarine (SSBN) project 096. The PLA Navy presently operates 4 094/094A SSBNs armed with the JL-2 SLBMs with a range of 7,400-8,000 km.

"In order to boost its sea-based strategic nuclear forces, China needs a missile with a range of 11,000-13,000 kilometers, preferably with a multiple independently targetable re-entry vehicle (MIRV)," said Vasily Kashin, a military expert and senior research fellow at the Institute for Far Eastern Studies of the Russian Academy of Sciences.

On August 2017, Chinese websites published pictures of the project 032 submarine, the world's largest conventionally powered submarine, undergoing tests and re-fitting work for bigger silos at a shipyard in Dalian. **sputniknews.com** 14:25 19.08.2017

4 pages 1,010 words 09.08.2017 11:57 22.08.2017 12:56 13:23 27.12.2017 21:48

6. Report by Yang Sheng, **GLOBAL TIMES (globaltimes.cn)** 2018/7/3
7. **nextbigfuture.com** June 22, 2018
8. 64-page testimony by Captain James Fanell (USN, Ret.), USN Intelligence Officer for 28 years: China's Global Naval Strategy and Expanding Force Structure: Pathway to Hegemony. 17 May 2018.

   intelligence.house.gov 17 may 18.pdf

9. **voanews.com** 06 August 2018
10. Steven Lee Myers **NYT nytimes.com** Aug 29, 2018

"… China's rapid buildup of the PLA Navy as a blue water force through its continued commissioning of highly capable multimission warships will give Beijing naval expeditionary capabilities deployable around the globe as early as 2025, well ahead of the PLA's broader 2035 modernization goal (to become a fully "modern" military by 2035)," the U.S.-China Economic and Security Review Commission reported to Congress on 14 November 2018. (11)

On China's military modernization, the Commission has observed that the Chinese strategy appears "designed to contest the U.S. military by developing high-technology weapons, such as maneuvering missiles capable of targeting ships at sea, space weaponry, cyber warfare tools and other advanced arms…"   02.04.2019 20:10

11. **2018 REPORT TO CONGRESS OF THE U.S.-CHINA ECONOMIC AND SECURITY REVIEW COMMISSION** 21.11.2018 02:05

AN UPDATE ON THE PLA NAVY (PLAN)

According to August 2018 Report to Congress by the US Department of Defense, the PLAN is the region's largest navy with more than 300 surface combatants, submarines, amphibious ships, patrol craft, and specialized vessels.

Currently operating 4 nuclear-powered ballistic missile submarines (SSBNs), 5 nuclear-powered attack submarines (SSNs), and 47 diesel-powered attack submarines, China's submarine force will expand to 69-78 submarines by 2020.

The Chinese navy is increasing its inventory of advanced anti-ship cruise missile (ASCM)-capable conventional submarines. Since the mid-1990s, the PLAN has purchased 12 Russian-built KILO-class SS units, 8 capable of launching ASCMs; and Chinese shipyards have delivered 13 SONG-class SS units (Type 039) and 17 YUAN-class diesel-electric air-independent power attack submarines (SSP) (Type 039A).

Over the past 15 years, the PLAN has built 10 nuclear submarines -- 2 SHANG I-class SSNs (Type 093), 4 SHANG II-class SSNs (Type 039A), and 4 JIN-class SSBNs (Type 049) to provide an underwater nuclear deterrence.

"Equipped with the CSS-N-14 (JL-2) submarine-launched ballistic missile (SLBM), China's four operational JIN-class SSBNs represent China's first credible, sea-based nuclear deterrent," the Pentagon reiterates in its 2018 report.

Construction of China's next-generation Type 096 SSBN, reportedly to be armed with the follow-on JL-3 SLBM, will likely commence in the early 2020s.

By the mid-2020s, China likely will build the Type 093B guided-missile nuclear attack submarine, the new SHANG-class SSN to enhance the PLAN's anti-surface warfare capability as well as to provide a more clandestine land-attack option.

In 2017, three new LUYANG III-class guided-missile destroyers (DDGs) (Type 052D) entered service, bringing the operational total to seven with at least six more under construction or outfitting. The

LUYANG III-class DDG has a multipurpose vertical launch system capable of launching ASCMs, surface-to-air missiles (SAMs), and anti-submarine missiles (ASMs).

China is also constructing the larger RENHAI-class Type 055 guided-missile cruiser (CG). The PLAN presently operates at least 24 JIANGKAI II-class guided-missile frigates FFG (Type 054A), and more than 35 JIANGDO-class corvettes (FELs) (Type 056) for anti-submarine warfare (ASW) with a towed-array sonar in littoral waters in the South China Sea and East China Sea.

Launched in 2017, China's first domestic aircraft carrier will likely enter service in 2019.

China is also expected to start building its first catapult-capable carrier in 2018.

Presently, the PLAN's fleet has 4 ballistic missile submarines (SSBNs), 5 nuclear attack submarines (SSNs), 47 diesel attack submarines, 28 destroyers, 51 frigates, and 28 corvettes.

According to Liu Zhen's report in **South China Morning Post** 10 Jan 2019. China's first indigenous aircraft carrier the Type 001A is expected to be delivered to the PLA Navy on Navy Day 23 April 2019. The 315 m (1,033 feet)-long flattop can carry 32 J-15 fighter jets -- 6 more than the Liaoning. And steam-turbine powered, the Type 001A has a ski-jump deck for take-offs.

China's current four Type-094 nuclear ballistic missile submarines (SSBNs) are each outfitted with 16 JL-2 missiles.

According to internet reports from China, the future Type-096 SSBNs will carry up to 24 missiles of the next-generation JL-3 SLBMs (slightly more than the US Navy's Ohio-class SSBNs armed with 20 missiles per boat).

9 pages 2,579 words 21.08.2018 05:59 10.09.2018 18:45 19:12 21.11.2018 03:09 02.04.2019 21:36
19.10.2018 00:12 21.11.2018 03:12 14.12.2018 01:05 03.04.2019 19:15

NEW CHINA B (8)
NAVAL MODERNISATION

China's Naval Modernisation: Towards Parity with the US by 2030

A. Rapid Progress

Chairman Mao Zedong was reported to have said in 1949, "to oppose imperialist aggression, we must build a powerful navy…"

The People's Liberation Army (PLA) Navy was founded on 23 April 1949 in the ancient city of Taizhou, south- central Jiangsu Province, East China – presently the HQ of the East Sea Fleet (China's first naval force). It had a very humble beginning with just nine warships and 17 boats obtained after a unit of the Kuomintang's second coastal defence fleet defected to the PLA. (1)

On its 68th anniversary in 2017, the Chinese navy has aircraft carriers (1 Type 001 in operation since 2012, 1 Type 001 launched on 26 April 2017, and 1 Type 002 under construction), nuclear submarines (4 ballistic missile subs/SSBNs) and 5 nuclear-powered attack subs/ SSNs), diesel-powered submarines (53 SSKs), squadrons of destroyers (41), landing ships and supporting ships in its three fleets.

China has 27 Type 054A guided-missile destroyers, including the Liupanshui launched on 1 April 2017. PLAN has 13 Type 052D guided-missile destroyers, including the Xining launched on 22 January 2017. And, the first new generation Type 055 guided-missile destroyer was launched on 28 June 2017.

The 255,000-strong navy is presently organised in three fleets: North Sea (Beihai), East Sea (Donghai), and South Sea (Nanhai). Main naval bases include those at Lushun (formerly known as Port Arthur) in Liaoning Province, Huludao (southwestern Liaoning), Qingdao (HQ of the North Sea Fleet) in eastern Shandong Province on China's east coast, Shanghai on China's central coast, Zhoushan in northeastern Zhejiang Province in eastern China, Wenzhou in southeastern Zhejiang Province, Xiamen in southeastern Fujian Province in southern China, Guangzhou to the west of Xiamen in southern China, Zhanjiang to the southwest of Guangzhou (HQ of the South Sea Fleet), and Yulin in southeastern Guangxi on the border with Guangdong in south China.

"China since the early to mid-1990s has been steadily building a modern and powerful navy. China's navy in recent years has emerged as a formidable military force within China's near-seas region, and it is conducting a growing number of operations in more-distant waters, including the broader waters of the Western Pacific, the Indian Ocean, and waters around Europe," the November 2017 CRS (Congressional Research Service) Report states in its Summary. (2)

"Observers of Chinese and U.S. military forces view China's improving naval capabilities as posing a challenge in the Western Pacific to the U.S. Navy's ability to achieve and maintain control of blue-water ocean areas in wartime – the first such challenge the U.S. Navy has faced since the end of the Cold War (1991).

"More broadly, these observers view China's naval capabilities as a key element of a broader Chinese military challenge to the long-standing status of the United States as the leading military power in the Western Pacific (and globally as well).

"The question of how the United States should respond to China's military modernization effort, including its naval modernization effort, is a key issue in U.S. defense planning.

"China's naval modernization effort encompasses a wide array of platform and weapon acquisition programs, including anti-ship ballistic missiles (ASBMs), anti-ship cruise missiles (ASCMs), submarines, surface ships, aircraft, and supporting C4ISR (command and control, communications, computers, intelligence, surveillance, and reconnaissance) systems.

"China's naval modernization effort also includes improvements in maintenance and logistics, doctrine, personnel quality, education and training, and exercises..."

On 9 April 2015 the Maryland-based Office of Naval Intelligence (ONI) published its report **The PLA Navy: New Capabilities and Missions for the 21ˢᵗ Century**. (3)

Explaining the significance of the highlights of the 49-page ONI report, noted military researcher and China analyst Dr Andrew S. Erickson wrote:

"...Accelerated modernization since roughly 2000 has put the PLAN "on track to dramatically increase its combat capability by 2020 through rapid acquisition and improved operational proficiency."

"On hardware side, it has done so in part by rapidly replacing older ships with larger, multi-mission, blue-water-capable variants…"

"ONI judges that "in the next decade, China will complete its transition...to a navy capable of multiple missions around the world'..." (4)

Beijing-based Jeremy Page of **Wall Street Journal** wrote on 10 April 2015: "According to the report, China's navy will soon assume a central role in the country's nuclear deterrence, launching ballistic missile submarine (SSBN) patrols with intercontinental range missiles.

""As we look ahead to the coming decade, the introduction of aircraft carriers, ballistic missile submarines, and potentially a large-deck amphibious ship will fundamentally alter how the PLA(N) operates and is viewed by the world," it says..." (5)   900 words 11.12.2017 09:19

B. Naval notches in 2017

Press Trust of India (PTI) in Beijing reported on 22 January 2017 the commissioning of the 31st Type-056 class corvette in the world's largest fleet of modern corvettes.

According to the **PLA Daily**, the CNS Ezhou with a hull number of 513 has a maximum speed of 52 km/h, good manoeuvrability, high-level automation and stealth capability, and is capable of hitting aircraft, ships and submarines. (6)

On 26 April 2017 China launched its first domestically-built Type 001A aircraft carrier. As reported in **Sputnik News**, it's 315 m long and 75 m wide, 70,000 tons displacement, with a cruising speed of 31 knots. It's expected to carry up to 36 Shenyang J-15 fighters.

China plans to put a third carrier into operation within the next three years.

According to **Sputnik**, China also plans to eventually field a total of six carrier battle groups, along with a series of naval bases around the globe. (7)

Led by its first aircraft carrier CNS Liaoning, China's sole carrier battle group conducted its maiden live-fire exercises in the Bohai Sea on November 2016 as well as take-off and landing drills in the South China Sea.

On 28 June 2017 China launched its first Type 055 guided-missile destroyer with a displacement of over 12,000 tons, in the same league as the US Navy's Arleigh Burke-class Fleet III multimission warships. (8)

"The Type 055 represents a large stride forward for the Chinese navy. When completed, that class (of heavy destroyers) will qualify among the best in the world, if not the most powerful overall," Stratfor (reputed American geopolitical intelligence platform and publisher) commented 4 May 2017 in a lengthy article on China's Navy in **WORLDVIEW**.

On 12 July 2017 Jeffrey Lin and P.W. Singer reported in **POPULAR SCIENCE** deployment of the XAC KJ-600 airborne early warning and control (AEW&C) plane (currently under development) on future, catapult equipped Chinese aircraft carriers.

Lin and Singer wrote, "...Given current Chinese combat datalinking capabilities and future plans, the KJ-600 will likely be able to guide aircraft as well as help target long-range Chinese missiles and integrate data from multiple platforms into a single stream (to detect stealth aircraft and boost ground-based systems as well)..." (9)

On 21 September 2017, **PTI** reported from Beijing the delivery of China's 69th submarine, a new nuclear-powered submarine, without categorising it (so it's the PLAN's 5th SSBN or 6th SSN). While all 70 US Navy's submarines are nuclear-powered, the Chinese Navy has only 10 of the kind.

According to a May 2017 report in **NextBigFuture.com**, China will have 12 nuclear-powered ballistic missile submarines (SSBNs) in 2030 – one more than the US (14 boomers in 2017).

In a very recent pictorial report/story documenting the phenomenal growth and modernization of the Chinese Navy (PLAN) since 2003 to 2016, Jeff Head detailed 86 major combatants:

26 x Guided missile destroyers, averaging two per year
26 x Guided missile frigates
34 x Light frigates over the last four years, averaging 8.5 per year.

Moreover, 41-44 other major vessels, including 14 Yuan class AIP SSKs (advanced conventional attack submarines), 6 Type 093 SSNs (nuclear-powered attack submarines), and 4 Type 094 SSBNs (Jin-class nuclear-powered ballistic missile submarines armed with CSS-NX-14/ JL-2 submarine-launched missiles/SLBMs).

"In the last 13 years (2003-2016), the Chinese Navy (PLAN) has really completed re-made itself from a coastal naval force of very many older, some would say antiquated vessels, to having added about 130 major, new, modern, and capable naval vessels," Jeff Head summed up. (10)

As reported by **Reuters** in Beijing, President Xi Jinping inspected navy headquarters on 24 May 2017, and he called for greater efforts to make China's navy world-class.

"Building a strong and modern navy is an important mark of a top ranking global military," the Defence Ministry paraphrased Xi as saying

"Innovation is key to improving and transforming the navy," Xi stressed. (11)

On 5 February 2018 **People's Daily Online** carried a report with photos on a military vessel reportedly equipped with a railgun on its bow.

On 6 February 2018 Jamie Seidel of **News Corp Australia's Network (news.com.au)** wrote on China's world-first deployment of an experimental electromagnetic rail gun (EMRG) on board an amphibious assault ship (Type 072III landing ship Haiyangshan 936).

On 14 March 2018 **ASIAN TIMES** reported a claim by lead engineer Zhang Xiao of China's "breakthrough" in EMRG after hundreds of failures and over 50,000 tests.

On 25 June 2018 Jared Keller reported in **TASK & PURPOSE (taskandpurpose.com)** that the Chinese railgun was first developed in 2011 and tested in 2014, followed by sea trials in December 2017.

Amanda Macias of **CNBC** reported on 21 June 2018 that China's EMRG, the world's most powerful naval gun is capable of striking a target 124 miles away at speeds of up to 1.6 miles per second. Mach 6 (4500 mph).

According to US intelligence, the Chinese railgun will be fielded by 2025.

Reported to be years away from being operational, the US Navy's railgun remains classified under the Office of Naval Research.   21.08.2018 02:52

C. Parity with the US by 2030

Long-time futurist and prolific website author Brian Wang has written that China's navy will be a Blue-Water Naval Power by 2030, with a two-ocean focus on the Pacific and Indian Oceans.

"The PLA Navy (PLAN) is in the midst of a massive shipbuilding program. If this program continues, China will surpass Russia as the world's second largest Navy by 2020, when measured in terms of submarines and frigate-class ships or larger," Admiral Harry B. Harris Jr, then US Navy Commander, US Pacific Command (USPACOM), stressed in his 56-page statement to the Senate Armed Services Committee on US Pacific Command Posture, 15 March 2018. **armed-services. senate.gov/03-15-18.pdf**

"The first Type 055 (Renhai) guided missile cruiser was launched in June 2017 -- the lead unit in a class of advanced multi-warfare ships that we expect will enter operational service next year (2019). At least four of these ships are under construction.

"Six Type 052 (Luyang III) Guided Missile Destroyers are operational, with another seven being built or fitted out.

"Amphibious capabilities are also growing. Four of an expected six Type 071 (Yuzhou) Amphibious Transport Docks have joined (p. 9) the fleet in the past decade, and the first Type 075 Landing Helicopter Dock is under construction.

"In October 2017 China launched the lead ship in the Type 901 Fast Combat Support Ship class, the first logistics ship specifically designed to support China's aircraft carrier(s); the second PLAN carrier is in the water at Dalian and progressing toward sea trials.

"New submarines under construction include five more Type 039A (Yuan) and four more Type 093 (Sheng)

Nuclear Attack Submarines (SSNs). All of these ships boast improved communications suites and defense systems, as well as more lethal and longer-range weapons...

"(p. 21) China has developed and fielded capability and capacity to challenge our regional maritime dominance.

"I need increased lethality, specifically ships and aircraft equipped with faster and more survivable weapons systems. Longer range offensive weapons on every platform are an imperative. We must also network this force and take advantage of man-machine teaming to improve our responsiveness...

"(p.25) China is improving the lethality and survivability of its attack submarines, building quieter, high-end diesel and nuclear powered submarines, and has placed in service four nuclear-powered Jin-class ballistic missile submarines (SSBNs). An armed Jin-class SSBN will give China an important strategic capability that must be countered..."

In testimony before the House of Representatives Permanent Select Committee on Intelligence, 17 May 2018, Richard D. Fisher, Jr, Senior Fellow at the International Assessment and Strategy Center, said:

"... By the early 2030s China could be deploying the world's first completely nuclear-powered aircraft carrier group: nuclear carrier, nuclear escort cruiser, escort nuclear attack submarine, and nuclear underway replenishment ship.

"Such a naval force will give the CCP leadership options for rapid deployment with far less reliance on a network of bases…" (p.6)
21.08.2018 03:47

"By 2030, many forecasts suggest that China will be qualitatively on par with the US," Brian Wang wrote. (12)

"By 2030, the existence of a global Chinese navy will be an important, influential and fundamental fact of international politics," said Patrick Cronin, director of the Center for a New American Security (CNAS)'s Asia-Pacific security program. (13)

"...They (the young PLAN officers) believe that China will soon end the United States' decades-long naval hegemony in the Western Pacific," award-winning Naval journalist Michael Fabey has narrated in his book **The Power Clash** (published October 24, 2017). (14)

On October 2017 Richard Fisher, Jr., a recognized authority on the PRC military, posted his article <u>The PLA Navy's Plan for Dominance</u>, based on a lecture on China's naval modernization delivered recently by retired Rear Admiral Zhao Dengping, former director of PLAN's Equipment Department.

Fisher concluded: "Former Vice Admiral Zhao's lecture is a very rare revelation, in perhaps unprecedented detail, of a portion of the PLA's future modernization's ambitions (including full nuclearization of the propulsion system of its submarine fleet, as well as acquisition of hypersonic, laser and microwave weapons).

"It confirms that many future PLAN modernization ambitions follow those of the U.S. Navy, possibly indicating that China intends to develop a navy with both the global reach and the high-tech weapons and electronics system necessary to compete for dominance with the U.S. Navy." (15)

19.09. 2018 22:23 6 pages 1,612 words 11.12.2017 17:47 03.04.2010 18:50

APPENDIX: CONTESTING US NAVAL SUPREMACY BY 2035

According to an announcement by China's missile force, five flight tests of the new submarine-launched ballistic missile (SLBM) known as the Julong (Big Wave)-3 (JL-3) were conducted on 20-23 November 2018. (16)

Bill Gertz, senior editor with **THE WASHINGTON FREE BEACON,** commented: "The flight test is a significant milestone for the Chinese strategic nuclear forces build-up -- the most lethal component of Beijing's large-scale military modernization program…"

When President Xi visited a submarine base in June 2018, he said that nuclear submarines are being upgraded rapidly among the country's key weapons systems.

"As a nation's ultimate instrument, submarines shall see great developments," Xi said. "Our seaborne nuclear forces need to advance by leaps and bounds…"

According to Chinese military commentator Wang Qiang, as reported in **Keji Ribao**, a publication of the State Science and Technology Commission (SSTC), the JL-3 SLBM will use advanced precision guidance technology with anti-jamming capabilities as well as missile-defense penetrating features including a variable trajectory, a radar-evading stealth warhead, and fast-burning motors to minimize the heat signature as well as advanced water-exit technology in underwater launches.

According to Rick Fisher, a China military analyst with the International Assessment and Strategy Center, when fully operational with a range of 7,456-8,700 miles, the JL-3 missile can reach most of the United States from underwater launch areas near the Chinese coasts.

Though it's expected to carry up to 10 multiple independently targetable reentry vehicle (MIRV) warheads, what's not known is the number of SLBMs that the next-generation nuclear ballistic missile submarine (SSBN) will carry, or how many of the new Type-096 submarines will be built.

China's current four Type-094 missile submarines are each outfitted with 16 missiles. According to internet reports from China, the future Type-096 SSBN will have up to 24 missiles (four more than the US Navy's Ohio-class).

"So it is possible that the Type 096 SSBN (fleet) could be equipped with hundreds of nuclear warheads," Fisher said.

The Type 096 is expected to become operational by the mid-to-late 2020s.

According to the National Air and Space Intelligence Center (NASIC), the present deployment of 48 JL-2 SLBMs on the Type 094 quartet of missile submarines has provided China with a significant nuclear strike capacity, which the Pentagon has described as "China's first credible, sea-based nuclear deterrent".

"By 2035, if not before, China will likely be able to contest U.S. operations throughout the entire Indo-Pacific region," stated the U.S.-China Economic and Security Review Commission in its 2018 annual report to Congress, released on 14 November 2018.

"As China continues to achieve its military modernization goals, the PLA will become increasingly capable of contesting all domains of warfare throughout the Indo-Pacific region and beyond…"

The Chinese strategy appears designed to contest the U.S. military by developing high-technology (HT) weapons, such as maneuvering missiles capable of targeting ships at sea, space weaponry, cyber warfare tools, and other advanced arms.

The rapid buildup of advanced naval forces is also a key feature, with deployment of large numbers of highly capable warships.

According to the Review Commission, the warships provide "naval expeditionary capabilities deployable around the globe as early as 2025, well ahead of the PLA's broader 2035 modernization goals…"

The Commission reported: "China's ability to threaten U.S. air bases, aircraft carriers, and other surface ships, presents serious strategic and operational challenges for the United States and its allies and partners throughout the Indo-Pacific…"   22.12.2018 04:50 05:15

Notes. NEW CHINA B (8) Naval Modernisation

1. Adapted from a report in **Global Times** 2017/4/23 on the 68th anniversary of the PLAN.
2. RL33153 posted on 1 November 2017 **everycrsreport.com**
3. The Office of Naval Intelligence (ONI) is the military intelligence agency of the US Navy. The oldest member of the American intelligence community, ONI was established on 23 March 1882 primarily to advance the USN's modernization. ONI serves as the nation's premier source of **maritime intelligence. Wikipedia.org last edited November 2017**
4. **andrewerickson.com 09 April 2015**
   Dr Erickson is a leading scholar on Chinese aerospace and maritime/naval policy and strategy at the Naval War College (NWC), the staff college for the US Navy at Naval Station Newport in Newport, Rhode Island. Erickson is Military Professor in the Asia-Pacific Center for Security Studies (APCSS), a DOD academic institute in Honolulu, Hawaii.

5. **wsj.com** April 10, 2015
6. **NEWS 18 news18.com** 22 Jan 2017
7. **sputniknews.com** 08.07.2017
8. Liu Zhen 29 Jun 2017 **South China Morning Post scmp.com**
9. **popsci.com**

10. **sinodefenceforum** last edited Sep 7, 2016
    Sino Defence Forum offers the place to discuss strategic Chinese defense, military, and geopolitical issues. In the SDF, Jeff Head is General, Staff Member as well as Super Moderator.
11. **Asahi Simbun asahi.com** May 25, 2017
12. **nextbigfture.com** May 2017
13. David Tweed and Adrian Leung Jun 01 2017 **bloomberg.com**
14. **The Power Clash Between the U.S. and China in the Pacific**, Scribner.
    Thomas E. Ricks Nov 2017 **foreignpolicy.com**
15. **maritime-executive.com** MarEx 2017-10-30 21:37:24
    Richard Fisher authored **China's Military Modernization, Building for Regional and Global Reach**, Stanford University Press.
16. Bill Gertz December 18, 2018 4.05 pm **freebeacon.com**
17. Bill Gertz November 14, 2018 3.00 pm **MUCK RACK muckrack.com**

12pages 3,381 words 12.12.2017 21.08.2018 03:56 10.09.2018 19:36 19.10.2018 00:27 22.12.2018 04:59
27.03.2019 03:42 03.04.2019 18:55

NEW CHINA (C) CHRONOLOGY

Milestones

21 September 1949	Mao Zedong declares to delegates of the Chinese People's Political Consultative Conference that "the Chinese people, (then) comprising one-quarter of humanity, have now stood up..."
1 October 1949	Mao proclaims the founding of the People's Republic of China (PRC) at Tiananmen Square in Peking/Beijing.
June 1950	Agrarian Reform Law redistributes land from landlords to peasants.
25 October 1949	China enters the Korean War in defence of North Korea.
1953	China's first modern census shows its population to be about 583 million.
September 1954	The first constitution of the PRC is adopted at the first meeting of the National People's Congress.
15 January 1955	Mao finally decides to go nuclear militarily with Project 02.
1956	*Hukou* (household registration) system is introduced in favour of urban proletariat.

| 1956 | "Hundred Flowers" campaign, sparking free debate and inquiry. |
| 27 February 1957 | Mao says: "...To make China rich and strong needs several decades of intense effort..." 21.12.2017 |

New China (C) Chronology/Milestones (2)

958-62	"Great Leap Forward" campaign for rapid industrialisation and collectivisation of agriculture with the audacious objective of "to catch up or exceed the UK" in industrial output in 15 years or more (to quote Mao).
28 July 1958	Central Military Commission (CMC) gives the green light to Project 09 for the dual development of nuclear submarine and its missile delivery system (the JL-1).
May 1964	First publication of **Quotations of Chairman Mao**.
16 October 1964	China's successful first test of a nuclear device (20 KT)
1966-76	Cultural Revolution
17 June 1967	China successfully detonates its first hydrogen bomb (3 MT), graduating in world record time from nuclear to thermonuclear class, and a year ahead of France.
14 July 1967	Both Mao and Zhou Enlai decide that China should not be left behind in the contrail of the US-Soviet space race.
24 April 1970 13:35 (UTC)	China successfully launches Long March-1 rocket with China's first satellite Dong Fang Hong (East is Red)-1.

| 1 December 1970 | China launches its first self-developed nuclear submarine. |
| October 1971 | The UN votes to give the PRC its seat in the world assembly, with permanent membership in its Security Council. |

NEW CHINA (C) Chronology/Milestones (3)

21-28 Feb 1972	President Richard Nixon meets with Chairman Mao on the first day of his historic visit to China.
29 March 1974	Farmers digging a well, uncover the terracotta army of over 8,000 life-size figures of warriors and horses near the ancient capital of Xian, buried with the first Qin emperor in 210-209 BCE.
August 1974	China commissions its first nuclear submarine.
January 1975	Zhou Enlai outlines the country's programme of Four Modernisations (agriculture, industry, national defence, science and technology) at the opening of the Fourth National Congress.
9 September 1976	Mao dies at the age of 82.
18-22 Dec 1978	Deng Xiaoping officially launches the Four Modernisations at the Third Plenum of the CPC's 11th Central Committee, marking the start of the "Reform and Opening Up" policy of national economic development, and sealing Deng's rise as the country's new paramount leader.
1 January 1979	Beijing and Washington normalise diplomatic relations.

| 1 May 1980 | Shenzhen becomes China's first Special Economic Zone (SEZ), followed shortly by three others in the cities of Zhuhai, Shantou and Xiamen in southern China. The quartet of SEZs are established to promote foreign investment and trade. |

NEW CHINA (C) Chronology/Milestones (4)

May 1980	Successful full-range (13,000 km) flight test of the DF-5 Intercontinental Ballistic Missile/ICBM (4-5 MT), followed by its deployment in 1981 to establish China's nuclear deterrent capability. 21.12.2017 10:40
1982	China's population exceeds one billion.
12 October 1982	First test of the JL-1 SLBM (submarine-launched ballistic missile.)
4 December 1982	Fifth National Congress adopts the current Constitution (the 12th since 1911).
April 1984	China establishes 14 more Special Economic Zones (SEZs) in the large coastal cities.
31 October 1988	Opening of China's first expressway Shanghai-Jiading.
May-June 1989	Student demonstrations at Tiananmen Square in Peking.
14 June 1989	Jiang Zemin succeeds Zhao Ziyang as CPC's General Secretary.
19 December 1990	First in New China, Shanghai Stock Exchange opens.
15 December 1991	China's first nuclear power reactor 288 MW PWR at Qinshan Nuclear Power Plant is connected to the grid.

1992   China's annual automobile production capacity exceeds one million. China makes over two million vehicles by 2000.

Before China's reform in 1979, its automotive industry produced fewer than 200,00 vehicles per annum.

NEW CHINA (C) Chronology/Milestones (5)

28 May 1993   Opening of Shanghai Metro, which becomes the world's largest in early 2010.

20 April 1994   China is connected to the Internet for the first time through a pilot network to serve education and scientific research via a special link in Zhongguangcun, Haidan District, northwestern Beijing, a notable technology hub since 1999.

14 December 1994   Start of construction of Three Gorges Dam, world's largest power station with 22,500 MW installed capacity.

Dr Sun Yat-sen was presciently right when he stated in 1919 that a dam capable of generating 30 million HP (22 GW) could be built downstream of the Three Gorges on the mighty Yangtze River.

1995   China's first website Yinghai wei Shikong is launched in autumn.

19 February 1997   Deng Xiaoping dies at the age of 92.

1 July 1997   Hong Kong becomes a Special Administrative Region (SAR) of China after 150 years of colonial rule.

1998   China's GDP exceeds one trillion dollars (USD), with a population of 1.24 billion.

| 20 November 1999 | Launch of Shenzhou-1 space capsule to mark 50th anniversary (Golden Jubilee) of the PRC's founding. |

| 11 December 2001 | China as world's 6th largest economy enters the World Trade Organisation (WTO) after16 years of negotiations – the longest in GATT history. China also enters on considerably harsher terms than other developing countries. |

NEW CHINA (C) Chronology/Milestones (6)

| 15 November 2002 | Hu Jintao succeeds Jiang Zemin as CPC's General Secretary. |

| 27 December 2002 | Official start of construction of the Eastern Route (Jiangdu-Tianjin) of the South-North-Water Diversion Project (SNWDP) to eventually supply 9.9 trillion gallons annually ("to borrow a little water", said Mao) to help meet demand in water-short northern China – the world's largest such project n human history. |

| 15 October 2003 | Launch of China's first manned spacecraft Shenzhou-5 0900 CST with the first Chinese taikonaut Yang Liwei in space. |

| 27 December 2003 | Start of construction of Central Route of North-South Water Diversion Project -- from Danjiangkou Reservoir in Xichuan, Henan Province, to Beijing. |

| 2004 | China's global trade exceeds US$1 trillion. |

| 2007 | With GDP of about US$3.5 trillion at end of 2007, China overtakes Germany to become the world's third biggest economy. |

2007	China overtakes the US to become the world's top emitter of greenhouse gases. In 2007 China becomes a net importer of food.
2007	China has the world's largest number of internet users –211,140,032 (16% of its population), considerably up from 138,126,944 (10.5% of population) in 2006, double that of 94,795,831 (7.3% of population) in 2004, and close to a 10-fold increase from 22,553,646 (1.8% of population) in 2000. Source: **internetlivestats.com**

NEW CHINA (C) Chronology/Milestones (7)

11 January 2007	China shoots down an old weather satellite, showing its anti-satellite (ASAT) capability.
18 April 2007	Hexia (Harmony) bullet trains inaugurate China's High Speed Rail (HSR) service.
October 2007	At the CPC's 17th National Congress, President Hu Jintao proposes concept and strategy of "ecological civilisation" for sustainable development of the nation.
24 October 2007	Chang'e-1 spacecraft, China's first to orbit the Moon.
18 April 2008	Start of construction of Beijing-Shanghai high-speed railway, the world's first HSR with designed speed of 380 km/h (236 mph).
7 August 2008	China Railway Corporation introduces its 350 km/h Beijing-Tianjin HSR service for 2008 Summer Olympics in Beijing.
7-24 August 2008	Beijing 2008 – Summer Olympic Games XXIX Olympiad

27 September 2008	Shenzhou-7 mission commander Zhai Zhigang becomes the first Chinese cosmonaut to spacewalk.
2009	China makes 13.83 million motor vehicles to be the world's top automaker.
2009	China overtakes Germany as the world's largest merchandise exporter worth US$1.2 trillion (9.5% of global). According to IMF data, China's exports grew by average of 17% annually in past 3 decades.
2009	China overtakes the US as the world's largest consumer of primary energy (2312 million/2.3 billion tons of oil equivalent).
April 2009	China displays its nuclear submarines for the first time.

NEW CHINA (C) Chronology/Milestones (8)

19 April 2009	Start of construction of world's first AP 1000 reactor (1250 MW Westinghouse) at Sanmen Nuclear Power Plant in Zhejiang Province. It's expected to be commissioned by end of 2017.
30 June 2009	At Three Gorges HEP, all 28 generators in full operation.
2010	China sells estimated 18 million cars to top the global market.
2010	With GDP of US$6.1 trillion, China surpasses Japan to become the world's second largest economy.
2010	China sails past South Korea to become the world's top shipbuilder.
2010	Shanghai overtakes Singapore to become world's busiest container port.

2010	China deploys its DF-21D "carrier-killer" missile, world's first anti-ship ballistic missile (ASBM).
November 2010	China's Tianhe (Milky Way)-1A supercomputer tops the computing world, operating at over 2.5 petaflops, 2.5 quadrillion per second.
2011	China overtakes the US to become the world's biggest PC market and also as the world's largest producer (7th in 1980) of manufactured goods.
11 January 2011	First flight test of 5-G stealth fighter Chengdu J-20.
July 2011	Start of construction of China's second aircraft carrier Type 001A.
29 September 2011	Launch of Tiangong-1 space laboratory.
31 October 2011	Unmanned Shenzhou-8 docks with Tiangong-1 space lab.
27 December 2011	Beidou Navigation Satellite System (BDS) inaugurates its regional high-precision positioning and navigation services to countries in the (Asia-Pacific.

NEW CHINA (C) Chronology/Milestones (9)

2011	China becomes the world's largest investor in infrastructure development, overtaking the US and the EU.
2011	Stretching 85,000 km/53,000 miles, China's highway system becomes the world's longest.
2011	Urban Chinese (51.27%, from 20.9% in 1982) outnumber rural Chinese in China's population of close to 1.35 billion
2011	China overtakes the US as world's largest producer of Manufactured goods.
18 June 2012	First manned docking with Tiangong-1 space lab.

24 July 2012	First test of the formidable DF-41 ICBM.
25 September 2012	Commissioning of China's first aircraft carrier Liaoning.
15 November 2012	Xi Jinping succeeds Hu Jintao as CPC's General Secretary and Chairman of the Central Military Commission (CMC).
29 November 2012	Xi Jinping's Chinese Dream of China's complete modernisation and rejuvenation.
2012	With a total installed generating capacity of 1000 GW/1 million MW (about one-fifth of the world's), China produces as well as consumes the most electricity in the world, overtaking the US in 2012. Also the most carbon emissions in the world.
14 March 2013	Xi Jinping is elected as the PRC's 7th President.
13 May 2013	DN-2 ASAT interceptor is tested at high altitude of over 18,600 miles in deep space.
11 June 2013	Launch of Shenzhou-10 with three astronauts on board.

NEW CHINA (C) Chronology/Milestones (10)

June 2013	Tianhe-2 tops the list of the world's most powerful supercomputers with a peak computing speed of 54.9 petaflops per second, and stays on top until mid-2016.
September 2013	**Air Pollution Prevention and Control Action Plan**
September 2013	China becomes the world's largest oil importer, importing 6.3 million barrels a day – 200,000 barrels a day more than the US.

17 October 2013   Inauguration of National Poverty Alleviation Day Based on international $1.90 a day poverty line, China alleviated 853 million poor in past three decades (from 88.3% in extreme poverty in 1981 to 1.9% in 2013). China aims "zero-poverty" by 2020.

2013   Deployment of the JL-2 submarine-launched ballistic missile (SLBM) delivers China's undersea strategic nuclear deterrence.

2013   China becomes the world's largest trading nation with its total external trade of US$4.2 trillion (exports of US$2.4 trillion and imports of US$1.8 trillion). 37 years ahead of Lee Kuan Yew's prediction in 2000 that China would become the world's largest or second largest trading nation in 2050.

2013   China overtakes Japan as world's largest market for industrial robots.

7 September 2013   Addressing students and faculty at the Nazarbayev University in Astana, capital of Kazakhstan, President Xi Jinping calls on countries in Central Asia to embrace Eurasia's "golden opportunity for development" and to jointly build an economic belt along the historic Silk Road.

This clarion call has launched Xi's signature BOR/BRI strategy of "win-win" international/regional cooperation and development.   10.09.2018 20:12

NEW CHINA (C) Chronology/Milestones (11)

3 October 2013	Addressing the Indonesian parliament, Dewan Perwakilan Rakyat, in Jakarta, capital of Indonesia, President Xi Jinping proposes joining hands with the countries in Southeast Asia to construct a new "Maritime Silk Road' from southern China to the Indian subcontinent and the two continents of Africa and Europe.
1 November 2013	Successful test of stealth combat drone "Sharp Sword".
November 2013	start of construction of China's first indigenously developed aircraft carrier the Type 001A at Dalian shipyard in NE Liaoning Province.
14 December 2013	Chang'e-3 soft-lands on the Moon to explore the the lunar surface.
9 January 2014	Successful first test of the WU-14/DF-ZF hypersonic glide vehicle (HGV), described as a game-changing prompt global strike (PGS) weapon.
March 2014	**National Plan on New Urbanisation (2014-2020)**
9 August 2014	Successful test of the new JL-3 submarine-launched ballistic missile (SLBM). For China's next-generation Type 096 SSBN.
27 December 2014	Opening of the Central Route of the South-North Water Diversion Project to start delivering water from Danjiankou Reservoir in Henan Province to Beijing.
December 2014	Number of high net-worth Chinese or superrich in China (having over 10 million yuan of investable assets) exceeds one million for the first time, twice as many as in 2010.

2014	Beijing makes breakthrough to the list of the top 10 globalised cities (ranked 8th).
2014	China's direct foreign investment of US$128 billion exceeds the US' $86 billion to top the global FDI list.
2014	China's GDP of 63.3 trillion yuan (US$10.2 trillion) with a population of 1.37 billion at the end of 2014; its growth rate of 7.4% in 2014 being the lowest in 24 years (9.2%+ in 1991). China's GDP is expected to reach 100 trillion yuan (US$16.1 trillion) in 2020 with per capita income of US$10,000.
January 2015	Following its successful latest test, the JL-2 SLBM is deployed in PLA Navy's 094 SSBNs (nuclear ballistic missile submarines) to give China "its first credible sea-based nuclear deterrent" (to quote the US Department of Defense). 1,826 words 22.12.2017 10:19
February 2015	First flight of high-altitude long-range stealth drone with special radars "Divine Eagle".
March 2015	Start of construction of China's third aircraft carrier Type 002.
30 March 2015	the first of five new-generation BeiDou satellites launched, and its 17th to initiate global coverage.
16 April 2015	**Water Pollution Prevention and Control Action Plan**

| April 2015 | China's record oil imports of about 7.4 million barrels per day (bpd) pips the US' estimated 7.2 million bpd to become the world's no. 1 crude oil importer for the first time. China is already the world's energy consumer (2009), and leads in consumption of almost allcommodities including coal, iron ore, and most metals. |

NEW CHINA (C) Chronology/Milestones (13)

May 2015	**Made in China 2025 (MIC 2025)**, a 10-year roadmap for industrial modernisation to promote intelligent, innovative and quality manufacturing to make China into a global manufacturing power.
June 2015	Asian Infrastructure Investment Bank (AIIB) established.
July 2015	**Internet Plus Plan (IPP)**, a development strategy to restructure China's economy and maintain its growth momentum at 6-7% per annum.
August 2015	China's foreign exchange reserves of US$3.56 trillion becomes the world's largest (China has come a long way from its GDP of US$35 billion in 1955).
September 2015	On display at the 2015 China Victory Parade in Beijing:
	DF-21D "carrier-killer" anti-ship ballistic missile (ASBM)
	JY-12 supersonic anti-ship cruise missile (ASCM)
	DF-26 dual-capable (conventional/nuclear) ASBM

15 September 2015	First flight test of PL-15 advanced air-to-air missile (AAM)
20 September 2015	Launch of new carrier rocket Long March (LM)-6
25 September 2015	Debut of solid-fuel carrier rocket Long March 11.
9 November 2015	First flight test of DN-3 direct ascent missile satellite-killer.
17 December 2015	Launch of "Wukong" (Monkey King) Dark Matter Particle Explorer (DAMPE), China's first space observatory and first astronomy satellite and space telescope to detect and record cosmic ray events, high-energy astronomy study of dark matter particles by high-resolution observations of high-energy electrons and gamma rays, and study of origin of cosmic rays.
December 2015	China emerges as the world's top photovoltaic (PV) country with installed capacity of 43 gigawatts (43,000 MW). In 2011, China blew away all other competitors to top in wind power (39 GW/39,000 MW).

NEW CHINA (C) Chronology/Milestones (14).

| 2015 | China surpasses the US to become the world's biggest market for new vehicles (electrics, plug-in hybrids, and fuel-cell cars). |
| January 2016 | Start of construction of the world's longest 1,100 kV (world's highest voltage) power transmission system (3,319 km) from Changji in Xinjiang Province in northwest China to Guquan in Anhui Province in east China. The UHV (Ultra High Voltage) project will be completed in 2018. |

31 January 2016	At the Institute of Plasma Physics in Hefei, capital of Anhui Province in east China, the Experimental Advanced Superconducting Tokamak (EAST) aka "artificial sun" HT-7U registers a breakthrough in fusion energy research by making a world record 102-second long pulse plasma discharge at over the central electron temperature (CET) of 50 million degrees.
	In operation since 2006, the 400-ton EAST has come one step closer to the critical goal of1000-seconds long pulse plasma discharge at 100 million degrees Centigrade for self-sustaining fusion reaction.
February 2016	New blueprint for more concentrated urbanisation
24 April 2016	China's first Space Day, declared and observed to mark the historic launching of Dong Fang Hong (East is Red) in 1970 which opened the Chinese space era.

NEW CHINA (C) Chronology/Milestones (15)

March 2016	**13th Five-Year Plan (2016-2020)** highlights technological innovation as the core of China's new development paradigm.
12 April 2016	7th test of the signature DF-41 ICBM
22 April 2016	7th test of the potential game-changer DF-ZF/WU-14 hypersonic glide vehicle (HGV).
25 June 2016	Maiden mission of new Wenchang Spacecraft Launch Site in Hainan, south China
26 June 2016	Debut of new carrier rocket Long March 7

16 August 2016	Launch of Mozi/Micius quantum communication satellite, the world's first, for its mission "Quantum Experiments at Space Scale" (QUESS), designed to establish "hack-proof" communications. China plans to globalize its quantum satellite system by 2030. 10.09.2018 21:12
15 September 2016	Launch of Tiangong 2 space lab
25 September 2016	Completion and opening for operation of China's FAST radio telescope, the world's largest single-dish radio telescope, after 22 years of development.
1 October 2016	Renminbi RMB/yuan is in the IMF's special drawing rights (XDR) basket, its share of 10.92% marking a milestone in the internationalisation of the RMB as well as in the global economy. China accounts for one-third of global economic growth.
10 October 2016	Launch of manned spacecraft Shenzhou 2
17 October 2016	First manned docking with Tiangong-2 space lab
8 December 2016	Plan (2016-2020) on intelligent manufacturing
23 December 2016	First flight test of 5-G stealth fighter FC-31 (formerly J-31)

NEW CHINA © Chronology/Milestones (16)

2016	China's investment of 1.57 trillion yuan (about US$240 billion) on Research & Development (R&D) in 2016 is 2.1% of national GDP, and world's second largest. China has made technological innovations and breakthroughs including high-speed rail (HSR), UHV (Ultra High Voltage) power transmission of up to 1,100 kV (world's highest voltage), hybrid rice, satellite navigation, and electric cars.

2016	China signs the Paris Agreement on Climate Change, pledging to cut its carbon emissions by 60-65% per unit of GDP by 2030.
January 2017	731 million internet users (53.1% of population) in China.
January 2017	Guidelines on Energy Development and Energy Industry Reform to promote and deepen China's "energy revolution".
15 January 2017	First test of DF-5C ICBM
17 January 2017	In his keynote address at the World Economic Forum in Davos, Switzerland, President Xi Jinping calls for joint responsibility to promote global growth, stresses his strong support for economic globalisation, and among other important things, he proposes innovation-driven growth, open and win-win cooperation, upholding multilateralism, and maintaining the Paris Agreement forfuture generations, and developing a balanced, equitable and inclusive development model for the people and common good. Xi invites people of other countries to come aboard "the express train (HSR Fuxing/ Rejuvenation) of China's development". China will keep its door wide open, Xi says, and he adds: "An opendoor allows both other countries to access the Chinese market and China itself to integrate with the world..."

1 March 2017	Three Gorges HEP (world's largest) generates 1 trillion kilowatt-hours (kwh) of electricity at 12.28 p.m. following 14 years of operation.
12 April 2017	Launch of the new communication satellite Shijian-13, China's first high-throughput with a transfer capacity of 20 Gyps and a designed 15-year orbital life.
20 April 2017	Launch of Tianzhou-1 cargo spacecraft, essential to construction to construction of China's multi-modular space station by 2022 and manned lunar exploration.
26 April 2017	Launch of China's second aircraft carrier Type 001A.
27 April 2017	the T'anzhou-1 cargo spacecraft successfully refuels the Tiangong-2 space lab in orbit.
5 May 2017	China's first home-built commercial passenger aircraft the C919 completes its maiden flight at 15:19 (7.19 am GMT) at the Shanghai Pudong International Airport. The 168-passenger narrow-body aircraft is in the league of Boeing new-generation 737 and Airbus updated A320.
May 2017	Debut of Caihong (Rainbow), China's largest and most advanced solar-powered unmanned aircraft.
14-15 May 2017	Participants from over 130 countries attend the first Belt and Road Forum for International Cooperation in Beijing, chaired by President Xi to forge win-win progress and build a global community with a shared future.

| 15 June 2017 | Launch of China's first space telescope "Huiyan" Hard X-ray Modulation Telescope (HXMT) for its interstellar mission of surveying the Milky Way galaxy to observe back holes, pulsars and gamma-ray bursts. |
| | The HXMT is one of only four telescopes in the world capable of detecting gravitational waves at high frequency and fielding/shooting the best image resolution. |

NEW CHINA (C) Chronology/Milestones (18)

19-25 June 2017	Public debut of China's state-of-the-art YLC-29 radar system at the 52nd International Paris Airshow.
28 June 2017	PLA Navy launches its first new-generation domestically designed and manufactured 10,000-ton missile destroyer at the Jianguan Shipyard
3 July 2017	China's experimental fusion device HT-7U EAST becomes the world's first tokamak to sustain H-Mode (steady-state high-performance) plasma for 101.2 seconds at 50 million degrees Kelvin, according to Chinese Academy of Sciences (CAS). Chinese scientists expect to operate a fusion power reactor by 2050
8 July 2017	**New Generation Artificial** Intelligence **Development Plan** and a Roadmap for China to lead the world in AI technology and Applications by 2030.
31 July 2017	Public debut of the DF-31AG ICBM in the massive military parade to mark the PLA's 90th anniversary.

1 August 2017	As Chairman of Central Military Commission (CMC) and Commander-in-Chief, President Xi tells military officials in Beijing that building a world-class military is central to China's rejuvenation.
1 August 2017	The PLA opens its first overseas support base in Djibouti in east Africa. China keeps a 8,000-strong standing peacekeeping force at the UN.
3 August 2017	**PLA Daily** declares that the DF-31AG ICBM represents China's status as a world power as well as its defence prowess.
21 August	Maiden run of the Fuxing (Rejuvenation) bulletin train at up to 350 km/h on the Beijing-Tianjin line to provide world's fastest commercial train service.
1 September 2017	The 29th Session of the Standing Committee of the National People's Congress (NPC) adopts China's Nuclear Safety Law, which will take effect on 1 January 2018.
13 September 2017	Cargo spacecraft Tianzhou 1 fast-docks with Tiangong 2 space lab.

NEW CHINA (C) Chronology/Milestones (19)

| 28 Sept 2017 | Commissioning of China's 5-G stealth fighter jet Chengdu J-20 |
| October 2017 | Opening of the world's first quantum communication trunk line, the 260km-long Shanghai-Hangzhou Quantum Communication Commercial Trunk Line. |

| 18 October 2017 | President Xi Jinping presents his report at the 19th CPC National Congress, stressing **China's three heroic tasks:** |

18 October 2017 — President Xi Jinping presents his report at the 19th CPC National Congress, stressing **China's three heroic tasks:**

    (1) **Advancing China's modernisation,**
    (2) **National reunification, and**
    (3) **World peace and common development**.

5 November 2017 — Launch of two third-generation BeiDou-3 satellites for global coverage.

10 November 2017 — First long-distance flight by the indigenous C919 from Shanghai to Xian over 1,300 km.

23 November 2017 — China's domestically-developed multi-pulse high-current accelerator "Shenlong-2", world's first of its kind, passes state-level on-site inspection, a milestone in development of linear induction accelerator and China's flash radiography technology.

28 November 2017 — China National Nuclear Corporation (CNNC) unveils its self-developed low-temperature heating reactor (400 MW) to supply heating needs of 200,000 three-bedroom families.

1 December 2017 — At the opening ceremony of the CPC in Dialogue with World Political Parties High-level Meeting at the Great Hall of the People in Beijing, President Xi expresses China's willingness to work with other political parties for world peace and global development with a shared future, upholding the international order, and building a better world. (The CPC keeps in close contact with over 400 political parties and organisations in more than 160 countries.)

4 December 2017   At World Internet Conference, China Electronics Technology Group Co. (CETC) unveils the world's fastest quantum random number generator (QRNG) -- the core device to realize quantum secure communication.

5 December 2017   Delivery in Shanghai by China State Shipbuilding Corporation of "Da Zhi", the world's first smart bulk carrier with up-to-date information technologies, including world's first self-learning information platform and China-built intelligent remote control system.

13 December 2017   Inauguration of the ARJ 21 (China's first domestic regional jetliner) commercial regional service on its destination route from Chengdu/Sichuan province to Shangrao City/Jiangxi province.

NEW CHINA (C) Chronology/Milestones (20) 26.12.2917

18:23

14 December 2017   Opening of the Beijing Academy of Quantum Information Science, designed to innovate in quantum communication, computing, and targeting.

14-15 December 2017   Xi'an hosts the 12th Confucius Institute Conference. Since its founding in 2004, there are 525 Confucius Institutes in 146 countries, including 53 im the Belt and Road Initiative.

20 December 2017   China launches its national carbon emissions trading scheme (CETS), initially with the power sector responsible for over 46% of carbon emissions, covering nearly 1,700 power plants in the country.

21 December 2017	Start of construction of the first phase 252-km line from Bangkok to Nakhon Ratchasima, in the planned 867-km Chinese-Thai railway from Nong Kuai on the Thai-Lao border to Rayong in eastern Thailand, for connection with China-Lao railway from Vientiane to Kunming in southeast China's Yunnan Province, and extension via Kuala Lumpur to Singapore.
24 December 2017	Maiden flight of China's first home-grown amphibious aircraft AG 600, the world's largest, joining the nation's "large aircraft family" after the Y-20 military freighter (Jan 2013) and C919 which made its first flight on 5 May 2017.
25 December 2017	Completion of the massive UHV power transmission project from Shanghaimiao (Inner Mongolia) to Linyi City (Shandong). 3,930 words

10.09.2018 23:59 19.10.2018 01:01
22 pages 4822 words 11.01.2019 06:33